Behind the Model

This ambitious book looks "behind the model" to reveal how economists use formal models to generate insights into the economy. Drawing on recent work in the philosophy of science and economic methodology, the book presents a novel framework for understanding the logic of economic modeling. It also reveals the ways in which economic models can mislead rather than illuminate. Importantly, the book goes beyond purely negative critique, proposing a concrete program of methodological reform to better equip economists to detect potential mismatches between their models and the targets of their inquiry. Ranging across economics, philosophy, and social science methods, and drawing on a variety of examples, including the recent financial crisis, *Behind the Model* will be of interest to anyone who has wondered how economics works – and why it sometimes fails so spectacularly.

Peter Spiegler is Assistant Professor of Economics at the University of Massachusetts, Amherst.

Strategies for Social Inquiry

Behind the Model: A Constructive Critique of Economic Modeling

Editors
Colin Elman, *Maxwell School of Syracuse University*
John Gerring, *Boston University*
James Mahoney, *Northwestern University*

Editorial Board
Bear Braumoeller, David Collier, Francesco Guala, Peter Hedström, Theodore Hopf,
Uskali Maki, Rose McDermott, Charles Ragin, Theda Skocpol, Peter Spiegler, David
Waldner, Lisa Wedeen, Christopher Winship

This new book series presents texts on a wide range of issues bearing upon
the practice of social inquiry. Strategies are construed broadly to
embrace the full spectrum of approaches to analysis, as well as relevant issues
in philosophy of social science.

Behind the Model

A Constructive Critique of Economic Modeling

Peter Spiegler

University of Massachusetts, Amherst

CAMBRIDGE
UNIVERSITY PRESS

CAMBRIDGE
UNIVERSITY PRESS

University Printing House, Cambridge CB2 8BS, United Kingdom

Cambridge University Press is part of the University of Cambridge.

It furthers the University's mission by disseminating knowledge in the pursuit of education, learning and research at the highest international levels of excellence.

www.cambridge.org
Information on this title: www.cambridge.org/9781107069664

© Peter Spiegler 2015

First published 2015

A catalogue record for this publication is available from the British Library

Library of Congress Cataloguing in Publication data
Spiegler, Peter.
Behind the model : a constructive critique of economic modeling / Peter Spiegler.
    pages   cm. – (Strategies for social inquiry)
Includes bibliographical references.
ISBN 978-1-107-06966-4 (hardback) – ISBN 978-1-107-67780-7 (paperback)
1. Economics.   2. Economics – Methodology – Evaluation.
3. Economics – Mathematical models.   4. Econometric models.   I. Title.
HB71.S735   2015
330.01–dc23

2015007320

ISBN 978-1-107-06966-4 Hardback

To David, Joyce, Lee, Benjamin and Miriam

Contents

Acknowledgments

During the long process of researching and writing this book, I have benefited greatly from the help and support of many friends, colleagues and institutions. I would like especially to acknowledge the Institute for New Economic Thinking for funding the research at a crucial stage, and for its role in supporting and promoting new scholarship in economic methodology more generally. I am very grateful also for support received from the Political Economy Research Institute at the University of Massachusetts, Amherst, which was especially helpful in bringing the book to completion, and to the University of Massachusetts, Boston, which provided funding that allowed me time to focus on research. A fellowship from the Harvard Center for Ethics and the Professions (now the Edmond J. Safra Center for Ethics) early in my graduate studies provided both funding and an environment in which to explore ideas across disciplines. I am very grateful to my fellow fellows, especially Tamara Metz and Bryan Garsten, and to the director of the program Arthur Applbaum.

I began writing systematically about economic methodology while studying economics and the history of economic thought with Stephen Marglin, and have benefited enormously over the years from his scholarship and mentorship as well as his steadfast support. I am very grateful also to Richard Tuck, whose teaching and writing on political theory and intellectual history have had a profound influence on me.

Daniela Cammack and David Grewal went to heroic lengths in their support during the editing stages of the project, not only painstakingly reading through every chapter and helping me to clarify the prose and the central ideas of the book, but also opening their home to me as I worked to incorporate their comments. I cannot overstate how grateful I am to both of them, for their lucid and incisive criticism and, above all, for their friendship. Sanjay Reddy has been a friend, interlocutor and intellectual fellow traveler since the very beginning of my economic methodology studies. He has taught me a great deal both about political economy and about scholarship in general, and I owe him great thanks. I am very grateful also to Will Milberg for his keen insights into economic methodology and the history of economic thought, and for graciously allowing me to include in chapters 4 and 5 of this book material that we wrote together. My thanks are due as well to John Gerring and Heike Schotten for reading early drafts and providing invaluable guidance, and to Sari Boren for helping me to rescue a disintegrating chapter. I would also like to express my profound gratitude to Hans Agrawal for his vital and long-standing support.

Various work that eventually made its way into this book was presented at several conferences and seminars, including the University of Chicago Metaphor Workshop in 2013, the 2012 conference of the European Network for the Philosophy of Social Science, the New School graduate economic methodology seminar in 2012 and 2011, the 2011 Tobin Project conference on financial reform, the 2010 Erasmus Institute for Philosophy and Economics Symposium on Economics-Made-Fun, the 2009 International Network for Economic Method conference, and the 2009 Allied Social Sciences Association conference. I am grateful for the comments of the participants, and would especially like to acknowledge Clifford Ando, John Cisternino, Francesco Guala, Karen Ho, Douglas Holmes, Vincent Lépinay, Caterina Marchionni, Corrado Matta, Mary Morgan, Annelise Riles and David Teira.

I am very thankful for the help I have received from many people at Cambridge University Press, and especially that of my editor John Haslam. I thank Carrie Parkinson, Gillian Dadd, Ed Robinson, and Charlotte Thomas for their help and encouragement, and Anne Valentine for her excellent and thorough copy editing.

I am very grateful as well to Michael Spiegler for his sage advice and guidance on writing, editing and publishing.

Finally, and above all, I would like to thank David, Joyce and Lee Spiegler, and Benjamin and Miriam Dembling for their patience, love and unwavering support.

Introduction

On December 5, 1871, John Stuart Mill wrote to his friend and disciple John Elliot Cairnes expressing dismay at the work of William Stanley Jevons, one of the pioneers of the new abstract mathematical style in economics. Jevons had "a mania for encumbering questions with useless complications," Mill wrote, "with a notation implying the existence of greater precision in the data than the questions admit of" (Mill 1972).

At the time of writing, Mill had not yet read Jevons' recently published *Theory of Political Economy*, but if he had, he would have found no reason to change his view. Jevons, for his part, was equally critical of Mill's work – and used remarkably similar language to make his complaint. According to Jevons, it was *Mill's* economic doctrines – and those of the then-dominant British Classical School more generally – that were unnecessarily complicated, because they were based on "mazy and preposterous assumptions" about the basic concepts of political economy (Jevons 1965: xliv).

What Mill and other classical political economists failed to see, Jevons argued, was that despite the apparent complexity of human social activity there was a fundamental simplicity and unity at its core. Standard economic notions such as utility, wealth, value, commodity, labor, land, and capital all reflected a single underlying theme: the basic human tendency to "satisfy our wants to the utmost with the least effort – to procure the greatest amount of what is desirable at the expense of the least that is undesirable – in other words, to maximise pleasure" (Jevons 1965: 37).[1] This tendency manifested itself in human behavior in a manner that was uniform across people, quantitatively (Jevons thought cardinally) measurable, and separable from influences that were more context-dependent, such as morality or culture. Recognizing this, Jevons argued, would allow many of the issues that had troubled classical political economists to be bracketed, enabling the

---

[1] Jevons borrowed this formulation (with acknowledgement) from J.-G. Courcelle-Seneuil (Jevons 1965: 41; Courcelle-Seneuil 1858: 36).

articulation of a precise "*mechanics of utility and self-interest*" on the model of physical mechanics (Jevons 1965: 21, emphasis original).

According to Jevons, the analogy with physical mechanics ran deep. The "laws and relations" governing utility mechanics had to be "mathematical in nature," because they "*dealt with quantities*," i.e. "things ... capable of being *greater or less*" (Jevons 1965: 3, emphasis original). These laws could also be isolated from potentially disturbing factors, not only conceptually but also empirically. Although the economist could not conduct controlled experiments to effect this isolation directly, Jevons believed that the effects of disturbing factors could be dealt with systematically, even when economists were largely in the dark about their nature and operation.[2]

Consequently, it seemed to Jevons that scepticism about the possibilities of a precise science of political economy, like that expressed by Mill in his letter to Cairnes, was merely conservatism standing in the way of progress. This sentiment was expressed clearly in the concluding comments to the *Theory of Political Economy*, in a section titled "The Noxious Influence of Authority" Jevons wrote:

I think there is some fear of the too great influence of authoritative writers in Political Economy. I protest against deference for any man, whether John Stuart Mill, or Adam Smith, or Aristotle, being allowed to check inquiry. Our science has become far too much a stagnant one, in which opinions rather than experience and reason are appealed to ... Under these circumstances it is a positive service to break the monotonous repetition of current questionable doctrines, even at the risk of new error. (Jevons 1965: 276–7)

Looking back on the disagreement between Mill and Jevons from the perspective of 2015, it would seem that Jevons has been vindicated. Contemporary academic economics is a thoroughly mathematical enterprise, reflecting many features of Jevons' approach. And one finds few doubts within the professional mainstream as to the aptness of the mathematical analysis of economic behavior.[3] To most contemporary economists, Mill's views on the methodology of political economy are at best an interesting piece of intellectual history. They are irrelevant to the actual practice of economics.

Yet Mill's skepticism toward Jevons' approach to political economy may be more than a mere historical curiosity. Mill's position, especially when

---

[2] See Jevons (1958: 376, 554–5) and Peart (1995: Section III).
[3] One may, however, find misgivings about the development of highly abstract mathematical models without clear empirical application – see, for example, Colander (2005b) for reflections on the discipline's changing views on the importance of empirical content.

understood in the context of his broader philosophy of science, poses a fundamental and formidable challenge to those who, like Jevons, would wish to use the power and precision of mathematics to investigate social phenomena. In fact, the issues Mill discerned continue to vex mathematical economics to this day. To see that, however, we need to understand the basis of his misgivings.

As a committed empiricist, Mill held fast to the value of experience. The general principles of science were, in Mill's eyes, contrivances in its service and subject to its discipline. Although abstractions were necessary to formulate general principles, Mill insisted that one must not make the mistake of taking the *abstractions* to be the object of scientific inquiry, rather than the phenomena they were supposed to represent. If a scientist lost focus on the actual phenomena of interest in that manner, the concepts advanced in their service might well become detached from them. It would then become unclear what, if any, epistemic value the principles formulated using those concepts would have. As Mill explained,

If any one, having possessed himself of the laws of phenomena as recorded in words, whether delivered to him originally by others, or even found out by himself, is content from thenceforth to live among these formulae, to think exclusively of them, and of applying them to cases as they arise, without keeping up his acquaintance with the realities from which these laws were collected – not only will he continually fail in his practical efforts, because he will apply his formulae without duly considering whether, in this case and in that, other laws of nature do not modify or supersede them; but the formulae themselves will progressively lose their meaning to him, and he will cease at last even to be capable of recognising with certainty whether a case falls within the contemplation of his formula or not. (Mill 1974: Bk. IV, ch. vi, sec. 6, 711)

Since experience can always reveal new possibilities and complexities, ensuring that abstractions remained firmly rooted in it required constant vigilance. "We must not only be constantly thinking of the phenomena themselves," Mill wrote, "but we must be constantly studying them; making ourselves acquainted with the peculiarities of every case to which we attempt to apply our general principles" (Mill 1974: Bk. IV, ch. vi, sec. 6, 710). To the extent that experience revealed that one's principles had become untethered from the subject matter they were supposed to represent, those principles would have to be revised accordingly.

Significantly, this requirement implied that the scientist must take care to articulate scientific principles in language that was *capable* of expressing whatever kinds of complexities might arise in relation to the phenomena under investigation. The more complex the subject matter, and/or the less known about what kind of complexities lay behind one's observations, the more important it was to maintain flexibility. This was why Mill was particularly concerned about Jevons' use of mathematical notation. Mill saw mathematical language as capable only of expressing relationships between purely quantitative concepts. Mathematical symbols, he wrote (by which he meant symbols denoting entities that take on values, such as variables and parameters, not operational symbols such as "+" and "−") are "mere counters, without even the semblance of a meaning apart from the convention which is renewed each time they are employed" (Mill 1974: Bk. IV, ch. vi, sec. 6, 708). As a language of empirical science, mathematics was for Mill sufficiently sensitive only in cases of purely "mechanical" subject matter, which he defined as "those of which the investigations have already been reduced to the ascertainment of a relation between numbers" (Mill 1974: Bk. IV, ch. vi, sec. 6, 710).

In other words, mathematical language was capable of representing adequately only subject matter constituted by strictly quantitative objects and relations. Moreover, this was in Mill's view a *practical* requirement. Even if one somehow *knew* that, for example, wealth-generating activity was (as Jevons supposed) intrinsically mechanical and therefore in principle open to mathematical analysis, mathematical language would still not be appropriate unless scientists themselves could discern that mechanical nature in their observations. The observer herself needed to be able to perceive quanta in order to gather the data necessary to put hypothetical mathematical principles to use and/or to test them (Mill 1974: Bk. IV, ch. vi, sec. 2, 877–8).

The prime example of mechanical subject matter, according to Mill, was the physical universe. In his view, it was appropriate to express (for example) Newton's principle of universal gravitation in mathematical language because human beings are capable of discerning specific quantities corresponding to "mass," "force," and "radius" (or, more generally "distance") with sufficient precision that there could be no relevant qualitative differences among observations within each category. From the standpoint of Newtonian mechanics, it would not matter if one set of forces, masses, and distances occurred in France and another in England (or on the Moon or anywhere else in the universe), or if one set of observations were associated with a morally reprehensible purpose and another not. The only relevant difference between observations of the same type was their magnitude.

When confident that one was dealing with mechanical subject matter, it was not only appropriate but ideal to articulate general principles in mathematical language. Doing so enabled scientists to take full advantage of its purely quantitative nature. In particular, they could use their observations to derive and test precise empirical laws from those general principles. This, for example, is what Henry Cavendish did when estimating the value of the gravitational constant, G, in Newton's principle of universal gravitation, $F = Gm_1\, m_2/r^2$ (which expresses the force exerted by a body of mass m_1 on a body of mass m_2, and vice versa, at a distance of r) (Cavendish 1798). That calculation would have been impossible – or rather, its result would have been meaningless – if Cavendish had not been warranted in taking each successive observation of mass (or the distance between the two objects, or the degree of displacement of the objects due to gravity) as qualitatively identical to his preceding observations.

Mathematical language is thus extremely useful in investigating mechanical subject matter. But, Mill argued, it would be perilous to use it to investigate subject matter that was not mechanical. There were two possible causes of concern. First, in such cases mathematical principles might simply project an underlying mechanical structure onto the subject matter whether or not the latter was mechanical in nature. That is, mathematical language might generate a purely quantitative conceptual map of the subject matter it purported to outline, with no way of telling whether the outlines on the map corresponded to the subject's own contours. As a result, scientists would not be able to feel confident that data gathered according to the conceptual map accurately reflected the underlying subject matter. And because of that, it would be inappropriate to interpret any apparently precise empirical laws derived from that data as empirical laws applying to *the actual subject matter*.

Second, and still more worryingly, Mill argued that the commitment to mathematical language could actually prevent scientists from detecting when their conceptual map had become untethered from the subject matter under study. As will be recalled, Mill's prescribed defense against this kind of detachment was ongoing close contact between the scientist and the object of study. But if exploration of the subject matter itself developed only through the lens of mathematical language – which necessarily obscured any qualitative distinctions among the observations being made within each category – then the scientist would become blind to signs of that mismatch arising. As a result, the mismatch might persist indefinitely. Because of this danger, Mill warned that when the scientist was not certain of the mechanical character of the subject matter, the language of any general principles "should be so constructed that there shall be the greatest possible obstacles to a merely mechanical use of it" (Mill 1974: Bk. IV, ch. vi, sec. 6, 707).

The risk that mathematical principles might ascribe mechanical features to non-mechanical subject matter, and thus become untethered from the subject matter they were meant to represent, was precisely what concerned Mill about Jevons' approach to political economy, and indeed about mathematical social science generally. Human social activity was, for Mill, a paradigmatic example of a non-mechanical subject. It was a realm of almost unfathomable complexity, in two important ways. First, social phenomena were subject to innumerably more causes than physical phenomena. And second, crucially, the operations of those causes were inextricably intertwined.

Whatever affects, in an appreciable degree, any one element of the social state, affects through it all the other elements. The mode of production of all social phenomena is one great case of Intermixture of Laws. We can never either understand in theory or command in practice the condition of a society in any one respect, without taking into consideration its condition in all other respects. (Mill 1974: Bk. VI, ch. ix, sec. 2, 899)

Thus, although Mill believed it was possible to form reliable general principles (perhaps even mathematical ones) about certain aspects of human nature in isolation, the fact that human beings always and only observe behavior in the welter of society meant it was impossible to discern whether and to what extent those general principles operated empirically. If indeed one knew, as Jevons presumed one would, that the influence of economic factors on human behavior was cleanly separable from the influence of all other factors, *and* one possessed a reliable method for screening off those influences, then a precise empirical science of political economy might be possible. But for Mill, whether the social world was parsable in this way was an empirical question – and, moreover, a question that could only be addressed through continual immersion in the social world itself – not a simple statement of fact or a self-evidently valid postulate, as Jevons assumed.[4] To take Jevons' route was to invite a split between model and target that would be undetectable using mathematical methods alone. One could go blithely on with mathematical explorations – gathering data, estimating the precise functional forms and parameters of the principles, and testing them against new data – unaware that in point of fact one had ceased to be exploring the phenomenon of interest in any meaningful way.

Mill's challenge to Jevons may seem distant from the modern discipline of economics. Yet it finds strong echoes in the debate over the implications for economic methodology of the recent financial crisis. A central question in

[4] See Jevons (1958: 2, 8).

that debate has been whether the highly abstract mathematical modeling methods that dominated macroeconomics in the years leading up to the crisis – in particular, Dynamic Stochastic General Equilibrium (DSGE) modeling – actively prevented economists from seeing the gathering storm. Critics of DSGE have charged that these models became untethered from the phenomena they were meant to represent in precisely the manner Mill feared. In a 2010 review of DSGE modeling in the *Journal of Economic Perspectives*, for example, Ricardo Caballero wrote that the practice of DSGE modeling "has become so mesmerized with its own internal logic that it has begun to confuse the precision it has achieved about its own world with the precision that it has about the real one" (Caballero 2010: 85). The primary culprits in that confusion, critics charged, were the extreme simplifying assumptions necessary to ensure the tractability of DSGE models – in particular, (i) the representation of aggregate economic activity as being generated by a small number of representative agents; (ii) the expression of the macroeconomy as a linear (generally log-linear) system; and (iii) the assumption of efficient financial markets. These assumptions rendered the model incapable of taking into account many kinds of complexity that turned out to be crucial factors in the crisis – for example, the perverse incentive structures at play in the financial sector in the late 1990s and 2000s. In effect, the models became mere mathematical exercises – toy models that were not models of the late 1990s–2000s economy in any meaningful sense.

Critics have also been concerned with the manner in which the mismatch between DSGE models and the actual economy gave rise to certain analytical blind spots. In a 2009 *New York Times Magazine* piece cataloguing the failures of economic methodology in the lead-up to the crisis, Paul Krugman argued that DSGE models caused a kind of tunnel vision in which the central causes of the crisis lay outside the realm of consideration. Conceiving of the economy through the lens of the model essentially required the economist to

[turn] a blind eye to the limitations of human rationality that often lead to bubbles and busts; to the problems of institutions that run amok; to the imperfections of markets – especially financial markets – that can cause the economy's operating system to undergo sudden, unpredictable crashes; and to the dangers created when regulators don't believe in regulation. (Krugman 2009)

As Willem Buiter pointed out: these assumptions not only prevented questions about insolvency and illiquidity from being answered, "[t]hey did not allow such questions to be *asked*" (Buiter 2009, emphasis original).

The concern with excessive abstraction in mathematical economic modeling is not new or unique to the post-crisis era. Indeed, it has been a persistent concern since the apotheosis of abstract modeling in the 1950s and has occasionally risen to the surface of intra-disciplinary discussion. In 1969, Frank Hahn used his presidential address to the Econometric Society as an opportunity to bring it to the fore. Commenting on the achievements of economic theory in the previous two decades, he argued that while they were "impressive and in many ways beautiful," there was nonetheless "something scandalous in the spectacle of so many people refining the analyses of economic states which they give no reason to suppose will ever, or have ever, come about." He added: "It is probably also dangerous" (Hahn 1970: 1). Wassily Leontief made a similar point in his Presidential Address to the American Economic Association the following year (Leontief 1971), as did Milton Friedman twenty years later in an article reviewing the trends in economics during the previous hundred years (Friedman 1991). Asked to reflect on the views expressed in that article in a 1999 interview, Friedman summed up his position as follows: "What I would say is that economics has become increasingly an arcane branch of mathematics rather than dealing with real economic problems" (Snowdon and Vane 1999: 137).

Yet the particular circumstances that gave rise to the current debate over DSGE modeling have brought out the perils of excessive abstraction with special clarity. Unlike previous discussions, this debate was precipitated by perceptions of a specific failure of economic methodology, and one with severe social consequences. It has even led to public calls for accountability.

Perhaps the most dramatic calling-to-account occurred on July 20, 2010, in a special hearing of the Science and Technology Committee of the US House of Representatives convened to investigate the failures of DSGE models. In its introductory statement, the committee commented on the inability of DSGE models to perceive the signs of the coming crisis, noting that "[t]he implosion of the subprime mortgage market came as almost a total surprise to most mainstream economists." And it noted that this blindness had affected even those explicitly charged with remaining aware of such issues: "The chief steward of the US economy from 1987 to 2006 [Alan Greenspan] said he was in a state of 'shocked disbelief' because he had 'found a flaw in the model that [he] perceived [to be] the critical functioning structure that defines how the world works'" (US House Committee on Science and Technology 2010: 3). But the committee also asked a broader question: essentially, given that DSGE models were so widely lauded within the discipline and that they seemed to have failed so spectacularly on such an important issue, why should anyone have confidence in economists' ability to assess their own models? The committee's words are worth quoting at length:

[T]he insights of economics, a field that aspires to be a science and for which the National Science Foundation (NSF) is the major funding resource in the Federal Government, shape far more than what takes place on Wall Street. Economic analysis is used to inform virtually every aspect of domestic policy. If the generally accepted economic models inclined the Nation's policy makers to dismiss the notion that a crisis was possible, and then led them toward measures that may have been less than optimal in addressing it, it seems appropriate to ask why the economics profession cannot provide better policy guidance. (US House Committee on Science and Technology 2010: 3)

Within the discipline, discussions of what went wrong and what (if anything) to do about it have mainly been couched in terms of the "realism" of the accepted models[5] – and, in particular, the need to incorporate into macroeconomic models certain features of the economy that were excluded from DSGE models but are now recognized to have been centrally important. The basic message in those prescriptions has been that while abstraction is a necessary, and indeed desirable, feature of any model, it is important to ensure that the information lost in that process is not essential. As Ricardo Caballero put it: "It is fine to be as 'goofy' as needed to make things simpler along inessential dimensions, but it is important not to sound 'funny' on the specific issue that is to be addressed" (Caballero 2010: 90).

Considered in the light of Mill's more general concerns, however, such prescriptions may seem inadequate. The goal of preserving essential information about the subject matter certainly fits well with Mill's understanding of the requirements of valid induction. But the approach advocated by Caballero and others leaves open two crucial questions: first how to determine what is essential, and second how to ensure that the representation of those features remains faithful to the underlying phenomena.

This book begins the work of answering those two questions. It starts, in Part I, with a detailed analysis of standard economic modeling practice, and finds an important cause for concern. The internal logic of mathematical economic modeling, I argue, entails a commitment to the view that the

---

[5] In the context of economics, the "realism" of a model generally refers to the extent to which the model accurately captures features of its target. This is in contrast to the way in which the term "(scientific) realism" is used in philosophical discourse – roughly, to denote the position that "the entities, states and processes described by correct theories really do exist" (Hacking 1983: 21). To capture this distinction, Uskali Mäki has referred to the first sense of the term as "realisticness" rather than "realism" (see, e.g., Mäki 1992; 1994).

phenomena under investigation are mechanical in the manner that Mill suggested. Yet there is no *ex ante* reason to suppose that that is the case – and, crucially, any mathematical model will itself be *inherently* incapable of proving the situation either way. If we have independent reasons to believe that the phenomena under investigation are mechanical in Mill's sense, well and good: mathematical modeling will prove an apt mode of representation (though this does not imply, of course, that any *given* model will be a *good* representation of the subject matter). But if we have independent reasons to believe that there is more going on in the phenomena under investigation than a mathematical model can suggest – that is, that the phenomena in question are *not* in fact mechanical in the required sense – then mathematical modeling will prove misleading. The result will be precisely the kind of mismatch between the principles discerned by the scientist and the phenomena under investigation that Mill and others warned about. Moreover, as will be discussed, the empirical assessment of such models using econometric methods will not be sufficient to reveal that mismatch.

Part II discusses some trends in recent economic research – including the reliance on DSGE models in the run-up to the financial crisis – in light of the analysis presented in Part I, and Part III argues that new research in the interpretative aspects of economics may be necessary to address the problems identified in Parts I and II. These problems cannot themselves be addressed through reforms to mathematical methods. That would simply be to produce a more refined version of the wrong tool for the job, like sharpening one's knife when what is needed is a spoon. Rather than striving to improve the quality of mathematical models *given* the assumption that the subject matter under investigation is mechanical in Mill's sense and therefore susceptible of mathematical analysis, we need to ask a prior question, which is whether there is sufficient reason to feel confident that the subject matter under investigation is mechanical in the first place. That means scrutinizing the subject matter in the first instance in non-mathematical ways.

In brief, this book argues that we as scientists must remain sensitive to information about the phenomena in which we are interested that lies outside our models' conceptual maps. In the case of economics, what this requires is a new field dedicated to qualitative empirical methods that would play a similar role to that played by econometrics in the matter of quantitative empirical methods. In closing, I provide concrete examples of current research in this field, and suggest avenues for future work.

Part I

A constructive critique of common modeling practice

1 Models and modeling

Economics, today, is a model-based science. Choose an article at random from one of the discipline's top journals, and you will almost certainly find a mathematical model acting – explicitly or implicitly – as the engine of the analysis. This is not coincidental. Economists are trained to see the economy through the lens of models. In Ph.D. programs, macroeconomic theory is taught through various versions of the Solow Growth model, riffs on the Friedman or Modigliani consumption model, the IS-LM interpretation of Keynesian theory, real business cycle and New Keynesian theory expressed as Dynamic Stochastic General Equilibrium models, and so on. In microeconomic theory, students are presented with Samuelsonian models of demand and utility, the Arrow–Debreu general equilibrium model, Nashian game theoretic models of strategic interaction, Akerlof and Stiglitz models of informational effects, trade theory based on the Edgeworth box, and more. The day-to-day practice of economists equally reflects this focus. Doing economics today effectively means constructing, manipulating, solving, estimating, and/or assessing mathematical models.

In light of this, it may come as a surprise to many economists that there is considerable controversy in the fields of philosophy of science and economic methodology over what models are and how they work. Indeed, one renowned scholar describes the term "model" as "surely one of the most contested in all of philosophy of science" (Godfrey-Smith 2006: 725). Accordingly, we must specify carefully what we mean by "modeling" before turning to the analysis of current economic practice. Providing that specification is the aim of this chapter.

I begin by laying out an account of modeling widely accepted by economists. Essentially, that account holds that models are hypothesis generators whose merit is and ought to be judged solely on the basis of the performance of those hypotheses in empirical testing. Since this view of models is a simplified version of that proposed by Milton Friedman (1953) in his essay "The Methodology of Positive Economics," I call it "Friedman-lite." I do not mean to suggest that precisely this view is held by all economists, but it is regularly appealed to when questions of the validity of economic methodology arise, and hence makes a good basis for discussion. Despite its popularity, however, it suffers from two serious shortcomings. First, it is based on an invalidly narrow conception of the aims of economic modeling. Second, it rests on a flawed conception of the possibilities of empirical testing – one that requires an unattainable level of objectivity in empirical observation. Moreover, although Friedman's actual position in the 1953 essay was more nuanced than Friedman-lite, the additional nuance ultimately fails to overcome these inadequacies.

The rest of the chapter develops what I call a "pragmatic" alternative to the Friedmanite account. According to this alternative account, models are not mere hypothesis generators, but rather representations of the target subject matter used by the scientist to explore puzzles about that subject matter. Viewed in this light, the merits of the model cannot be assessed by establishing the truth or falsehood of hypotheses generated by it, but only by the success of the model in achieving the stated aims of the modeler, judged against the pragmatic norms of her discipline. In Section 1.2, I provide a basic sketch of the pragmatic account; Sections 1.3 and 1.4 fill out that sketch by explaining precisely how modelers use models to achieve their purposes. The key concept here is *representation*, explored in Section 1.3. Models *represent* their targets in a manner that allows the modeler to draw inferences about the latter by reasoning about the former. I discuss two views of the nature and functioning of representation, and consider what is required for successful representation, including in the kind of scientific modeling exercises developed by economists.

1.1 The fallacies of the instrumental-positive standard

Let us begin by considering the possibility that an extensive investigation of the nature of modeling is unnecessary for economists. After all, what real use does it have? Surely economists need only be expert in the *practice* of modeling; the philosophical underpinnings can be left to philosophers. And for practical purposes, a perfectly serviceable understanding of models is already available: roughly, that given by Milton Friedman in his 1953 essay "The Methodology of Positive Economics."

To address this objection, we must first be clear about Friedman's view. Put briefly, Friedman argued that what is important about economic models[1] is not their *content* but their *products* – namely, their empirically testable implications or "hypotheses." Models are mere tools for generating and articulating hypotheses, and are deemed to be "good" or "successful" to the extent (and only to the extent) that their hypotheses correspond to empirical reality. "Viewed as a body of substantive hypotheses," Friedman wrote,

theory is to be judged by its predictive power for the class of phenomena which it is intended to "explain." Only factual evidence can show whether it is "right" or "wrong" or, better, tentatively "accepted" as valid or "rejected." . . . the only relevant test of the *validity* of a hypothesis is comparison of its predictions with experience. (Friedman 1953: 8–9, emphasis original)[2]

An important corollary of this view is that there is little to talk about when it comes to the construction of models. Specifically, models need not be "realistic" in the sense of representing empirical reality faithfully. The only relevant discussion to be had about the correspondence of a model to the real world is with respect to the hypotheses it generates. The proof of the pudding, as the saying goes, is in the eating: we have no warrant to make *a priori* pronouncements about the merits of a model. The only proper standard is the *a posteriori* correspondence of its implications to empirical reality. We may identify this view as "instrumental-positive," and the standard for assessing the merits of a model it suggests, the "instrumental-positive standard."[3]

In the course of the essay, Friedman qualified his position in several important ways. For now, though, we may stick to considering the less qualified version. For one thing, its shortcomings, not surprisingly, are easier to see than those of the more nuanced version. For another, and more importantly, Friedman's qualifications actually reveal the difficulties in his position more than they address them. In the end, the shortcomings of the less nuanced position are the same as those that undo the more nuanced one.

For the sake of concreteness, let us consider the simple model of economic growth presented in Solow (1956). Solow's purpose in the paper was

---

[1] Friedman actually spoke of economic 'theory' rather than 'models,' and it is true that the distinction between the two is significant in the philosophy of science (see, e.g., Suppe 1989; Herfel *et al.* 1995; Bailer-Jones 1999). However, Friedman's usage does not reflect that distinction, and contemporary economists tend to use the terms interchangeably. For this reason, it seems acceptable to conflate the two concepts here.

[2] Friedman was not the first economist to make this argument. Jevons anticipated him by nearly eighty years, writing in the first edition of his *Principles of Science* that "*[a]greement with fact is the one sole and sufficient test of a true hypothesis*" (Jevons 1958: 138, emphasis original). Economists today, however, generally look to Friedman's articulation.

[3] It is "instrumental" in the sense that the model is viewed merely as an instrument for generating hypotheses. It is "positive" in the sense that it is only the model's correspondence with empirical reality that is deemed relevant to assessing its merits.

to counter the Harrod–Domar depiction of the economy as operating on a knife-edge where any deviation of critical parameters from the level required to equilibrate the "natural" and "warranted" rates of growth would lead to ever-increasing unemployment or inflation.[4] In the paper, Solow demonstrates, mathematically, that the knife-edge result is an artifact of Harrod and Domar's use of a particular production function – specifically, the fixed proportions production function of the form $Y = \min\{K/a, L/b\}$. Using alternative functional forms, Solow demonstrates that it is possible for an economy to exhibit stabilizing dynamics, with out-of-equilibrium input levels gradually adjusting toward a steady state equilibrium in the long run.

For Solow, as for Harrod and Domar, long-run steady state equilibrium occurs when the warranted growth rate equals the natural growth rate, which will occur when both the capital stock and labor stock are growing at that long-run growth rate – or, put another way, the growth rate of the capital-labor ratio will be stable at zero.

Solow represents this mathematically as follows. He begins with the following expression of the time path of the capital stock:

$$\dot{K} = sF(K, L_0 e^{nt}) \tag{1.1}$$

where K is the capital stock, $\dot{K}$ the time derivative of K, L_0 the initial labor stock, n a population growth parameter, s the fraction of output saved, and $F(K, L)$ a production function. If we define r as the capital-labor ratio, then $K = rL = rL_0 e^{nt}$. Taking the time derivative gives $\dot{K} = \dot{r}L_0 e^{nt} + nrL_0 e^{nt}$. Substituting this into expression (1.1) gives

$$\dot{r}L_0 e^{nt} + nrL_0 e^{nt} = sF(K, L_0 e^{nt}) \tag{1.2}$$

Because, by Solow's assumption, F exhibits constant returns to scale, we can divide both arguments by $L_0 e^{nt}$ and multiply F by the same factor. A bit of algebra produces the canonical statement:

$$\dot{r} = sF(r, 1) - nr \tag{1.3}$$

which implies the steady state condition

[4] The Harrod–Domar model refers to the system articulated in Harrod (1939) and Domar (1946). The "natural" rate of growth is "the maximum rate of growth allowed by the increase of population, accumulation of capital, technological improvement and the work/leisure preference schedule, supposing that there is always full employment in some sense" (Harrod 1939: 30). The "warranted" rate of growth is defined as "that rate of growth which, if it occurs, will leave all parties satisfied that they have produced neither more nor less than the right amount" (Harrod 1939: 16).

$$sF(r^*, 1) = nr^* \tag{1.4}$$

For a wide class of constant returns-to-scale production functions, statement (1.3) gives the result that at least one stable r^* exists – stable in the sense that out-of-equilibrium values of r adjust over time toward r^*.

Under the instrumental-positive standard, the Solow model can be deemed successful if, and only if, its implications (i.e. hypotheses) coincide to a sufficient degree with empirical reality. But, as we shall see, using the instrumental-positive standard to assess this model does not result in a clear evaluation of its merits. Rather, it reveals fundamental problems with the instrumental-positive standard itself.

Problem 1: Unwarranted restriction of the aims of modeling

The first and most obvious problem with using the instrumental-positive standard to assess the Solow model is that the version of the model reviewed above (that of the 1956 paper) does not clearly issue in empirically testable hypotheses. Nor is it meant to do so. The purpose of the paper is to demonstrate that it is possible to construct a formal version of the economy along Harrod–Domar lines that does not exhibit the knife-edge character-istics of the Harrod–Domar model (Solow 1956: 91). Solow's model, that is to say, is meant to tell us something about the Harrod–Domar model of the economy, not the economy itself, and Solow explicitly states this. As such, it is unclear how the instrumental-positive standard could even apply to Solow's model, let alone what its application would reveal.

In fact, the non-applicability of the instrumental-positive standard is com-mon to all "theoretical" models – that is, those that are not articulated in an immediately testable form, as opposed to "empirical models" which *are* imme-diately testable. As we shall see, the line between these two categories is quite fuzzy, but it is helpful to make the distinction if only because it is part of the standard vocabulary of economists. It may be objected that the "non-testability" of theoretical models such as the 1956 version of the Solow model is not problematic because they are not meant to be tested empirically. This is a reasonable claim (at least *prima facie*), and one that will be familiar to econo-mists with respect to the nature and uses of theoretical models. However, we should notice that it immediately calls into question the adequacy of the instrumental-positive standard in that it implies that a model can be "success-ful" even if it cannot be tested, which implies, in turn, that accurate prediction/retrodiction is not the only legitimate goal of an economic model.

One could object that the non-testability of the Solow (1956) model is acceptable only provisionally, contingent upon its being used as a source of testable hypotheses. This is essentially the position articulated by Paul Samuelson in *Foundations of Economic Analysis*, in which he argues that a model or theory must be testable only *in principle* in order to be meaningful.[5] But this elaboration does not save the instrumental-positive standard for two reasons. First, it would seem to require a much higher standard for the validity of theoretical work than currently exists in economics. In order for a theoretical model to be deemed valid, its author would need to argue explicitly for its in-principle refutability. Even if the model's implications were later found not to be refutable, current acceptance of its validity would depend upon its having been accepted as in-principle refutable given the available knowledge. In practice, however, we find that theoretical models can be deemed acceptable (judging, for example, by their publication in reputable journals) even when no explicit case is made for their testability, as in Solow (1956). It is possible that this is because the standard is actually looser than its formal expression would suggest, along the lines of "innocent until proven guilty": a theoretical model is given the benefit of the doubt as long as it is not clear that its implications *cannot possibly* be refuted. But even in such a case, there would have to be some other reason to value the model in spite of its potential violation of the central requirement of refutability.

All this points to a more straightforward explanation for the ostensible validity of the Solow (1956) model. In actual practice, models are used for many purposes, of which prediction/retrodiction is only one.[6] As such, a model may be deemed not only valid but useful and successful even if its primary purpose is not empirical testing and even if it is not immediately clear whether or not its implications are testable in principle. Theoretical models are regularly used as heuristic devices, as a means of orienting ourselves in relation to a given subject. They can give us a shared framework and conceptual vocabulary for thinking and talking about the object of inquiry. And while it is true that economists do generally seek to generate versions of models that are testable, it is not the case that the original model will necessarily be quarantined subject to the outcome of those tests. The

---

[5] Samuelson defined a meaningful theorem as "a hypothesis about empirical data which could conceivably be refuted, if only under ideal conditions" (Samuelson 1947: 4). Terence Hutchison had articulated essentially the same sentiment several years earlier in *The Significance and Basic Postulates of Economic Theory*, writing that "if the finished propositions of a science ... including Economics, are to have any empirical content ... then these propositions must *conceivably* be capable of empirical testing *or be reducible to such propositions* by logical or mathematical deduction" (Hutchison 1938: 9).

[6] See, e.g., Morgan (2008).

literature on growth accounting and convergence attests to this. Both of these were explicit attempts to put the Solow (1956) model to empirical use. Growth accounting, however, was essentially a re-description of data according to the framework of the Solow model rather than a test of it (see, e.g., Solow 1957). It *applied* the model despite its not having been tested or even having been shown to be refutable. The work on convergence was a more explicit attempt to "test" the model which ultimately led to the conclusion that there was little evidence to support it (see Baumol 1986; DeLong 1987). Yet the basic Solow (1956) model is still an integral part of the graduate economics curriculum. Under the instrumental-positive standard, this ought simply to be considered a mistake. And, of course, one is free to take that view. What is important for our purposes, however, is that economics as a discipline does *not* take that view – neither with respect to the Solow model nor with respect to theoretical models more generally. And this suggests that the instrumental-positive standard does not adequately reflect the actual standards of economic practice.

Problem 2: Practical impossibility of applying the standard

The unwarranted restriction of the aims of modeling implied by the instrumental-positive standard thus looks like a significant problem. Still, one could object that although it may *appear* that theoretical models are being given a pass with respect to the instrumental-positive standard, this is never actually the case. Under such an objection, any theoretical model judged (either currently or retrospectively) to be either irrefutable or refuted *must* be considered invalid. And to the extent that some models seem to skirt this demand, their apparent acceptance must be understood as provisional and probationary. Moreover, any seeming merits of the model beyond its predictive/retrodictive success will become irrelevant if it is refuted or found to be irrefutable.

But this position is also unsustainable, and for reasons that must ultimately sound the death knell for the claim that economics operates under the instrumental-positive standard. The standard fails because it is impossible to apply, at least without additional qualifications. This is an implication of the so-called Duhem–Quine thesis, named after the French physicist and philosopher Pierre Duhem and the American philosopher Willard Quine. The central tenet of this thesis is that empirical tests of scientific hypotheses are always *underdetermined* in the sense that they are never tests of a single, isolated hypothesis, but rather joint tests of that hypothesis along with "the whole theoretical scaffolding" used by the scientist in constructing the hypothesis in question (Duhem 1954: 185). Consequently, one can never interpret the results of a hypothesis test simply as an assessment of the predictive/retrodictive success of the hypothesis ostensibly being tested. As Duhem explains, the only thing that a hypothesis rejection teaches us is that "among the propositions used to predict the phenomenon and to establish whether it would be produced, there is at least one error; but where this error lies is just what it [the experiment] does not tell us" (Duhem 1954: 185).

Underdetermination is a serious problem from the point of view of the instrumental-positive standard, as it implies that individual hypotheses are irrefutable. If every hypothesis test is actually a joint test of multiple hypotheses, a rejection presents the scientist not with a definitive judgment but with a choice: interpret the rejection as a rejection of the hypothesis ostensibly in question, or cling to the hypothesis and blame any number of auxiliary hypotheses for the failure. Of course, in some cases auxiliary hypotheses may legitimately help to justify the rejection. For example, a rejection of the hypothesis of a zero-valued Ordinary Least Squares coefficient could well result from an omitted variable or data gathering mistakes. The problem is that there is no definitive standard for distinguishing between legitimate questioning of auxiliary hypotheses and the dogmatic commitment to a favored hypothesis.[7]

A further, and related, problem is that our observation of empirical "facts" is always done from within the perspective of the theory that we are ostensibly testing. That is, observation is always *theory-laden*. This idea lies at the heart of Thomas Kuhn's conception of the scientific "paradigm," introduced in his influential 1962 work *The Structure of Scientific Revolutions*. As Kuhn explains, a "paradigm" comprises the set of shared beliefs and values around which a scientific community is organized and by which it is distinguished. Put another way, it comprises answers to questions such as: "What are the fundamental entities of which the universe is composed? How do these interact with each other and with the senses? What questions may legitimately be asked about such entities and what techniques employed in seeking solutions?" (Kuhn 1996: 4–5). Kuhn argues that answers to such questions are not *targets* of scientific inquiry, but rather the *prerequisites* for conducting it. "Effective research scarcely begins," he writes, "before a scientific

---

[7] Karl Popper and Imre Lakatos attempted to provide such standards – Popper through the requirement of a critical rationalist attitude (Popper 1968: Chapters 5, 10) and later through the application of the "rationality principle" and "situational analysis" (Popper 1994), and Lakatos through the concept of the "progressive scientific research programme" (Lakatos 1978). See Hands (2001: Chapter 7) and Hacking (1983: 112–28) for a discussion of some of the difficulties with these attempts.

community thinks it has acquired firm answers" to these kinds of questions (Kuhn 1996: 4). One must know the answers to these questions before engaging in science because they establish what doing science *means*. The prospective scientist, that is, must first learn how to see the world *as a scientist* – to recognize which aspects of experience correspond to which scientific concepts and problem types, and to learn how to bring those problem types to an acceptable conclusion (Kuhn 1996: 109, 190–4).

One major implication of this is that scientific activity is (always and only) a means of organizing our perceptions of the world according to a particular world view, and not (ever) a means of ascertaining "truth" or "falsity." Although it is certainly the case that scientific activity involves "empirical testing" of various sorts – i.e. comparisons of theoretical and empirical statements – it is wrong to interpret these as moments of verification or falsification of theory relative to objective fact. This is because what would be taken as objective facts in such tests are in reality simply statements whose meanings derive entirely from the world view within which a test was conceived (Kuhn 1996: 80). For example, Gross Domestic Product time series data from the Bureau of Economic Analysis are not a list of facts about the world, because "Gross Domestic Product (GDP)" is a concept of the scientific paradigm of contemporary economics rather than a natural feature of the world. The GDP data cannot, therefore, be used to test whether or not a real business cycle model, for example, is "true," but only to test whether or not it has succeeded in addressing a puzzle – say, whether or not the government spending multiplier is greater than 1 – from within the perspective of the given paradigm. Indeed, on Kuhn's account, there is no such thing as answering this question objectively. It is a question "for whose very existence the validity of the paradigm must be assumed" (Kuhn 1996: 80). Theory-ladenness is thus one cause of underdetermination which it is impossible to avoid. While it may be possible in principle to suppress *some* auxiliary hypotheses, one cannot undertake empirical observation without imposing onto empirical reality some theory of its constitution.

One could object that the Duhem–Quine thesis and the problem of theory-ladenness are fatal only for a very strict and narrow version of the instrumental-positive standard and that actual economic practice cleaves to a more sophisticated position. Indeed, Friedman himself acknowledged the force of these problems in his 1953 essay. In particular, he added several caveats to the Friedman-lite position. A single case of rejection, he suggested, is not (and apparently *ought* not to be) enough to dismiss a hypothesis. A hypothesis "is rejected if its predictions are contradicted ('frequently' or more often than predictions from an alternative hypothesis)" (Friedman 1953: 9). This implies that there is some reason to be wary of regarding individual economic hypothesis tests as crucial tests, and indeed Friedman argued that economic data are not as clean as those produced by the laboratory experiments of the natural sciences. The kind of evidence afforded to economists, namely that "cast up by experience" as opposed to that of "contrived experiments," is "difficult to interpret," "frequently complex," and "always indirect and incomplete." As such, its collection is "often arduous" and its interpretation "requires subtle analysis and involved chains of reasoning." Still, Friedman also claimed that this difficulty "does not hinder the adequate testing of hypotheses." Rather, it only "renders the weeding-out of unsuccessful hypotheses slow and difficult" (Friedman 1953: 9–10). This conclusion does not sit well, however, with his acknowledgement of the more radical problem of the inherent theory-ladenness of data. "A theory is the way we perceive 'facts'," he wrote, "and we cannot perceive 'facts' without a theory" (Friedman 1953: 34). But this observation was made in connection with a different issue – his assertion that the apparent complexity of economic phenomena is really just a case of our not yet having an adequate theory to explain it – and Friedman did not seem to recognize its significance for the interpretation and significance of empirical testing of hypotheses.

Friedman also discussed the importance of pragmatic standards to supplement the ostensibly objective standards of hypothesis testing. To begin with, the discussion in the paragraph above about the messiness of economic data implicitly invokes the need for pragmatic standards, if only to judge when a rejection of a hypothesis in a given test is not sufficient to reject the hypothesis *tout court*. Next, he notes that in cases where multiple hypotheses seem to agree with the data, we must turn to other standards to choose between them.

The choice among alternative hypotheses equally consistent with the available evidence must to some extent be arbitrary, though there is general agreement that relevant considerations are suggested by the criteria "simplicity" and "fruitfulness," themselves notions that defy completely objective specification. (Friedman 1953: 10)

What is interesting for our purposes about these invocations of pragmatic assessment standards is that Friedman presents them as essentially auxiliary to the ostensibly objective standards of hypothesis testing. They are training wheels that, at least in principle, can be progressively done away with over time as continued testing weeds out competing hypotheses, models, and theories on the sole basis of their correspondence with empirical fact. This position is a necessary consequence of Friedman's view of economics as inherently a positive science to be judged solely on the correspondence of its hypotheses to empirical reality. "Its task," he wrote,

is to provide a system of generalizations that can be used to make correct predictions about the consequences of any change in circumstances. Its performance is to be judged by the precision, scope, and conformity with experience of the predictions it yields. (Friedman 1953: 4)

In Friedman's vision, there is no independent role for pragmatic standards to determine, for example, the extent to which the instrumental-positive goal of economics should be weighed against other goals or constraints. Presumably, this is why Friedman did not deem it necessary to provide a separate account of the pragmatic standards involved in deciding when a rejected hypothesis might nonetheless be retained.

Arguably, both Friedman's invalidly narrow conception of the aims of economic modeling and his dubious account of the possibilities of empirical testing stem from an inadequate engagement with the actual practice of economic modeling. Economic models are not only used for generating hypotheses subject to empirical testing, they are also a source of conjectures meant to be assessed in a less strict manner and the basis of thought experiments. And this does not inherently disqualify these models. On the contrary, many well-regarded and influential models fit this description. Accordingly, there must be some basis on which such models are judged successful or not, and the logic of assessment proposed by Friedman is arguably inadequate to the task. Friedman himself implicitly accepted the need for pragmatic rather than objective standards as a means of assessing the output of modeling exercises, though he did not attempt to specify them. Developing an account of modeling that makes room for that specification is our next task.

1.2   Introducing the pragmatic account

Our goal is to develop an account of model-based scientific practice that resembles current norms more closely than Friedman-lite, particularly in respect of the deployment of pragmatic standards of model assessment. We can begin with the basic structure of model-based science. Like Peter Godfrey-Smith (2006) and Michael Weisberg (2007a), I take the core of model-based science to be its indirect method of exploring the target subject matter: the modeling scientist seeks to illuminate aspects of the target not by exploring it directly, but by deliberately exploring a distinct entity – the model. In the course of this exploration, the model represents the target. Just what this representation involves is a contested issue and will be explored in detail below. For present purposes, we can simply say that the model represents the target in some as yet unspecified way. This yields the following initial articulation of the basic framework of the pragmatic account:

M (the model) represents X (the target)

Yet this is not a complete description of modeling practice. As a practical tool, the model is used *by* someone *for* some purpose. Solow (1956), for example, indicates that he will use his model to probe some of the implications of the Harrod–Domar model:[8]

> The characteristic and powerful conclusion of the Harrod–Domar line of thought is that even for the long run the economic system is at best balanced on a knife-edge of equilibrium growth. Were the magnitudes of the key parameters – the savings ratio, the capital-output ratio, the rate of increase of the labor force – to slip ever so slightly from dead center, the consequence would be either growing unemployment or prolonged inflation ...
>
> But this fundamental opposition of warranted and natural rates turns out in the end to flow from the crucial assumption that production takes place under conditions of fixed proportions. There is no possibility of substituting labor for capital in production ...
>
> The bulk of this paper is devoted to a model of long-run growth which accepts all the Harrod–Domar assumptions except that of fixed proportions. Instead I suppose that the single composite commodity is produced by labor and capital under the standard neoclassical conditions. The adaptation of the system to an exogenously given rate of increase of the labor force is worked out in some detail, to see if the Harrod instability appears. (Solow 1956: 65–6)

The recognition of the modeler and his or her intentions gives the following augmented version of the basic framework, suggested by Giere (2004):

[1] S (the scientist) uses M to represent X for purposes P

Note that we are not assuming that the purpose of the modeling exercise must be to generate empirically testable hypotheses about X.

To this augmented framework, we need to append one additional element: the norms by which one may judge the success of S in achieving the intended purpose. This is essential because these norms not only guide the scientist in the construction and manipulation of the model, but also determine the epistemic status of the model (i.e. whether it is found to produce knowledge

---

[8] See Harrod (1939) and Domar (1946) for the two independent statements of the basic model.

in the appropriate way). Holding fast to the pragmatic perspective, we place the source of these standards within the practice itself, i.e. as (intersubjectively) constructed by the relevant scientific community. The full basic framework is then as follows:[9]

[2] S uses M to represent X for purposes P
    The success of S in accomplishing P is judged against norms N

The framework articulated in statement [2] provides a very basic map of the territory of modeling practice. In particular, it highlights the centrality of representation and its complex relationship to the other elements of the modeling process. Representation is the link between model and target in the sense that it is by virtue of its representing the target in some way that the model helps to illuminate the target. And it is also the link between the model, the scientist's purposes, and the norms of the scientific community – in the sense that the latter two factors inform and constrain what is demanded of the representational relationship between model and target. I will follow Michael Weisberg (2007b: 648–9) in referring to this conception of the goals of a modeling exercise as the "representational ideal" of that exercise.

To see what must be added to the basic framework to give a more complete picture, we may consider what questions we would like an account of modeling to be able to answer. Essentially, while the basic framework gives the "what" of model-based science, a more complete account will add the "how" and the "why." As the basic framework suggests, the core of model-based science is the representational capacity of the model, which is deployed to serve the modeler's purpose with the norms of the discipline in mind. But until we have defined more clearly how representation works, we shall not be able to assess the merits of specific modeling exercises. We need more information on three fronts. First, with respect to the norms of the discipline, we need to know how success is defined and how it will be assessed. Next, with respect to the scientist's purposes, we need to know whether these purposes comport with the discipline's norms and whether the particular modeling strategy chosen is up to the task. Finally, we need to understand more about the capabilities of any given model. For example, with respect to the Solow model, we know that the author intends the model to illuminate aspects of the Harrod–Domar model. The question is, by virtue of what is this possible and how we know when it has been successful.

---

[9] This depiction is similar to that proposed by Uskali Mäki (2009a) in his account of models as isolations and surrogate systems.

The answers to these questions will lead us toward a more plausible and comprehensive account of modeling. We shall find that the practice of modeling is constrained in distinct but interrelated ways by the norms of the scientist's discipline and the representational capabilities of the model. While disciplinary norms indicate the tasks that modeling must fulfill in order to be considered knowledge-generating, we must look carefully into the nuts and bolts of the modeling process to ascertain what is necessary for the model to be able to represent the target in a manner that conforms to disciplinary norms. We can begin by exploring the mechanics of representation.

1.3   A closer look at representation

When we say that a scientific model *represents* its target, what do we mean? The precise answer to this question will vary from model to model, but we can say something general about how representation works in model-based science simply by virtue of what a model is and how the scientist uses it. Loosely speaking, representation is the special kind of relation between model and target that transforms the model from an otherwise unrelated object into a tool with the potential to illuminate the target. Tightening this characterization, however, is no simple matter.

We may deal with one source of confusion right away. In common usage, as well as in the day-to-day practice of science, "representation" refers to at least four distinct things. First is the *intension* of representation, that is, how we specify the concept, or the set of criteria through which we decide that something is a representation. Second is the *extension* of representation, that is, all instantiations of the intension; a single element of that set may be referred to as *an* extension, or "a representation." For example, to the extent that the Solow model represents some aspects of a real economy, it is an element of the extension of representation, or "an extension of representation," or "a representation." And it belongs to this set by virtue of its possessing the characteristics specified by the intension of representation. Next, representation in each of these senses may be used either as a success term or as a neutral one. That is, "representation" may refer to something that succeeds at doing what representations are supposed to do, or it may refer to something that attempts to do what representations do, even if it is not successful.

These four senses of "representation" are depicted in Figure 1.1 below. (Note that the contents of each quadrant are not definitions, but simply clarifications.)

	Success Term	Neutral Term
Intension	A two-place relation $R_s(A,B)$	A two-place relation $R_n(A,B)$
Extension	All entities A standing in relation $R_s(A,B)$ with some B	All entities A standing in relation $R_n(A,B)$ with some B

Figure 1.1   The four senses of "representation"

R_s, here, is a relation of successful representation and R_n what Gabriele Contessa (2007) refers to as representation *simpliciter* – a representational relation that may or may not succeed at whatever it is that representations are supposed to do. If we take representation to be inherently a success term, then R_s and R_n are identical. If we do not, then the extension of R_s (i.e. all As that stand in relation R_s to some B) will be a subset of the extension of R_n.

The account of representation we will develop focuses on the upper half of the figure: the intension of representation, that is, the specification of the criteria that must be met in order for something to be deemed a representation. We will begin by exploring representation in a neutral sense, and then consider what is required for successful representation, which is of course the scientist's ultimate goal. Regarding distinctions between intension and extension, although we will use the term "representation" for both, extensions will generally be preceded by a definite or indefinite article or will be in the plural.

Let us begin by examining the function of representation in model-based science. The purpose of model-based science is to employ models in a manner that results in the illumination of the relevant targets. In practice, this involves reasoning about a model and drawing inferences about the target from this reasoning. Along these lines, following Mauricio Suárez's "inferential" account of representation (Suárez 2004), we can offer a preliminary characterization of representation as follows:

[Rep. 1]   A model represents its target only if it allows competent and informed agents to draw specific inferences regarding the target.[10]

---

[10] This is one of the two necessary conditions for representation suggested by Suárez. The second is that the "representational force" of the model "points toward" the target. Suárez includes this qualification to make clear which object is the representation and which is the target. For purposes of brevity, I simply assume that the direction of representation is not in question.

To fix terms, we may refer to the practice of drawing inferences about a target in this manner – i.e. by reasoning directly not about the target but about a surrogate – as "surrogative reasoning."[11]

[Rep. 1] is a basic version of a "functional account" of representation – i.e. an account that tells us only what representations *do*, and deliberately makes no claim about the exact relation that a model must have to its target in order for it to be a representation even in the neutral sense.[12] If we take functional accounts to characterize representation adequately, then we are suggesting that there is nothing more to be said about representation beyond what it does. An alternative is to adopt a "thicker" account of representation, according to which models must possess specific features in order to fulfill their functions. On such accounts, an adequate characterization of representation must specify not only what representations do, but also how they do it. Before discussing such thicker accounts, however, we will consider functional accounts on their own, to see why a thicker account may be desirable.

Consider again the model of economic growth presented in Solow (1956). As discussed above, Solow uses the following statement to represent the time path of the capital stock:

$$\dot{K} = sF(K, L_0 e^{nt}) \tag{1.1}$$

where K is the capital stock, $\dot{K}$ the time derivative of K, L_0 the initial labor stock, n a population growth parameter, s the fraction of output saved, and $F(K, L)$ a production function.

If we say that statement (1.1) *represents* some aspect of the economy, what are we saying? According to [Rep. 1], we are saying only that a competent and informed agent – for example, a macroeconomist – can use it to draw specific inferences about some aspect of the economy. But this, on its own, is not enough. Models are used for a specific purpose, and their merits are assessed according to the norms of the relevant scientific community. In light of this, an adequate account of representation needs to specify that the *right kinds* of inferences can be drawn – i.e. the kinds of inferences that are necessary for the scientist to achieve the intended purposes. Further, in order for the

---

[11] See Swoyer (1981) for a detailed and technical (set-theoretic) account of surrogative reasoning. For a less technical account, see, e.g., Mäki (2009a).

[12] If these latter issues are left unaddressed because the theorist claims that they are outside the scope of representation – i.e. that representation is a purely functional concept and that there is no deeper characteristic that is the source of "representationality" – then the account would be *deflationary*. If the issues are left aside because, although there may be such deeper characteristics, they are being left aside either for the sake of simplicity or, perhaps, because the characteristics are epistemically inaccessible to us, then the account would be *minimalist*.

representation to be successful, it must be the case that such inferences can be drawn in a manner consonant with the relevant norms of assessment. Armed only with [Rep. 1], it remains unclear what would make an inference even potentially successful, let alone actually successful.[13] We therefore need answers to two further questions. (1) What properties must a model possess in order to be a representation in the neutral sense? (2) What properties must a model possess in order to be a successful representation?

Contessa (2007) proposes an answer to the first question in his "interpretive account" of representation. Essentially, he argues that what makes a model a potential representation is a unique, one-to-one correspondence between the objects and relations of the model, on the one hand, and those of the target, on the other. Formally, we can express this by saying that the functions that map from objects and relations of the model to objects and relations of the target are *bijective* (or *one-to-one* and *onto* – i.e., if A is the relevant set of elements and relations in the model and B the set of relevant elements and relations in the target, then the mapping $f: A \rightarrow B$ has the property that $\forall a, a' \in A$, if $f(a) = f(a')$ then $a = a'$ and if $a = a'$ then $f(a) = f(a')$).

The basic idea of the interpretive account is that a model is a representation if and only if everything that happens in the model has one and only one equivalent in the target. With such clear correspondence, the model becomes a tool for navigating the target in the same way that a subway map is a tool for navigating an actual subway system. Every dot on the map corresponds to a subway stop, and the relations between dots on the map correspond to relations between the corresponding subway stops. On a New York subway map, there will be dots corresponding to the stations at Union Square, Times Square, and Rockefeller Center, and because a single line connects Union Square and Times Square I know that I can get there on one train whereas the fact that no single line connects Union Square and Rockefeller Center means that I will have to change trains to make that trip.

This is an improvement over Suárez's inferential account in that it allows us to say not only *that* a representation allows surrogative reasoning, but also *why* it does so. As Contessa points out, Suárez's account takes the inferential capacity of a representation to be simply "a brute fact, which has no deeper explanation," thereby making "the performance of valid surrogative

---

[13] It might be argued that requiring "competent and informed" agents to be the ones making the inferences takes care of this problem, but at best it simply kicks it down the road – we need to understand what kind of competence and information these agents possess that sets them apart as potentially successful wielders of representations.

inferences an activity as mysterious and unfathomable as soothsaying or divination" (Contessa 2007: 61). Contessa's interpretive account, on the other hand, tells us additionally what a scientist takes herself to be doing when she is using a representation to draw inferences about a target: namely, utilizing the bijective correspondence between model and target as the central bridging mechanism of surrogative reasoning. And, indeed, this comports with what we find in the actual practice of scientific modeling. Generally, by introducing a model, the scientist will make clear which target objects and relations are meant to be represented by the objects and relations in the model, and will explicitly use these correspondences in drawing inferences from model to target.

For example, in the following passage from Solow (1956) the author clarifies exactly how various objects in his model are meant to correspond to actual economic phenomena:

There is only one commodity, output as a whole, whose rate of production is designated $Y(t)$. Thus we can speak unambiguously of the community's real income. Part of each instant's output is consumed and the rest is saved and invested. The fraction of output saved is a constant s, so that the rate of saving is $sY(t)$. The community's stock of capital $K(t)$ takes the form of an accumulation of the composite commodity. Net investment is then just the rate of increase of this capital stock dK/dt or $\dot{K}$, so we have the basic identity at every instant of time:

(1) $\dot{K} = sY.$

Output is produced with the help of two factors of production, capital and labor, whose rate of input is $L(t)$. Technological possibilities are represented by a production function:

(2) $Y = F(K,L).$
       (Solow 1956: 66)

In doing this, Solow implicitly sketches the path that his surrogative reasoning will follow. Every element of the target that is of direct interest to Solow has a *doppelgänger* in the model. For example: $Y(t)$ is the rate of production of an output commodity, L is the amount of labor inputted into the production of Y, and so on.

But the interpretive account misses something important. To see this, we need to delve a bit deeper into the distinction between neutral and successful representations. First, some vocabulary. As noted above, the interpretive account concerns representation used in a neutral sense. Any representation that fulfills the conditions specified by this account – i.e., roughly, bijective correspondence – Contessa calls an *epistemic representation*.[14] Such a representation is taken by the scientist to represent the target in the sense that its bijective correspondence with the target gives a clear guide for how inferences in the model lead to inferences about the target. Contessa calls such an inference a *valid* inference. Crucially, a valid inference about the target need not be correct for the model to be an epistemic representation in Contessa's sense. Of course, it *might* be, and, if it is, then it is a *sound* inference (in addition to being valid). An epistemic representation that leads to at least some sound inferences about the target is a *partially faithful* representation. One whose inferences are *all* sound is a *completely faithful* representation. Faithfulness of representation varies along a continuum, and significantly, the continuum includes the extreme point where *none* of the inferences about the target is sound.

The fact that a model that enables *no* sound inferences can still be deemed a representation shows how thin the concept of representation is in the interpretive account. In fact, all that is required for representation seems to be that the candidate model and target share the same number of objects and relations and that the modeler assert a bijective correspondence between them. For example, Contessa suggests that Rutherford's model of the atom could also be a valid representation of a hockey puck moving over a frozen lake.

Suppose that, according to the new interpretation, the electron in the model denotes the puck and the nucleus denotes the surface of the ice. According to the general interpretation, it would then be possible to infer from the model that, say, the puck is negatively charged and the ice is positively charged, that the puck orbits around the ice surface in circular orbits, etc. If the account of scientific representation I propose is correct, it would seem that, under these circumstances, the Rutherford model of the atom is an epistemic representation of the system in question. (Contessa 2007: 62–3)

There is nothing invalid about this usage of Rutherford's model, according to the interpretive account. Yet equally, the interpretive account does not give us any grounds for judging whether or not we might *want* to use Rutherford's model in this way. Granted that Rutherford's model offers a partially faithful representation of a hockey puck moving over a frozen lake, but exactly what makes the model partially faithful is left unexplored, and even seems to have no relation to the concept of representation as such. In the end, even Contessa seems to have a difficult time imagining what is left of the concept

---

[14] This is to differentiate it from something like a corporate logo, which, in common parlance, is understood to be a representation, but does not produce knowledge in the way that surrogative reasoning is supposed to.

of representation if it is as thin as this. In arguing that the bare fact of a model's being able to enable surrogative reasoning is a sufficient condition for its being a representation, he adds an extra feature that thickens the concept enough to nudge it along the continuum toward faithful representation. "For example," he writes,

suppose that a scientist proposes a *bona fide* model of a certain system that, upon investigation, turns out to misrepresent every aspect of the system. Even if, gradually, we might discover that all the inferences that are valid according to its standard interpretation are unsound, that model still seems to be an epistemic representation of the system, though an entirely unfaithful one. (Contessa 2007: 63, emphasis added)

But what makes a model a "*bona fide*" model? Contessa seems to suggest that it is one offered in good faith as a partially faithful representation. But the grounds on which the scientist believes this to be true are left unstated. The interpretive account, then, like Suárez's inferential account, leaves the nature of *successful* representation in the realm of the mysterious.[15]

What prevents the interpretive account from saying more about successful representation is its lack of substantive engagement with the target and its relationship to the model. All that is required of a model *qua* representation under the interpretive account is that each object or relation in the model correspond to one and only one object or relation in the target. The particular correspondence need have nothing to do with the actual nature and dynamics of the target. This is the sense in which the Rutherford model of the atom can represent the hockey puck on the ice, and why it would represent the hockey puck on the ice equally well if we randomly re-assigned each element in the model to a different element in the target. The target is merely a collection of elements that stand in no particular relationship to the model or to each other. No regard is given to the precise manner in which those elements *constitute* the target.

But this does not entirely accord with the actual practice of scientific modeling. Scientists generally construct their models with direct reference to their understanding of (and conjectures about) the constitution of the target, that is, the precise way in which the objects and relations that the target is composed of relate to each other. Correspondences between the model and the target are thus not merely asserted, but rather embody particular conjectures about similarities between target and candidate model.

---

[15] This is not necessarily a failing of the interpretive account, but rather a reflection of its taking representation in the neutral sense as its target.

The assignment of particular elements in the model to particular elements of the target is meant to reflect a match of their underlying constitutions. It is no accident, for example, that Solow assigns the function Y to production and the functional arguments K and L to capital and labor. He does so *because* it is his conjecture that, like the mathematical objects K, L, and $Y=f(K,L)$, capital, labor, and production mutually contribute to the constitution of the economy by (in part) standing in a relation of input, input, and output to each other, respectively. His hope in deploying the model is that it will reveal aspects of the functioning of the target that would otherwise be hidden or obscure.

Moving beyond the interpretive account, then, requires us to say something about how the modeler thinks about the constitution of both model and target, and how to draw correspondences between them so that surrogative reasoning will illuminate obscure or puzzling aspects of the target. The paradigmatic example of such an account is the "semantic view" of scientific theories. According to this view, models are *structures* that exemplify theories. This definition contains two parts: the concept of a "structure" and the idea that models "exemplify theories."[16] A structure is a formal object, for example a set-theoretic n-tuple or a system of equations, that specifies a set of elements and the kinds of relations that obtain between them. In non-technical language, a structure is an abstract representation of the dynamics (more formally, the "relational properties") of a system. We can view the Solow model, for example, as such a structure. Its elements (or objects) are mathematical variables and parameters, and its relations include both (a) the combinatorial and compositional rules of algebra, calculus, and differential equations, and (b) the specific relations defined in the model itself, such as the production function. Leaving aside any notion of the target to which the model is meant to apply, the Solow model, in this view, simply depicts a set of objects and their relations.

According to the semantic view, models "exemplify theories" in the sense that they define systems within which a theory is true. For example, the Solow model is a system in which neo-classical macroeconomic theory is true. (This says nothing, yet, about the connection of the theory or the model to empirical reality, only that the structure defined by the model is one in which the axioms of the governing theory are true.) An individual model represents just one such system, and a full articulation of a theory is the set of

---

[16] The seminal account of the semantic view of theories is that of Patrick Suppes (e.g., Suppes 1960, 1962, 1967). Later influential accounts include Suppe (1989), van Fraassen (1980), and Giere (1988). Suppe (1989) provides a very helpful history of the early development of the semantic view.

all models of the theory. The model of Ricardian equivalence (Barro 1974) is another example of a model of neo-classical macroeconomic theory.

Models become tools of discovery, under the semantic view, when the scientist posits that a particular target (a set of empirical phenomena) possesses the structure embodied by the model.[17] For example, one could posit that the economy of the United States possesses the structure exemplified in the Solow growth model – i.e. that it is constituted by objects and relations similar to that of the latter. And it is here that we see that the semantic view operates with a conception of representation that is more substantive than merely functional accounts like that of Contessa and Suárez. On the semantic view, the scientist is not merely asserting correspondences between individual objects and relations of model and target. Rather, she is positing a correspondence of integrated *structure*. The model is meant not merely to allow one to draw inferences about objects and relations in the target in the brute force manner of Contessa's interpretive account of representation, it is meant as a kind of map of the territory of the target.

How do we determine whether or not a model is successful, from the semantic view? Very generally, we can say that a model is successful only if its structure is sufficiently similar – i.e. similar *enough* and *in the right ways* – to the target it is meant to represent. In part, this is an empirical matter: our conjecture about the shared structure of model and target must be borne out by empirical observation. But as we saw in Section 1.1, empirical testing is never an entirely empirical matter. Pragmatic considerations must be brought to bear on several levels. Most obviously, the inherent theory-ladenness of the data makes objective evaluations of the truth of model-based conjectures about the target impossible. As Kuhn suggests, what we are doing when we conduct an empirical "test" is determining whether or not our suggested solution to the particular puzzle we have taken up is a proper solution under the operative paradigm – that is, we are answering the question: "Is this putative solution to the chosen puzzle valid and correct *given* the validity of the operative paradigm?"[18] In Section 1.1, this picture of the inherent embeddedness of scientific activity in a paradigm helped us to see the shortcomings of the Friedman-lite account of modeling. Essentially, the problem is that because the scientist only sees the world through the lens of the paradigm within which she operates, empirical testing according to the accepted methods and standards of the paradigm will be adequate only if that

---

[17] See, e.g., Hausman (1992: 74–5), Giere (1979: Chapter 5).
[18] The paradigm can change, of course, in large and small ways. But, as Kuhn points out, all scientific activity takes place within *some* paradigm (Kuhn 1996: 16–17).

lens is not distorted in ways that fundamentally frustrate her purposes. This is so for the same reasons, and in the same way, that a New York City subway map will be helpful in achieving the purpose of navigating from Grand Central Station to the Brooklyn Bridge *only if* the map is faithful to the physical subway system with respect to the relevant path of travel.

The foregoing helps us to understand what is involved in answering the question of what kind (and what extent) of similarity must obtain between model and target. We can see that this is not simply a question of the relationship between model and target, but more broadly a question of the relationship between the model-target dyad, the purposes (P) of the particular modeling exercise, the manner in which the scientist uses the model to achieve those purposes, and the norms (N) governing the construction, use, and assessment of models. That is, a model must be sufficiently similar to the target to accomplish the goals of the modeling exercise given the norms governing how such things proceed and are judged. Note that this statement is consonant with the view of modeling associated with the instrumental-positive standard discussed in Section 1.1, but is not limited to it. That said, the statement is still quite general and vague at this point. We must now make it more concrete.

1.4   Completing the pragmatic account

In Section 1.3, we focused on the central role of representation in modeling. I argued that for a model to be a successful representation of its target, it is necessary for there to be a relation of similarity between the two. Just what kind and what degree of similarity is required is not a question that can be answered for models in general. As Ronald Giere suggests, what is required is "similarity in relevant respects," and what counts as relevant depends on the purpose of the modeling exercise and the norms of modeling practice under which the scientist is operating. Accordingly, "what makes a model a successful representation *in general*?" would seem to be the wrong question. Rather, to understand what is necessary for a model to be successful we must shift our focus from the level of modeling in general to that of the individual modeling exercise – i.e. to ask: "What is necessary for a particular model to be a successful representation in a particular modeling exercise *given* the purposes of the scientist, the manner in which she purports to use the model, and the norms of modeling practice under which she is operating?" In what follows, I will refer to this conception of successful representation as "apt

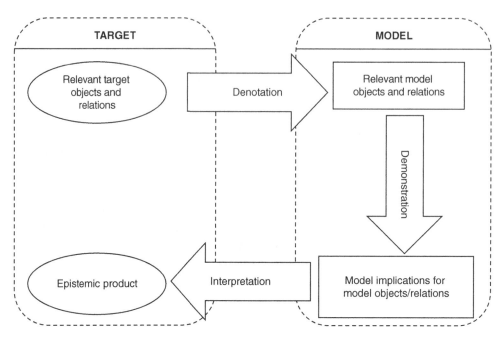

Figure 1.2   The DDI model

representation" to reflect its grounding in the particular purposes of the modeling exercise.

We may thus complete the explication of the pragmatic account of modeling by exploring what is required for a model to be an apt representation of its target. Concretely, this means making clear the role of purposes (*P*), norms (*N*), and model usage in model-based science. It will be helpful to begin by providing a framework depicting the relevant elements and their relations. R.I.G. Hughes' (1997) simple DDI model provides a good foundation. It is essentially a schematic depiction of the surrogative reasoning process. Its three components – Denotation, Demonstration, and Interpretation – identify the three phases of surrogative reasoning: assigning correspondences between elements of the model and elements of the target, tracing out implications of the model's structure for the model elements, and drawing inferences about the target based on inferences about the model (see Figure 1.2). The output of surrogative reasoning is the set of inferences that result from the Interpretation phase.

The DDI model is a helpful visual depiction of the phases of surrogative reasoning, and therefore of representation *simpliciter*. Like the Suárez and Contessa accounts discussed above, however, the DDI framework does not explicitly address the influence of the elements of practice with which we are concerned here. These will need to be added by incorporating an account of modeling practice that brings the modeler and her discipline into the foreground.

Mary Morgan's (2001) account of the use of *stories* in modeling is helpful for this purpose.[19] The crux of Morgan's account is that models themselves do not explain but merely embody certain structures. They become explanatory tools, Morgan argues, only when the scientist uses that structure to address a question about the target in which she is interested. This is done through the construction of a story about the model which, it is hoped, will illuminate the target. In effect, the story is the vehicle that operationalizes the model's illuminative capacity.

There are two parts to this process. First, there is the "motivating question" of the modeling exercise which transforms the model from a dumb object into a potential tool of explanation. In Morgan's words: "The story is suggested by a question, or by an ad hoc observation, which needs accounting for, or by a supposed change to some term in the model, or by the modification of an assumption. This 'question' begins the work done by the model" (Morgan 2001: 366–7). The second part of the process concerns the content of this work. The work done by the model – or more precisely by the modeler with respect to the model – takes the form of a story about the target based on the structure and "internal dynamic" of the model.[20] There are two distinct aspects to this story. The first corresponds roughly to what Hughes (1997) calls "Demonstration" – namely, the tracing out of selected implications of the model structure for the relevant model elements. In the case of a mathematical model, for example, this would correspond to solving the model. Using terminology from the work of Louis Mink, Morgan refers to this aspect of the story – which I will call the "model narrative" – as being told in "the theoretical mode of natural science" (Morgan 2001: 377). I will use the term "formal" instead of "theoretical" in what follows, in order to emphasize that the pathways along which this part of the story can unfold are given entirely by the form of the model. The second aspect of the story – which I will call the "target narrative" – is a conjectural narrative about the target that reconfigures it using the structure of the model narrative as a guide. Put another way, the target narrative is an "interpretation" of the model narrative, in a sense that will be made clearer below.

---

[19] Morgan's account builds on earlier suggestive accounts by Gibbard and Varian (1978) and McCloskey (1990). Subsequent accounts of the role of stories in modeling have sometimes used the term "commentary" instead of story – e.g., Mäki (2009b) and Bailer-Jones (2003).

[20] "Internal dynamic" is Hughes' (1997) term, also employed by Morgan.

Significantly, Morgan points out that what is being interpreted is not simply the *result* of the model narrative – i.e. not just the solution of a model as a specific statement about some or all of the target elements – but, in addition, the dynamics of the model that brought the solution about. Put another way, inferences about the target cannot be understood as isolated objects, but must be understood as part of a narrative – specifically, the narrative proposed by the modeler as an interpretation of the model story. Referring to James Meade's model-based exploration of parts of Keynes' macroeconomic theory, Morgan remarks that: "The stories enabled him to tell not just the outcomes, but also something of the processes by which the results were arrived at, and the side effects involved." And she elaborates, quoting Barthes: "meaning is not 'at the end' of the narrative, it runs across it" (Barthes 1982: 259, quoted in Morgan 2001: 372).

Morgan's account helps to clarify what is necessary for apt representation. It makes clear the central role of the modeler's purpose (*P*) in modeling. Represented by the "motivating question," this purpose both sets the modeling process in motion and suggests what features the model must have. The model is, as Morgan puts it, an inherently "purpose-built entity." And as the purposes of modelers are varied, so is the nature of model construction. The modeler may cobble together the model from whatever materials fit the bill – fragments of theories, stylized facts, parts of other models – within the strictures of the relevant norms of the paradigm within which she operates. Marcel Boumans (1999) likens the process to baking a cake without a recipe. One knows what the desired outcome is (the modeler's purpose), one has various relevant ingredients and tools available, and one is free to combine and process them in whatever way one thinks best to achieve the desired outcome (constrained, of course, by their physical properties and the laws of chemistry and physics).

This conception of models as inherently purpose-built suggests they do not simply exemplify theories, as proponents of the semantic view argue.[21] They are not constrained, that is to say, by any given set of axioms, but only by the modeler's purposes in pursuing a given modeling exercise, congruent with the norms of the discipline.[22] Yet – as Morgan's account also implies – the requirements of model-based story-telling themselves impose

---

[21] The later work of Ronald Giere, which takes a view that is more consonant with that of models as purpose-built entities, is an exception. Giere marks the distinction by referring to this later view as "model-based" rather than "semantic" (Giere 1999; 2004).

[22] This is especially important for the study of economic models, as very little of what economists would refer to as "economic theory" is axiomatized or perhaps even axiomatizable.

considerable constraints on both model and modeler. We can see this by considering the additions we must make to Figure 1.2 to accommodate the role of stories. As discussed above, the DDI model depicts the basic phases of the surrogative reasoning process. It shows us how the modeler can use a model to move from a question about the target to an answer phrased in terms of objects and relations in the target. The process involves a double translation: first, a translation of the relevant target objects into the language of the model, and then – after following a model narrative to its conclusion – a re-translation back into the terms of the target. The translation and re-translation are both effected using the initial denotations – i.e. the asserted correspondences between target and model.[23] As such, we arrive at an answer to the initial question without having had to consider how (or whether) we could have arrived at this answer by reasoning about the target *directly*. That is the point of surrogative reasoning.

But we cannot entirely avoid direct consideration of the nature and dynamics of the target, and Morgan's account helps us to see why. As discussed above, Morgan points out that the model narrative allows the scientist to say something not only about the answer to the initial question, but also something about "the processes by which the results were arrived at." The model narrative plays this latter role when we translate aspects of that narrative into the terms of the target, using the initial denotations as a guide. The translated narrative is essentially a *projection* of the model narrative onto the target, and it can relate to the motivating question in one of two ways. When the motivating question is of the form, "what are the relations between the different objects in the target?" (e.g., "what is the connection between wages and unemployment?"), the target narrative supplies the answer to the motivating question. When the motivating question is of the form "what is the result when the target is in a certain condition?" (e.g., "what level of unemployment can we expect when wages are at a certain level?"), the target narrative supplies the background story necessary to reach the answer provided by the model. Either way, the target narrative constitutes a response to the motivating question strictly in terms of the target (see Figure 1.3). Yet this gives rise to a further significant constraint on the modeler. The modeler must ask whether the proposed target narrative is actually *possible* in respect of the target, when that target is considered on its own terms and not simply as a projection of the model. Note that this is a very minimal requirement: we are not (yet) asking that the proposed target narrative be deemed a *good* response to the motivating question. It must simply seem

---

[23] See Dennis (1982a, b) for an interesting discussion of this process of double translation.

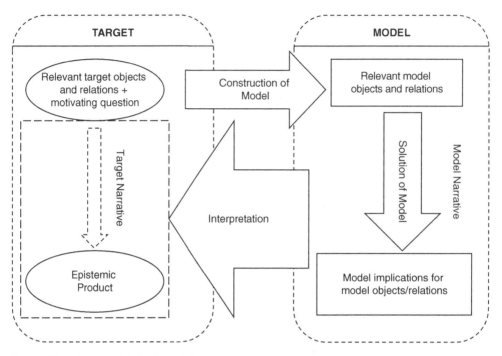

Figure 1.3   The role of stories in modeling

allowable when the nature and dynamics of the target are taken into consideration. Another way to put this is that there must be conceivable processes within
the world of the target to justify the target narrative.

Chapters 2 and 3 will argue this point in more detail. For now, we need
only clarify why it is crucial. To do this, we may go back to the Friedman-lite
account of modeling with which we began this chapter. According to that
account, the only proper standard for assessing the merits of a model is the *a
posteriori* correspondence of its implications (i.e. hypotheses generated by it)
to empirical reality. In terms of our diagrams, all that matters is the correspondence of the result of the model to the relevant data about the target. The
actual path by which the target is supposed to have arrived at that result is not
directly relevant. As Milton Friedman famously suggested, the target need
not actually be configured exactly like the model, it must only behave "as if" it
were. Friedman's example of the pattern of leaf-growth on trees succinctly
illustrates the point. A utility-maximization model may well provide good
predictions about foliage patterns, and this would make it a successful model
irrespective of the fact that each leaf is not *consciously* maximizing its
exposure to sunlight. We can simply interpret the leaves as acting "as if"

they were conscious sunlight-maximizers. In this case, what we have labeled the "Target Narrative" in Figure 1.3 would be a narrative about the leaves maximizing their sunlight exposure. Something along the lines of: The leaves get utility from sunlight exposure. They can put forth effort to gain sunlight by using their inputs of food and water, but the latter are in scarce supply. And so forth.

This narrative contains an element that is (as far as we know) literally false – the consciousness of the leaves. In this sense, taken as a whole, the proposed target narrative is not a possible account of the leaves' behavior; yet, as Friedman argues, the model may still be able to generate accurate predictions about the target. How then can this be? A closer look at Friedman's example reveals two important points. First, Friedman himself dismisses the "as if" story about the leaves' consciousness as soon as he begins to consider the nature of tree growth directly. A more plausible narrative, he suggests, is that the leaves' behavior reflects a passive, rather than an active or "conscious" adaptation to the availability of sunlight. Since this is a preferable narrative, the prior version may be dismissed. And what *this* shows is that the prior version – that is, the narrative in which the leaves acted "as if" they were conscious – is not, in fact, doing any work in Friedman's hypothetical modeling exercise. The construction of a *plausible* target narrative is, in fact, far more important than a superficial reading of Friedman's account would suggest. And numerous other examples could also be adduced to illustrate this. Many modeling exercises take the creation of a plausible narrative – as opposed to merely a specific prediction/retrodiction – as their primary purpose. Solow (1956) is one such case. It does not issue in specific empirical implications susceptible to testing, though it can still be a successful modeling exercise on the basis of its ability to support thought experiments about the implications of neo-classical macroeconomics. The relationship of these thought experiments to the possible dynamics of actual economies is crucially important to Solow, as he makes clear in the paper. He is not merely doing math problems, he is doing economics. And this is a general feature of economic analyses *qua economic* analyses.

Second, even in cases where mere prediction is the ostensible goal, the relation of the model narrative to the narrative possibilities of the target remains crucially relevant. A mere predictive machine is of only limited value, even if initially it seems a reliable one. Without any consideration of the possible dynamics actually generating the outcomes in the target, the reliability of the model is a complete mystery and we have no grounds for ruling out mere coincidence in the generation of appropriate-looking results.

In practice, we do not see scientists resting content with such models. Reliable prediction without any sense of what dynamics could be generating the result is a spur to further research. One reason for this, as Hausman (1984) points out, is that if such a model ceased to make accurate predictions we would have no idea how to make sense of this, and thus no idea how to build a more successful model. This is not to say that we require models to reflect the dynamics of the target completely faithfully – this is obviously not the case, as all models are unfaithful descriptions in some respects. But, as I will explore in detail in the next two chapters, it *is* necessary for the model to be faithful in *some specific respects*. Just which respects and what extent of faithfulness we require will depend upon the purposes of the modeling exercise, the manner in which the scientist uses the model, and the relevant norms of assessment.

A final reason that the narrative possibilities of the target remain relevant even for mere prediction/retrodiction is that empirical testing of predictions/retrodictions always necessarily presumes the validity of the paradigm within which the test has been formulated and the data gathered, as discussed above. At most, the test itself will suggest whether or not our answer to the initial question about the target is adequate given our conceptual map of the target. The testing process itself cannot be relied upon to detect a flawed conceptual map. To address this issue, we need to use resources and methods that do not themselves rely upon the validity of that paradigm. In Chapters 6 and 7, I will explore what sorts of resources and methods may be used.

Conclusion

This chapter began by outlining an account of modeling widely accepted by economists, a simplified version of that advanced in Friedman's 1953 essay "The Methodology of Positive Economics." On inspection, that account was found to have two shortcomings: an invalidly narrow conception of the aims of economic modeling and a flawed conception of the possibilities of empirical testing. Neither was mitigated by Friedman's own attempts to develop a more nuanced position. We then turned to the development of a more plausible "pragmatic" account, first in a basic outline and then, through careful consideration of the nature of representation, in a more complete picture. Morgan's account of stories in modeling provided the final piece of the jigsaw, and moreover helped us to see some of the issues that will be central to the analysis of current economic modeling practices presented in the next two chapters.

We began with the general statement:

[2] S uses M to represent X for purposes P
    The success of S in accomplishing P is judged against norms N

We may now add some detail to this basic framework. The scientist's purpose motivates the modeling exercise and guides the construction of the model. Specifically, the scientist constructs a model with an eye toward making available model narratives that enable the modeler to produce an answer to the motivating question in terms of the target. The model acts as a surrogate for the target in this process. In order for the surrogative reasoning to be successful (i.e. to achieve the modeler's purpose in a manner consonant with the relevant disciplinary norms), certain kinds of similarity between model and target must hold – just those similarities that allow the chosen model narratives to be possible pathways in the target. To the extent that the disciplinarily prescribed methods of model assessment themselves rely on the validity of the operative paradigm – as, for example, econometric assessment methods do – we must look to other resources and methods to assess the plausibility of the conjectured target narratives.

2 The use of mathematics in theoretical modeling

The previous chapter developed a pragmatic account of scientific modeling, and with it a new standard for assessing the merits of a scientific modeling exercise. Specifically, it argued that for a modeling exercise to be successful, the model has to be an *apt representation* of the target. And that, in turn, means that the model narrative generated in the modeling exercise must also be possible in respect of the target.

This chapter uses that standard to assess the modeling process commonly followed by economists. As noted, this modeling process centers on mathematics. Mathematical models are not the only conceivable way one might choose to represent economic activity; one might construct a physical model, for example, or a narrative in ordinary language. But economics today is unquestionably a mathematical-model-based science, and this has been the case since at least the mid-twentieth century.[1] Broken into its component parts, this process involves (a) the use of mathematical models (b) to represent social phenomena[2] (c) for the purpose of illuminating aspects of the latter (d) through the production of inferences about the latter.

I will argue that this process rests on a crucial presupposition: that the social phenomena under study can be adequately represented in the language of mathematics. More specifically, it presupposes that mathematical models can be used as *metaphors* for human social activity. This chapter will defend

---

[1] See, e.g., Lawson (2003: 3–8).

[2] It may be argued that not all economic models take social phenomena as their target. For example, one may think of counterfactual models (such as toy theoretical models and simulations) or econometric models which aim simply to characterize the shape of the data. It is true that these modeling exercises are some distance from the social phenomena that they represent. But they are still pursued in the hope of illuminating real social phenomena and to that extent necessarily take social phenomena as their *ultimate* referent. Counterfactual economic models are not models of arbitrary systems, but rather of social systems in which some (but not all) features are counterfactual. Such models import essential features of social phenomena into their construction, and are pursued in the hope of illuminating these and other aspects of the social world. Econometric modeling exercises aimed at characterizing the shape of the data (i.e. "letting the data speak for themselves") are not merely characterizing the internal structure of matrices of numbers, but rather of matrices of numbers that represent social phenomena. This is discussed in more detail in Chapter 3. See also Lawson (1997: 110).

the characterization of economists' use of mathematical models as metaphorical, and consider the implications of that characterization for economics. Its purview will be limited in one respect. In the interests of clarity, only theoretical modeling exercises – i.e. those that do not include empirical testing – will be explored at present. Empirical modeling exercises – i.e. those that engage directly with data – will be discussed in the next chapter.

As argued in the previous chapter, scientific modeling embodies a general *representational ideal* of the modeling process, which is to illuminate a given target in a manner that addresses the motivating question of the given exercise. In economics, the models in question are typically mathematical, and the manner in which the motivating question is addressed is generally through the production of inferences that are at least in principle testable (though as we saw, this is not always the case). The exact process of economic modeling has four parts (discussed in detail below), and any modeling exercise that conforms to this process will share the representational ideal of modeling in general. The question I wish to consider is: What is required for such modeling exercises to be capable of realizing that ideal? That is, what are the conditions under which a mathematical model can perform the task set for it by the economist? In keeping with the account presented in the last chapter, this is a *pragmatic* assessment standard, in that we take the scientist's representational ideal as our ultimate criterion (rather than, for example, "truth" or "verisimilitude").[3] And we will find that mathematical economic modeling exercises can accomplish their purpose only when the target phenomena constitute what Mill called a "mechanical" system, i.e. one in which "the investigations have already been reduced to the ascertainment of a relation between numbers." In other words (as discussed in the Introduction), mathematical language is capable of representing adequately only subject matter constituted by strictly quantitative objects and relations.

More specifically, in the terminology I will use, this means that:

(1*) the objects under investigation must plausibly be *stable, modular,* and *quantitative*, with no qualitative differences among instantiations of each type;

(2*) the relations between them are plausibly *fixed* and *law-like* throughout the context under study in the modeling exercise.[4]

---

[3] Using a pragmatic standard does not, of course, make the assessment itself subjective; we judge the capacity of the model to do its job irrespective of the scientist's beliefs or claims.

[4] The qualification that the objects under study must *plausibly* – as opposed to *actually* – possess these properties indicates that this is a pragmatic rather than a realist standard. The question of what constitutes plausibility must be a disciplinary matter. This is discussed in detail in Chapter 7.

The chapter proceeds as follows. Section 2.1 introduces the standard mathematical modeling process followed by economists. Section 2.2 defends the claim that mathematics is used as a metaphor in this process, and Section 2.3. explores the commitment this implies and its implications for successful economic modeling.

2.1   Mathematical modeling: a four-part process

Mathematical modeling follows the general pattern of scientific modeling outlined in Chapter 1. The scientist identifies a puzzle to investigate, supplies a mathematical construct to represent the set of phenomena under investigation, and demonstrates how the association between the phenomena under study and the mathematical construct solves the puzzle identified at the outset.

We may use a slightly altered version of the Hughes (1997) DDI model presented in the previous chapter to depict this process as conceived and practiced by economists. One alteration is to include the initial identification of the phenomena to be investigated and the formulation of the motivating question as an explicit part of the process. I will refer to this as the "Delimitation" phase. The other alteration is a slight change in terminology: from "Demonstration" to "Solution," since that is the term standardly used by economists. With these alterations, mathematical modeling as commonly practiced by economists may be presented as comprising the following four phases:

1. *Delimitation*, in which the set of social phenomena under study is delimited and a research question is articulated;
2. *Denotation*, in which a mathematical construct meant to represent these phenomena and their interactions is formulated;
3. *Solution*, in which the mathematical construct is brought to a solution;
4. *Interpretation*, in which the mathematical solution and its implications are interpreted with respect to the motivating research question.[5]

This four-part process is followed in most contemporary economic research. Indeed, many research papers follow these four phases not only in their gestation, but in their published presentation as well. And laying out the phases in this way calls attention to an important point: the modeling

---

[5] This framework also draws on work by Black (1962: esp. pp. 224–5, 230–1).

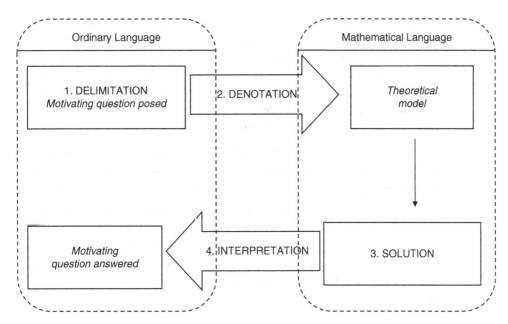

Figure 2.1   Mathematical modeling in economics: a four-part process

process entails twice crossing a significant linguistic divide. The economist begins with ordinary language in the presentation of the social phenomena to be investigated. Economists are interested in real-world puzzles, and the description of the real world is presented in the first instance in the form of natural language, that is, in a language developed in an unpremeditated way for the purposes of communication with other human beings.[6] The real-world puzzle is then translated into mathematical language. Finally, in the last stage of the process, the mathematical solution is translated back into ordinary language for the purpose of answering the initial research question.

Figure 2.1 presents this process in graphical form.

Let us consider an example of this modeling process in action: Carl Shapiro and Joseph Stiglitz's seminal work in efficiency wage theory, "Equilibrium Unemployment as a Worker Discipline Device" (1984).

In the Delimitation phase of their analysis, Shapiro and Stiglitz identify as a puzzle the persistence of unemployment. They delimit unemployment and related social phenomena as the set of social phenomena with which their analysis will be concerned:

---

[6] See Lycan (1999).

Involuntary unemployment appears to be a persistent feature of many modern labor markets. The presence of such unemployment raises the question of why wages do not fall to clear labor markets. In this paper we show how the information structure of employer-employee relationships, in particular the inability of employers to cost-lessly observe workers' on-the-job effort, can explain involuntary unemployment[7] as an equilibrium phenomenon. Indeed, we show that imperfect monitoring necessitates unemployment in equilibrium. (Shapiro and Stiglitz 1984: 433)

We may note that the quotation above is not solely focused on the task of delimiting the phenomena under investigation. Alongside their introduction of the object of study, the authors give an intimation of the approach they will use to examine it (an "asymmetric information" model) and the conclusions they will reach (that imperfect monitoring necessitates unemployment). Their primary task at this stage, however, is to specify their objects of interest. And these objects of interest are presented in ordinary language. The authors refer to labor, unemployment, employers, employees, and so on as they are conventionally understood by other members of the English-speaking community. Later, Shapiro and Stiglitz will provide mathematical analogues for these concepts. But the paper is first and foremost a study of social phenomena as they are experienced and conceived in a broader linguistic community. The elements of the Delimitation phase must be understood in this light.

The Denotation phase involves connecting the delimited social phenomena to a mathematical model. This typically involves at least two parts. First, the formal structure of the model is described informally using (mostly) the ordinary language names of the phenomena under study:

There are a fixed number ... of identical workers, all of whom dislike putting forth effort, but enjoy consuming goods ...

Each worker is in one of two states at any point in time: employed or unemployed. There is a probability b per unit time that a worker will be separated from his job due to relocation, etc., which will be taken as exogenous. Exogenous separations cause a worker to enter the unemployment pool. Workers maximize the expected present discounted value of utility with a discount rate $r > 0$.

The only choice workers make is the selection of an effort level, which is a discrete choice by assumption. If a worker performs at the customary level of effort for his job, that is, if he does not shirk, he receives a wage of w and will retain his job until exogenous factors cause a separation to occur. If he shirks, there is some

---

[7] The following footnote appears in Shapiro and Stiglitz (1984: 433): "By involuntary unemployment we mean a situation where an unemployed worker is willing to work for less than the wage received by an equally skilled employed worker, yet no job offers are forthcoming."

probability q ... per unit time, that he will be caught. If he is caught shirking, he will be fired, and forced to enter the unemployment pool. The probability per unit time of acquiring a job while in the unemployment pool (which we call the job acquisition rate, an endogenous variable calculated below) determines the expected length of the unemployment spell he must face. While unemployed, he receives unemployment compensation of $\overline{w}$. (Shapiro and Stiglitz 1984: 435)

These statements combine elements of the formal model and the phenomena under study as conventionally described. The authors use terms that will have many and varied connotations for readers – workers, employment, enjoyment, shirking, etc. – but they also gesture toward an analytical structure that belongs to the world of the formal model they will later introduce. Significantly, although the authors will ultimately want to claim that this structure also represents the causal dynamics underlying the social phenomena under investigation, that claim is still conjectural in statements like the one quoted above. In this kind of modeling exercise, presentations of the structure of the model using ordinary language are deemed to be *only* conjectures until a formal argument has been made establishing the truth value of the conjecture.[8]

In the second part of the Denotation phase, the formal model is fully presented. The authors provide mathematical analogues to the phenomena under study, formal definitions of these mathematical analogues, and a solution concept for the model described by this collection of mathematical objects and relations. The full version of the model used in Shapiro and Stiglitz (1984) has many elements – too many to present here. We may, however, consider a few. The following passage provides mathematical names for work-related enjoyment, wage, effort (where lack of effort is understood to be shirking), employment and unemployment:

We write an individual's instantaneous utility function as $U(w, e)$, where w is the wage received and e is the level of effort on the job ...

The worker selects an effort level to maximize his discounted utility stream. This involves comparison of the utility from shirking with the utility from not shirking, to which we now turn. We define V_E^S as the expected lifetime utility of an employed shirker, V_E^N as the expected lifetime utility of an employed nonshirker, and V_u, as the expected lifetime utility of an unemployed individual. The fundamental asset equation for a shirker is given by

$$rV_E^S = w + (b + q)(V_u - V_E^S) \qquad (2.1)$$

while for a nonshirker, it is

---

[8] The importance of this will become more apparent in the discussion of the Interpretation phase below.

$$rV_E^N = w - e + b(V_u - V_E^N) \tag{2.2}$$

The worker will choose not to shirk if and only if $V_E^N \geq V_E^S$. (Shapiro and Stiglitz 1984: 435–6)

By the end of the Denotation phase we have three articulations of the phenomena under investigation. The two least ambiguous are (1) the "ordinary language articulation," as presented in the Delimitation phase, and (2) the "formal model," whose referents are mathematical objects formally defined. The claim that the latter articulation aptly represents the phenomena of interest is still a conjecture at this point. There is also (3) a hybrid articulation that we may call the "proto-model," which expresses the structure of the model using the ordinary language names of the phenomena of interest. This articulation effectively embodies the conjecture that the model represents the phenomena of interest. Its referents are thus ambiguous. Sometimes the authors appear to be referring to the social phenomena conceived in ordinary language, and sometimes to the mathematical analogues.

Table 2.1 summarizes some of the Denotation phase elements of the statement quoted above in a "catalog of correspondences" between the social phenomena and the formal model.

The final entry in the table is particularly important in that it articulates the solution concept for this portion of the model. It tells us not only the authors' intended representation of one of the social elements of their model (as all the entries in the catalog do), but also how and for what purpose the model's dynamics will be set in motion.

The Solution phase is the most straightforward, as it resides purely in the mathematical realm and involves only the working out of the mathematical model according to the formal definitions and solution concept specified in the Denotation phase. As long as the model has been appropriately articulated, mathematically speaking, then either a solution (or solutions) exists, a solution does not exist, or it is not possible to determine whether or not a solution exists. In empirical research, the Solution phase will involve econometric analysis of data, which requires an expansion of the kind of catalog of correspondences shown below to include two extra layers of representation; such cases will be discussed in Chapter 3. In purely theoretical analyses, the Solution phase involves working out the implications of the model's mathematical structure in a manner that need not issue in immediately empirically testable statements. This is the case with Shapiro and Stiglitz (1984). Their Solution phase does not involve actual empirical testing, but only working

Table 2.1 Selected correspondences of Shapiro and Stiglitz (1984)

Social phenomena (ordinary language)	Proto-model (mixture of languages, informal statement of formal structure)	Formal model (mathematical language)
Work-related enjoyment	The assessment along a single value scale of the relative effects on one's enjoyment of consuming goods from one's wages and dislike of putting forth effort.	$U(w, e)$
Expectations of lifetime work-related enjoyment if one shirks	Expected lifetime utility of a shirker, understood as a return on an investment.	$rV_E^S = w + (b + q)(V_u - V_E^S)$
Effort	The worker's sole input into the work process, which s/he dislikes performing.	$e \in \mathbb{R}_+$
An individual's decision about how to comport himself/herself at work	The choice of a non-negative real-valued level of effort to maximize expected utility as a function of (and only of) wage and (generic) effort	$\text{Argmax}_e (V); V \in \{V_E^N, V_E^S\}$

out the implications of the structure and dynamics of the terms of the formal model. One such implication presented by the authors is:[9]

(For $e \in [0,\infty)$), e will be at some positive level $e' > 0$ if and only if:

$$w \geq rV_u + (r + b + q)e'/q \equiv \hat{w} \tag{2.3}$$

This is an entirely mathematical statement. It can be understood with reference to the mathematical construct *only*, independently of the social phenomena under investigation.

In the Interpretation phase, in order to re-connect the analysis to the question initially posed, the authors must utilize the correspondences already established to interpret the mathematical result of the Solution phase in terms of the social phenomena identified in the Delimitation phase. The following statement exemplifies this kind of interpretation.

---

[9] Equation (2.3) is a slightly modified version of equation (5) from the text of the Shapiro–Stiglitz paper. Where I have written e' in (2.3), they have written e. That is, in the paper, (2.3) is: $w \geq rV_u + (r + b + q) e / q \equiv \hat{w}$. I am taking the statement out of its context, and the modification is necessary to ensure that (2.3) here has the same meaning as does equation (5) in the Shapiro-Stiglitz paper.

Statement 2.1:

Equation [(2.3)] has several natural implications. If the firm pays a sufficiently high wage, then the workers will not shirk. The critical wage, $\hat{w}$, is higher:

(a) the higher the required effort (e),
(b) the higher the expected utility associated with being unemployed (V_u),
(c) the lower the probability of being detected shirking (q),
(d) the higher the rate of interest (i.e. the relatively more weight is attached to the short-run gains from shirking (until one is caught) compared to the losses incurred when one is eventually caught),
(e) the higher the exogenous quit rate b (if one is going to have to leave the firm anyway, one might as well cheat on the firm). (Shapiro and Stiglitz 1984: 436)

One final point is worth noting here. Though Shapiro and Stiglitz characterize Equation (2.3) as having several "natural" implications, there is nothing "natural" about these implications absent the correspondences established earlier in the modeling process. That is, without *independent* work connecting the mathematical construct to the social phenomena under investigation, the implications in *Statement 2.1* do not arise. This suggests that the process of establishing the correspondences does a good deal of work in the analysis. The nature of that work will be discussed in more detail below. For now, it is sufficient simply to recognize the above statement as an example of activity associated with the Interpretation phase.

2.2 Mathematical models as metaphors

As described above, mathematical modeling exercises involve two distinct linguistic realms: that of ordinary language and that of mathematical language. Specifically, mathematical modeling exercises generate results by positing an analogous relationship between the dynamics of the mathematical construct, on the one hand, and the dynamics of the social phenomena under investigation, on the other. It will now be argued that mathematical language, in this process, is best understood as *metaphorical*. That is (to build on the account of modeling given in Chapter 1), the mathematical model is a metaphor for the target and the modeling exercise consists in an exploration of the metaphor.

A metaphor is "a figure of speech (or a trope) in which a word or phrase that literally denotes one thing is used to denote another, thereby implicitly comparing the two things" (Audi 1999: 562). For example, the term "wolf" literally denotes the non-human animal *canis lupus*, but in the metaphor "man is a wolf" it denotes humans. This denotation is strictly speaking false, but the metaphor invites us to consider in what sense men can be understood as wolves by "projecting" attributes of the latter onto the former. Such metaphorical "projection" is a complex process, and one that gives considerable leeway to the interpreter, since the particular qualities that one language user associates with "wolf" may not be the same as those immediately conjured by another. For example, one language user may associate "wolf" primarily with voraciousness, another with pack hunting. Nonetheless, whatever connotations the word "wolf" presents to different language users, the process of making sense of the metaphor will be the same. The field of associations (or "interpretive framework") relating to "man" in the mind of the interpreter will be temporarily overlain by the field of associations relating to "wolf." Making sense of the juxtaposition of these two fields requires drawing connections between them, with a view to illuminating some qualities of the concept "man."

The constructs produced in mathematical modeling exercises work in the same way. Consider the following passage from Shapiro and Stiglitz (1984: 435): "We write an individual's instantaneous utility function as $U(w,e)$, where w is the wage received and e is the level of effort on the job." The authors indicate that w "is" the wage received, and that e "is" the level of effort on the job. But this is literally false. w is a mathematical variable, as is e. "Wage received" and "effort on the job" (as introduced in the Delimitation phase) are ordinary language items denoting social phenomena in a way familiar to the community of English speakers. In what sense, then, "is" w the wage received and e the level of effort on the job? As with "man is a wolf," the statements are not meant literally. Rather, they invite us to consider how we could conceive of wages and effort on the job (understood in their social context), on the one hand, and the mathematical variables e and w, on the other, as capable of being understood in the same terms. In effect, we are invited to project the attributes of mathematical objects onto these social entities: to "see" social phenomena through the overlay of mathematical relations. This is not to imply that the social world literally *is* populated by mathematical relations, only that we are invited to consider what insights can be gleaned by imagining it in such a light. This is what it means to deploy a metaphor.

By construction, then, mathematical modeling is inherently metaphorical.[10] But how exactly do metaphors work, and what does their usage imply? Mary Hesse provides a helpful account of the mechanics of metaphor specifically in the context of scientific modeling.[11] In Hesse's view, metaphors are a type of proposition. They comprise two entities: a "primary subject" (i.e. the thing being modified) and a "secondary subject" (i.e. the thing metaphorically denoting the primary subject)[12] that are similar in some ways and dissimilar in others. What is proposed is that there is more similarity between the two than there seems to be *prima facie*. Specifically, Hesse argues that the illumination provided by metaphors draws on three types of analogy between the primary and secondary subjects: (1) positive analogy, i.e. the ways in which the two entities are similar; (2) negative analogy (or disanalogy), i.e. the ways in which they are dissimilar; and (3) neutral analogy, i.e. the ways in which the entities may possibly be similar. We first satisfy ourselves (by considering the positive and negative analogies) that there is enough relevant similarity and sufficiently little relevant dissimilarity between the two subjects for their conjunction to be fruitful, and then we see what insight can be gained from thinking of the neutral analogies as positive analogies.

As an illustration, we may return to the example "man is a wolf." Here "man" is the primary subject and "wolf" the secondary subject. Obvious similarities, or positive analogies, between the two include various physical characteristics: animal, vertebrate, mammal, and so on. Obvious differences, or negative analogies, include the fact that one is human and the other not; one civilized, one wild; one biped, one quadruped, and so on. And possible neutral analogies include characteristics like uncontrollably voracious, pack hunter, and instinctively hierarchical.

Hesse argues that in order for a metaphor to get off the ground there must be *some* positive analogy between the two subjects, and the negative analogies must not include *essential* properties of either subject.[13] The second of these two conditions – that there be no *essential* differences between the primary

---

[10] It may be asked why I use the term metaphor here rather than analogue. While economic models are certainly meant to be analogous to their targets in some sense, the characterization of an economic model simply as an analogue does not, I think, sufficiently capture the complex ways in which the analogical relationship between model and target is drawn upon in the process of gaining epistemic access to the latter through the former. Following, e.g., Black (1993: esp. 28–30), Hesse (1966: 157–77), McCloskey (1983) and Bailer-Jones (2002), I consider that the concept of metaphor offers a more faithful rendering of this process, as I will argue below.

[11] See especially Hesse (1963).

[12] "Primary subject" and "secondary subject" are Max Black's terms. See Black (1993: 27).

[13] See, e.g., Hesse (1963: 38, 102, 108).

and secondary subjects – is crucial, so we must specify clearly what it means. We may do this via another illustrative example.

Imagine three college students, Audrey, Bert, and Caroline. Audrey is in a troubled relationship with Bert, whom she has known since high school. She goes to Caroline for relationship advice, telling her that the relationship is in difficulty because she and Bert only spend time together in large groups: they seldom see each other alone any more. Caroline, who is an expert chess player, sees strategic interaction at play, and suggests that the relationship is like a particular chess match she remembers. She tells Audrey that the following correspondences apply. Audrey is the white King; Bert is the black Queen; Audrey and Bert's friends are the black pawns. Caroline then sets up a chess board to play out the match she has in mind, demonstrating that the black pawns isolate the white King, forcing him into a corner until he is checkmated owing primarily to lack of space. Caroline suggests that the solution to the relationship problem is the same as the solution to the white side's predicament. White should use its pieces to thin out black's pawns. That is, Audrey should find ways to divert their mutual friends so that she has more space to operate.

Now, several questions arise concerning Caroline's metaphor and the advice she gives. One is whether or not the advice she ultimately gives seems helpful. Importantly, her advice may seem helpful *regardless* of what one thinks about the aptness of the metaphor that preceded it. It is entirely possible, for example, that Caroline, as a chess expert, finds it so natural to conceive of all relations through the lens of chess that she tends to deploy chess as a metaphor even when it is not necessary to reach her conclusion – even, perhaps, when she has already arrived at her conclusion on other grounds. That is to say, it is possible that Caroline, without herself relying internally on the chess metaphor to reach her conclusion, might yet offer a chess metaphor as a kind of *post-hoc* rationalization of the advice she independently prefers. That preference might be unconscious, and she might even believe that the metaphor generated the advice in a direct way (and feel awed, as a result, by what she sees as the illuminative power of chess). Nonetheless, there may be no *necessary* connection between the chess metaphor she uses and her subsequent advice. We may therefore assess the merits of the advice independently from that of the metaphor.

Another question is whether a chess metaphor is an apt way of thinking about romantic relationships in general; and still another, whether the metaphor Caroline uses is an apt way of thinking about this *particular* relationship. Again, these questions are independent. One might feel that since chess aims not at the harmonious coexistence of the white and black pieces but rather the defeat of one side by the other, the metaphor risks sending us down the wrong path from the outset. Or one might feel that since a chess metaphor cannot accommodate the issue of Bert's volition – that is, whether he *wants* to spend time alone with Audrey – it cannot possibly succeed. Nonetheless, that claim might be too hasty. One can imagine circumstances in which Caroline's metaphor might prove a good fit. If Audrey and Bert's friends really were terrible hangers-on, for example, and/or if Bert had chronic difficulties with self-assertion, such that he didn't know how to make it clear either to his friends or to Audrey that he would like more time alone with her, the metaphor might well seem apt. The only way to know whether this is the case is to gather further information about the situation. Suppose, for instance, that Audrey now tells Caroline that their relationship has always been difficult because, having been friends for such a long time, what they actually want from each other is uncertain. In fact, she's not even sure that she wants a romantic relationship with him most of the time – she just wishes that he would pay her more attention. If this is the case, Audrey having "more space to operate" would make next to no difference to the relationship itself. The issue is not really how much time or space she and Bert have together, but something rather more complicated. If so, the relevance of Caroline's chess metaphor will seem very dubious indeed.

This reveals an important point. The fit between the metaphor and the situation it is meant to illuminate depends crucially on the particular circumstances of the case, and requires familiarity with the target on its own terms. Another point – which follows – is that the final question posed above is more important than the second. It is more important to consider in what ways a mooted model is an apt representation of a particular target than it is to arrive at conclusions about *kinds* of models, such as chess metaphors, conceived generally. Sometimes a chess match may be an apt way to represent a romantic relationship; sometimes it may not. It all depends on the nature of the relationship and the particular purpose of the exercise. Finally, we can say that what makes a given model apt is its capacity to reflect properties of the target that are *essential* in light of the purpose of the modeling exercise. If it is the case that what Audrey and Bert want from each other is uncertain, this ambiguity represents an essential dissimilarity (negative analogy) between their relationship and the chess match Caroline has in mind. An essential characteristic of the world of chess is that the relations between the pieces are unambiguous and that each side's goals are well-defined. Since it is essential to the goal of giving advice about Audrey and Bert's relationship that the relationship between them be properly conceived, reading a greater level of clarity into it than it really possesses can only weaken the usefulness of the advice given. In other words, because there are essential negative analogies in this case between the primary subject (the relationship) and the secondary subject (the chess match), Caroline's metaphor cannot fulfill its particular purpose of reliably generating insight into Audrey and Bert's relationship.

This gives rise to another significant question. Given the risk of a mismatch between the primary and secondary subjects in *any* metaphorical exercise – that is, the existence of one or more essential negative analogies between the two subjects – why, we may ask, should we deploy metaphors at all? Why might one wish to say "war is hell," for example, rather than "war is horrible and violent and goes on and on"? One possibility is that the two modes of expression are identical, and that employing metaphors is simply a matter of taste. But that view of metaphor - known as the "substitution view" – falls short of the mark.[14] What it misses is what is gained by overlaying the interpretive framework (or field of associations) associated with one item with that of another.

In the case of "man is a wolf," as we saw, what the metaphor does is to project the field of things associated with "wolf" onto "man." At first, many features of wolves may flash through the mind of the interpreter: animal, furry, terrifying, pack hunter, big teeth, mammal, rapacious, quadruped, and so on. But the task of making sense of the metaphor – of "trying it on" – leads us to allow obvious dissimilarities or negative analogies to fade into the background: "furry" and "quadruped" might be among these. What remains are obvious (and therefore uninteresting) similarities, such as "animal" and "mammal" (positive analogies), and other less obvious (and therefore interesting) possible similarities, such as "terrifying," "pack hunter," and "voracious" (Hesse's "neutral analogies"). It is this last set of features that shows the usefulness of metaphors. What they do is draw attention to those aspects of two subjects that are (a) shared and (b) whose commonality is easily overlooked. What one ends up with is an image of the primary subject that focuses us on neutral analogies, at least some of which may be highly revealing about the primary subject in ways we might otherwise not have considered.

---

[14] See, e.g., Black (1993: 27; 1962: 31–4).

In this respect, one may conceive of the field of associations of the secondary subject as a kind of polarizing light filter. An apt metaphor helps us to see certain things about the primary subject more clearly. It cuts down on extraneous "glare" and reveals features of the target that had previously been difficult to see, just as a good pair of polarized sunglasses does. But polarized sunglasses are not intrinsically apt tools of clarification. They will be potentially helpful when we wish to investigate aspects of the world that are otherwise obscured by glare. But if our goal is, for example, to detect light sources with a polarization opposite to that of the sunglasses' lenses, or to read fine print on a smartphone screen, the sunglasses will be inherently ill-suited to the job. In these cases, the sunglasses themselves are not the problem: the problem is wearing them in the wrong conditions. In the same way, a metaphor may be very useful in certain circumstances and yet fail completely when the context changes. If a given secondary subject is different from the primary subject in some *essential* respect, the metaphor will simply distort or obscure rather than illuminate the target subject matter. And there is a further point of commonality. The sunglasses *themselves* cannot draw the wearer's attention to the difference between the view of the world with shades on and that without. The only way to become aware of the difference is to take the sunglasses off. In the same way, the only way to become aware of any essential negative analogies between a model (or secondary subject) and target (or primary subject) is to examine the target through lenses other than those of the model.

What this implies for the success of any given mathematical model is twofold. First, there must not be any essential negative analogy between the model and its target. That is, there must not be any dissimilarity between the two subjects so profound such that one's conception of the target is obscured rather than illuminated. We may call this fit "essential compatibility." Second, one must not become fixated on the model to the exclusion of direct interest in the target under investigation. One has to relinquish the model from time to time, to re-ascertain that what is looked at really is clearer using the model than without it, in case either the objects examined or the relations between them have changed. What this implies for mathematical modeling exercises in economics is explored in the next section.

Before turning to this exploration, however, I would like to address a potential objection to the "no essential negative analogies" condition. Specifically, one might object that it is too restrictive in denying *any* possibility that an essential negative analogy between model and target could prove illuminating and therefore actually aid the modeling exercise rather than doom it.[15] We can explore this possibility by considering a historical example in which a negative analogy played an important role in the development of a successful model: Irving Fisher's mechanical balance model of the quantity theory of money, developed in his 1911 work *The Purchasing Power of Money*.[16]

In the 1911 work, Fisher sought to illustrate the accounting identity embodied in his equation of exchange – $MV = PT$ – by drawing an analogy to a mechanical balance. The equation of exchange is an expression of the quantity theory of money, which posits a relationship of equality between the product of the amount of money in the economy (M) and the velocity of money (V), on the one hand, and the product of the average level of prices (P) and the quantities of goods traded (T, for "transactions"). Significantly, the equality between MV and PT was a necessary one – an accounting identity. Fisher presented a mechanical balancing scale as a representation of the equation, with the following correspondences: M and T are the weights on the left and right sides of the scale, respectively; V and P, respectively, are the distances from the fulcrum at which the weights are attached.

There are two clear positive analogies that aid us in using the mechanical balance to gain insight into the workings of the equation of exchange: First, like the variables in the equation, the weights and their placement on the fulcrum can vary quantitatively and continuously (bounded below by zero); and, second, the equality of the two sides of the equation corresponds to the balancing of the two sides of the scale. But, as Morgan (1997: S307) notes, there are also two important negative analogies. First, whereas the scale, when perturbed from balance, will oscillate through out-of-equilibrium states until eventually reaching a new equilibrium, the equation of exchange, as an accounting identity, must adjust instantaneously. Second, it is possible for the scale to come to rest without the two sides balancing exactly, whereas this is not possible for the equation of exchange.

Far from rendering the models invalid or inherently unilluminating, however, these negative analogies required Fisher to think creatively about their implications and ultimately come to an insightful resolution. As Morgan explains, Fisher:

reintroduced the accounting identity to hold over the mechanical balance as a kind of higher order constraint; and redefined the nature of that identity. He assumed that the identity holds not exactly all the time, but in the nature of a tendency of the

---

[15] I thank Mary Morgan for bringing this objection to my attention.
[16] The following explanation of Fisher's model follows Morgan (1997).

elements in the system towards an equilibrium at the equity point of balance. So the accounting identity is reestablished, but is reinterpreted as an equilibrium tendency, and it no longer constrains so tightly as before: the balance never is exactly in equity. (Morgan 1997: S307)

This innovation, spurred by the recognition of a negative analogy, improved the insight-generating potential of the equation of exchange by clarifying its relation to economic dynamics.

The foregoing example does not, however, demonstrate that the no essential negative analogies condition is overly restrictive, for two reasons. First, the no essential negative analogies condition does not preclude the possibility that the recognition of negative analogies – even essential ones – between model and target can be helpful in the course of developing a model. Indeed, the process of ascertaining the points of positive and negative analogy between model and target is a fundamental part of any modeling exercise.

Second, the no essential negative analogies condition relates to the use of a model *in a specific modeling exercise*. In particular, the "essential" properties of a model for the purposes of a specific modeling exercise are those which are required in the model narrative constructed to address the motivating question of that exercise. In the case of Fisher's models, the question of whether the *necessary* equality of *PV* and *MT* constituted an essential negative analogy with its target would depend upon the specific use to which one was putting it. The equation of exchange would still be inherently inapt despite Fisher's innovation if, for example, one were seeking to characterize out-of-equilibrium macro-dynamics. The important point here is that negative analogies *per se* between model and target are not problematic and will often even be important to the development of a good model, but *essential* negative analogies between model and target will always render the model inapt for the purposes of the particular modeling exercise in question.

2.3 The presuppositions of mathematical modeling

The central implication of the previous section's discussion is as follows. In order for a given mathematical modeling exercise to be even potentially successful in fulfilling its purpose, the social phenomena under investigation and the mathematical construct said to represent them must be essentially compatible. That is, there must be some positive analogies, some neutral, and no essential negative analogies between them. Only in these conditions can the model narratives generated by the modeler be interpreted as possible narratives about the target.

This brings us to a crucial question. In what respects must a mathematical model and its target be essentially compatible in order for the model to function as a potentially successful representation of the target for the purposes of a given modeling exercise? Or, to put the question slightly differently, what features must a set of social phenomena possess in order for it to be essentially compatible with, and hence aptly represented by, a mathematical construct?

To answer this question, we may begin by recalling that the crux of mathematical modeling is the interpretation of a mathematical model narrative as a possible narrative about the target. It is by means of this projection of the chosen model narrative onto the target that the modeling exercise yields illumination. Or, put in the terms used above to describe the four-part process of mathematical modeling, it is by means of projecting the solution of the model onto the target that the modeling exercise yields illumination. The fundamental payoff of using a mathematical model, rather than examining the target on its own terms, lies in this Solution phase. Having translated the target into a mathematical construct (in the Denotation phase), the modeler can (in the Solution phase) construct a model narrative (i.e. solve the model) with reference only to the relevant rules of mathematics and with no separate regard for the characteristics of the target. If there is the right kind of correspondence between model and target, then any valid mathematical manipulations will correspond to an analogous narrative in the target. As such, we may undertake the mathematical manipulations freely, following the mathematical narratives wherever they may take us, confident that the corresponding target objects can follow. This allows the modeler to pursue possibilities that may not obviously present themselves (or may even seem inconceivable) in respect of the target. It is difficult to see, for example, what it could mean to divide wages by effort when we conceive of those concepts in their own terms, but when we re-imagine them as the mathematical variables w and e, we are free to proceed with that and any other valid mathematical operation we choose. But what is it about the variables w and e that allows them to be manipulated in this way?

Let us consider the following Solution phase statement from Shapiro and Stiglitz (1984: 436):

(For $e \in [0,\infty)$), e will be at some positive level $e' > 0$ if and only if:

$$w \geq rV_u + (r + b + q)e'/q \equiv \widehat{w} \tag{2.4}$$

There are several points worth observing about this mathematical statement. For one, every object within it has a *precise* and *stable* meaning throughout the context under discussion. This is true by definition, since, as with all mathematical objects, each is formally defined. Moreover, that meaning is inherently quantitative: that is, each variable will be defined over some numerical set, with no qualitative differences among realized values of each type. Another point is that each object may be detached from every other with no loss of meaning: that is, each may be manipulated independently of the others, provided, of course, that the manipulation obeys the relevant rules of mathematics. An alternative way of putting this is to say that the construct is made up of strictly *modular* parts. Finally, the construct is constrained solely by the relevant rules of mathematics (i.e. the rules of mathematics that govern the kinds of objects defined in the model). This fact is what underpins the modeler's capacity to manipulate the model objects solely as mathematical objects once they are defined, but it also limits the meaning of each of the variables to what can be conceived mathematically. In other words, the elements of the model are open to (and only to) strictly mathematical comprehension: they relate to one another in fixed ways, given by the relevant rules of mathematics and the definitions of the model.

These properties of w and e – precise and stable meaning, modularity, and uniform rule-following – are not peculiar to w and e, but rather are necessary properties of the objects of mathematical models in general. It is by virtue of possessing these features (though not only these) that the objects can be used by the modeler to construct mathematical (solution) narratives. They are thus *essential* features of the model. And since apt representation requires essential compatibility of model and target, it follows that the target, too, must share in these essential properties if it is to be aptly represented by the model. If any of the above features of mathematical constructs seem implausible in terms of the target – that is, if any of them constitute an *essential negative analogy* between model and target – then the model solution narrative (which *required* that the elements of the narrative possess these properties) cannot be interpreted as a plausible target narrative.

Using a mathematical model to illuminate a target thus commits the modeler to assuming certain things about the target. To be precise, mathematical modeling entails a commitment on the part of the modeler to the claim that it is *plausible* that the essential properties of mathematical constructs outlined above are also properties of the target. In other words, mathematical modeling presupposes that: (1*) the objects under investigation are plausibly *stable, modular,* and *quantitative,* with no qualitative differences among instantiations of each type; and that (2*) the relations between these objects are plausibly fixed and law-like throughout the context under study in the modeling exercise.[17]

We may return to Shapiro and Stiglitz (1984) to illustrate these points. Recall the following statements from the Denotation, Solution, and Interpretation phases:

Denotation:

Solution concept: $Max_e (V(e, \bullet))$; $V(e, \bullet) \in \{V_E^N(e, \bullet), V_E^S(e, \bullet)\}$; subject to $e \in [0,\infty)$, $w \in [0,\infty)$.

Solution:

(For $e \in [0,\infty)$), e will be at some positive level $e' > 0$ if and only if:

$$w \geq rV_u + (r + b + q)e'/q \equiv \hat{w} \qquad (2.3)^{18}$$

Interpretation:

Equation (2.3) has several natural implications. If the firm pays a sufficiently high wage, then the workers will not shirk. The critical wage, $\hat{w}$, is higher:

(a) the higher the required effort (e),
(b) the higher the expected utility associated with being unemployed (V_u),

---

[17] Cf. Lawson's conditions of "intrinsic closure": "A first constraint to impose, or seek to guarantee in the course of economic reasoning, is that of *intrinsic constancy*: that the internal, or intrinsic, structure of any (delineated state of any) individual of analysis be constant. The second obvious requirement (of any theoretical construction that is to satisfy the intrinsic condition for a closure) is *reducibility*: that the overall outcome event, for any state description, be reducible to the system conditions obtaining" (Lawson 1997: 98). A central difference between these conditions and conditions (1*) and (2*) above is that Lawson's conditions are pitched at the level of ontology – i.e. they are about the (real) nature of the analysands – whereas conditions (1*) and (2*) deal with the plausibility of claims and are therefore essentially pragmatic conditions. The subject of the content and development of the standards for judging the plausibility of such claims is discussed in Chapter 7.

[18] As noted above, (2.3) is a slightly modified version from how this equation appears in the text of the Shapiro–Stiglitz paper. Where I have written e' in (2.3), they have written e. I.e., in the paper (2.3) is: $w \geq rV_u + (r + b + q) e / q \equiv \hat{w}$. I am taking the statement out of its context, and the modification is necessary to ensure that (2.3) here has the same meaning it does in the Shapiro–Stiglitz paper.

(c) the lower the probability of being detected shirking (q),
(d) the higher the rate of interest (i.e. the relatively more weight is attached to the short-run gains from shirking (until one is caught) compared to the losses incurred when one is eventually caught),
(e) the higher the exogenous quit rate b (if one is going to have to leave the firm anyway, one might as well cheat on the firm). (Shapiro and Stiglitz 1984: 436)

Suppose we learned that, within the target under study, "wage" and "effort" seemed not to satisfy (1*) and (2*). For example, suppose we learned the following two things: first, that effort means different things in different contexts (specifically, that there are qualitative differences between different instantiations of it); and, second, that the relationship between effort and wage (and work-related enjoyment) would likely be affected by the kind of adversarial environment between management and workers envisioned in the Shapiro–Stiglitz model.

Regarding the first item, it is obvious that "effort" on the job comprises a wide range of qualitatively different activities – effort on an assembly-line, for example, differs significantly from effort in the context of, say, an advertising firm. But even if we limit ourselves to looking within job types that seem similar, what it means to put forth more effort may differ in important ways depending upon, for example, the particular work environment and managerial strategy of the organization in question. This was, in fact, one of the common themes to emerge from Truman Bewley's discussions with a wide range of managers (118 in all) about the plausibility of efficiency wage theories (Bewley 1999: 110–16). In such circumstances, it is question begging to represent effort with an object that does not admit qualitative distinctions among its instantiations. The referent of the term "effort" in a statement such as "the critical wage will be higher the higher is the effort required" is quite unclear unless we presume that such a quantitative concept is available to us in referring to the social phenomenon Shapiro and Stiglitz mean to refer to when speaking of worker effort in ordinary language.

One might object that we could imagine a kind of index of worker effort whose construction does not require the combining of qualitatively different objects – for example, a measure of the ratio of an individual's effort to the average effort of others doing similar jobs (or the minimum required effort) in similar work environments. But such a measure would still presume the possibility of a unidimensional measure summarizing the totality of the contribution of each worker to the work process that is qualitatively identical across the workers being compared. This would present a particular problem in workplaces that encourage creativity and innovation. In such cases, the very idea of what constitutes effort may itself be somewhat plastic, and in any event would be unlikely to admit a meaningful unidimensional interpretation.[19]

The second item – that the relationship between effort and wage (and work-related enjoyment) would likely be affected by the kind of adversarial environment between management and workers envisioned in the Shapiro-Stiglitz model – also raises interpretive challenges. The central conclusion the authors draw from their modeling exercise is that "the inability of employers to costlessly observe workers' on-the-job effort, can explain involuntary unemployment as an equilibrium phenomenon" (Shapiro and Stiglitz 1984: 433). In the model, the meaning of q, e, w, and V and the relationship between them is (necessarily) precise, fixed, and uniformly applicable throughout the modeling exercise. As model objects and relations, they have no connotation beyond their formal definitions. In actual workplaces, a given relationship between the ostensible counterparts of q, e, w, and V (which we might call a "monitoring regime") is not simply a passive fact of the world, but rather something actively constructed, implemented, and enforced by management with-respect-to/against workers. Put another way, such regimes are a kind of social gesture. As such, they will likely have connotations beyond their formal structure that may affect workers' reactions to them. A regime such as that depicted in the Shapiro-Stiglitz model, for example – i.e. one in which monitoring serves the sole purpose of detecting fireable offenses, and in which the judgment that such an offense has occurred is immediate and not subject to appeal – may be interpreted as adversarial, mistrustful, or even hostile.[20] A regime in which responsibility for monitoring is devolved to worker groups, on the other hand, might be interpreted as collegial and trusting. And these interpretations will likely also be shaped by the social context within which the regime is implemented – for example, the current state of labor relations and class relations, the extent of income inequality, and the prevalence of stigma against fired workers and/or the unemployed in general.

The point is that we cannot know *a priori* how the connotations of a monitoring regime will affect the functioning of that regime. We do know *a*

---

[19] See also Lawson (1997: 129).

[20] Indeed, this was another common theme to arise from Bewley's conversations with managers. See Bewley (1999: 110–16).

priori, however, that the effect of q on e and V in the model is fixed and *cannot* be affected by the possibly multifarious connotations of q (because q cannot have multiple connotations). This has significant consequences for how we may validly apply the model. To the extent that it is important to us (in a given modeling exercise) that we leave open the possibility of multiple connotations of monitoring regimes, the Shapiro–Stiglitz model will be inapt. Another way to put this is that the model can only be apt with respect to targets (specifically, to motivating questions about those targets) for which the possibility of multiple connotations of monitoring regimes may be ignored.

It might seem that by pointing this out I am restating a commonplace of economic modeling: that *ceteris paribus* conditions accompany the inter-pretation of all economic models, and the implications of a model are meant to hold only in situations in which the *ceteris* are indeed *paribus*. But I am saying something a bit more specific – namely, that among the things assumed to be held equal we need to pay special attention to those that are essential to the unfolding of the model narrative. Concretely, the theoretical modeler needs to explore the possible correspondences between target and model in order to judge when the use of a mathematical variable – with all the restrictions internal to the deductive system of mathematics – is apt or inapt in any particular case.

It might seem that this requirement places a heavy burden on theoretical modeling. Specifically, it would seem to restrict the modeler's freedom to engage in model-based thought experiments that leave to one side the question of the essential compatibility of model and target. Moreover, this restriction may seem unnecessary and inappropriate to the extent that one accepts an instrumental-positive standard of assessment (see the discussion in Chapter 1). Recall that under that standard, models can and should be assessed with reference to their predictive/postdictive capacity alone, and any other assessment of the correspondence between model and target is beside the point. To the extent that a model is not an apt representation of its target, the inaptness will reveal itself empirically in the failure of the model's implications to match the data (in a manner detectable econome-trically). But carrying out such an empirical assessment is the province of empirical modeling rather than theoretical modeling.

There are two reasons to resist this view. The first is that the division of labor between theoretical and empirical models it suggests is too starkly drawn. While theoretical economic modeling exercises do not involve econo-metric analysis of data, they still ultimately refer to the social world and are justified on the basis of their ability to represent (or to develop tools to help us represent) aspects of that world, however loosely. For example, it is a common trope of theoretical modeling exercises to begin by citing a "stylized fact" about some aspect of the economy and to present the exercise as developing a possible explanation. Theoretical modeling exercises may vary in how much they foreground the questions about the target world that ultimately motivate the exercise, but some recourse of this kind is implied whenever these exercises are presented as economically relevant (as opposed to simply mathematical exercises) (see footnote 2, above). This matters because it suggests that even highly abstract theoretical models are ultimately justified on the basis of their correspondence to some features of the target world. My argument in this chapter has tried to excavate this largely unarticulated feature of theoretical modeling and present the conditions under which it may prove tenable.

Second, as I will discuss in detail in the next chapter, the aptness of empirical models depends upon essential compatibility with their targets for precisely the same reasons (and in precisely the same manner) as is the case for theoretical models. Empirical and theoretical modeling exercises follow the same illuminative process: a motivating question about some aspect of the social world is explored through analysis of a mathematical model (i.e. a purely quantitative representation). Significantly, economic data are quantitative representations of the underlying social objects of interest, just as the variables and parameters of theoretical models are, and are thus model objects. Recognizing this allows us to see that inferences about the data are entirely *model* narratives. And as such they can provide answers to questions about the social world only to the extent that the model (*including the data*) is essentially compatible with the target. Thus empirical testing, in itself, is neither an adequate means of assessing the aptness of a model nor a means of escaping the necessity of establishing the essential compatibility of a model and its target. The arguments of the next chapter seek to substantiate these claims.

Conclusion

In this chapter, I have argued that in order for a mathematical modeling exercise to illuminate its target the following two conditions must be met: (1*) the objects under investigation must plausibly be *stable*, *modular*, and *quantitative*, with no qualitative differences among instantiations of each type; and (2*) the relations between them must be *fixed* and *law-like* through-out the context under study in the modeling exercise. This is because mathematical objects and the relations between them are of this type. If the social phenomena ostensibly represented by a mathematical model do not share those characteristics, the claim that the modeling exercise offers any information about the social phenomena the model is supposed to represent will be false. Moreover, this conclusion is derived not from an independent or objective standard of good scientific practice, but rather from the internal logic of mathematical modeling itself. Mathematical modeling practice embodies a representational ideal that requires mathematical models to generate inferences about social phenomena, and this representational ideal cannot be achieved if conditions (1*) and (2*) are not satisfied.

The foregoing analysis focused solely on theoretical modeling practice. Empirical economic modeling involves additional complexity, and it is to this that we now turn.

3 The use of mathematics in empirical modeling

The last chapter analyzed the use of mathematics in theoretical economic modeling exercises, paying close attention to a single paper, Shapiro and Stiglitz (1984). It concluded that further work would need to be done in order to establish that the social phenomena modeled by Shapiro and Stiglitz are essentially compatible with the authors' model. This chapter will extend that analysis by considering the use of mathematics in empirical economic modeling exercises, again by engaging carefully with a single paper: Sushil Wadhwani and Martin Wall's "A Direct Test of the Efficiency Wage Model Using UK Micro-Data" (1991).

By empirical modeling exercises, I mean those that confront the inferences drawn from a mathematical model with empirical data, whether gathered through passive observation or actively generated in laboratory or field experiments. This process represents an important test of the argument made in the last chapter, because empirical modeling exercises are sometimes thought to prove their own adequacy in the extent to which they successfully predict or retrodict the data they seek to represent. Nonetheless, I will argue that the "testing" process within empirical modeling is insufficient to overcome the limitations of mathematical modeling as already outlined in relation to theoretical modeling exercises. Exactly the same kind of objections apply to both. Showing this, however, requires addressing a set of significant additional complications. Specifically, the question of what is meant by "model" and "target," and the related question of what things are representing and what things being represented, are less straightforward in the case of empirical modeling than in the case of theoretical modeling. In the latter case, the representational process includes only two subjects: the model and the target. In empirical modeling exercises, however, additional subjects come into play, each with a key role in the process. In total, we will have to account for at least three and sometimes four separate entities: namely, the underlying phenomena of interest (i.e. the delimited social phenomena), the data, the empirical model used to analyze the data, and often (though not always) a theoretical model from which the empirical model is derived in some manner.

Understanding the use of mathematics in empirical economic modeling exercises requires that we are first clear on the respective roles and relations of all these entities. This is the goal of Section 3.1. That section describes the conceptual landscape of econometric modeling in general – whether the data being analyzed are gleaned from passive observation or actively generated in an experimental context – and argues that, notwithstanding the additional complexities involved, the underlying logic of the illuminative process of empirical mathematical modeling is conceptually parallel to that of theoretical mathematical modeling, and, therefore, that conditions (1*) and (2*) are also necessary conditions for the aptness of empirical mathematical modeling exercises. I illustrate these points in Sections 3.2 and 3.3. In Section 3.2, I examine an empirical mathematical analysis of efficiency wage theory using passive observation data – Wadhwani and Wall (1991). In Section 3.3, I consider the case of empirical modeling exercises using data that are actively generated in laboratory and field experiments.

3.1   Introducing empirical modeling

Econometrics was born in the 1930s as a means of formally characterizing the causal dynamics of business cycles.[1] The primary innovation of the early econometricians was to bring together mathematics, economics, and statistics in a manner that (ostensibly) not only mapped regularities but also provided a causal story about economic dynamics. Using Boumans' (2005) terminology, we can describe their approach as comprising two main elements: mathematical shaping and statistical verification.

Mathematical shaping involved choosing a mathematical form capable of capturing apparent features of the business cycle. Before the introduction of econometric analysis, such features were understood via "*a priori* considerations about what explanatory variables are to be included ... based on economic theory or common sense" (Tinbergen 1935: 10) and observation of the movements of these variables over time. A mathematical form could then be proposed that matched the features of these time series. A common early form was equations with lag schemes, as these were known to be able to produce cyclical behavior. Tinbergen noted, however, that cyclical behavior

[1] For an excellent account of the history of econometrics, see Morgan (1990).

was also produced by other mathematical forms, such as second-order differential equations. In the latter, the character of the cycle is affected not only by past values of the variable but also by differential and integral terms. Adding these features into a lag scheme produced a mathematical form capable of expressing the impact of several different kinds of influences on cyclical behavior.

The next step was to estimate the parameter values of the mathematical form implied by actual data. Essentially, this process provided an answer to the question: Assuming that the data were generated in line with the general mathematical form proposed, what specific version of that form did the data imply? The estimation process was understood by the early econometricians as providing information about both the magnitude and the significance of the parameter estimates. To the extent that certain features of the mathematical form seemed to contribute little or nothing to the observed shape of the data, they could be discarded and the estimation could be repeated without them in order to sharpen its focus on the significant factors. Tinbergen, for example, dropped the differential and integral terms in his business cycle equations on this basis.

The purpose of these early business cycle econometric exercises was to identify and quantify the "mechanism" (to use Tinbergen's term) that generated the business cycle. The means of doing so was to propose a candidate mechanism, and then use the data to refine (or "tune") the mechanism. And the aim was to produce a tuned mechanism that corresponded to the mechanism actually in operation in "the economic community to be considered in our theory" (Tinbergen 1935: 242).

Although econometrics has advanced prodigiously since these early business cycle exercises, its basic goal remains the same: namely, to analyze data in a manner that allows the economist to draw inferences about the aspects of the economy that the data ostensibly represent. The central challenge in doing so is overcoming the inherent epistemic limitations of economic data. Most immediately, the data are usually passive observations of particular realizations of states of the world.[2] In order to infer something about economic relations from them, we must impose additional structure. Tinbergen did so through mathematical shaping and tuning, interpreting the data as realizations of a particular mathematical process with well-established properties. This interpretation provided enough extra

---

[2] Actively generated data come with their own epistemic limitations. I will discuss these and other issues related to actively generated data in Section 3.3.

information to construct a causal story about the observations. The imposition of structure need not be as explicit as Tinbergen's imposition of a specific, determinate functional form: the probability-based approach introduced by Haavelmo, for example, imposed structure by reading the data as a single observation "of n variables (or a 'sample point') following an n-dimensional *joint* probability law" (Haavelmo 1944: iii, emphasis original). This structure, along with details about the probability law, provide the information needed to draw probabilistic inferences about causal relations of the variables.

One cost of the need for additional structure is that inferences drawn from the data using that additional structure are conditional on the additional structure. For example, suppose we wish to empirically assess a New Neoclassical Synthesis (NNS) model of the macroeconomy by estimating a Dynamic Stochastic General Equilibrium (DSGE) model, and suppose that the estimated model fits the data well (as in, e.g., Smets and Wouters 2007). From this alone, it would not be appropriate to infer, for example, that any of the particular behavioral assumptions of the NNS model have been vindicated (as in, e.g., Cogan *et al.* 2009), or that we can use the model as a tool for assessing the likely impact of a particular policy on the economy. The parameter estimates answer the question: assuming that the data are related in the manner depicted in the model, what parameter values would best describe these relationships (see, e.g, Sims 2007: 153). If the data are not related in this manner, then we cannot know what, if anything, the parameter values and the goodness of fit of the model imply about the data.

The question of what kind of correspondence between data and model is necessary for us to be able to draw valid inferences about the former from the latter is parallel to the questions we asked in Chapter 1 regarding modeling in general and in Chapter 2 regarding theoretical mathematical economic modeling. And, indeed, I will suggest that the answer here is parallel to the answer given in Chapter 2. The extra complication involved in addressing it in the case of empirical mathematical economic modeling arises from the fact that we cannot be concerned only with the relationship between the data and the empirical model, we must additionally consider the relationship of these things to economic theory and the social phenomena with which it is concerned (and which the data are meant to represent).

To see how and why these must be taken into account, consider again the case of empirical DSGE modeling. We may begin by asking what kind of match there must be between an empirical DSGE model and the data used to estimate it in order to be able to draw valid inferences about the latter from the former. Katarina Juselius and Massimo Franchi (2007) explore precisely this question in their paper "Taking a DSGE Model to the Data Meaningfully." The goal of the paper is to make explicit and to test the statistical assumptions underlying an empirical DSGE model (specifically the model of Ireland 2004). Doing so is crucial, the authors argue, in order to know what information, if any, the estimation of the DSGE model can give us about the meaning of the data: "The reported estimates [in Ireland (2004)] are claimed to be maximum likelihood estimates. These estimates, however, are only relevant given that the assumed model is a correct representation of the data" (Juselius and Franchi 2007: 7).

To perform this kind of assessment, we would ideally like a method that allows us to characterize the data in a way that does not impose a particular structure onto them. Juselius and Franchi (2007) use a Vector Autoregression (VAR) model for this purpose. The main impetus for, and primary virtue of, using VAR in macroeconometric modeling is that it imposes few restrictions on the data. In particular, it does not require "restrictions based on supposed a priori knowledge" (Sims 1980: 15) of the data's structure, such as restrictions imposed by the form of a particular economic theory. Because of this, proponents of VAR argue that it simply "represents the information in the data" – that is, it allows the data to speak for themselves (Juselius and Franchi 2007: 3, 1). Juselius and Franchi estimate a VAR model of the time series used to estimate Ireland's DSGE model, and analyze this characterization of the data to determine whether the restrictions implied in Ireland's model are consistent with it. They render a negative verdict with respect to the restrictions, and thus a negative verdict on the use of Ireland's model as a valid source of inferences about the data:

most of the assumptions underlying the DSGE model were testable and . . . most of them were rejected. The story the data wanted to tell, when allowed, was in fact very different from the [Real Business Cycle] story. (Juselius and Franchi 2007: 33)

What is important for our purposes is the question of what this process tells us about the validity of Ireland's model as a source of inferences about the ultimate target of interest: the social phenomena ostensibly underlying the data. This is a question not only of whether the restrictions of Ireland (2004) are consistent with the data, but also of the connection between the data and the phenomena they are meant to represent. In their introductory remarks about the procedure and aims of the paper, Juselius and Franchi make it clear that they are ultimately aiming past the data at this latter target:

we use the statistical model to find out, prior to the specification of the economic model, which assumptions are tenable with [respect to] the *economic reality*. The advantage is that it allows us to modify the untenable parts of the theory model (or choose another model altogether) so as to bring the model closer to the *economic reality*. (Juselius and Franchi 2007: 1, emphasis added)

But even if we accept that VAR modeling provides an accurate characterization of the statistical properties of the data, this in itself tells us nothing about what it implies for the phenomena that Juselius and Franchi refer to as "economic reality." Put another way, even if VAR lets the data speak for themselves, whether the data speak for the phenomena they are meant to represent remains an open question. It is one we must address, however, in order to understand the meaning of any econometric analysis.

To understand the relationship between economic data and economic phenomena, it is helpful first to be clear about what we mean by each of these terms. Following Jim Woodward (1989), we can characterize "phenomena" as features of our experience that we take to be "relatively stable" and "which are potential objects of explanation and prediction by general theory." The phenomena themselves are in general not directly observable, and so in order to investigate claims about them, we require some observable representation. Data play this role. And although it is a crucial role, it is a supporting rather than a starring role. As Woodward suggests, "data are typically not viewed as potential objects of explanation by or derivation from general theory; indeed, they typically are of no theoretical interest except insofar as they constitute evidence" for claims about the phenomena (Woodward 1989: 393–4). Data are simply matrices of numbers. Economically speaking, characterizing the internal relations of a matrix of numbers is not of inherent interest. It only becomes so when we claim that the numbers represent *in some way* actual phenomena of interest.

What is the nature of this representation? Data are, in a sense, meant to be a quantitative crystallization of the phenomena. In order to determine what will count as data for a particular phenomenon or set of phenomena, one must specify particular observable and quantifiable features of the world that can capture the meaning of the phenomena adequately for the purposes of one's particular inquiry. This is essentially, as Marcel Boumans (2005) has argued, a problem of *measurement*. In brute terms, measurement is simply "the assignment of numerals to objects or events according to rule – any rule" (Stevens 1959: 19; cited in Boumans 2005: 110). But ideally we would like the measurement to be reliably associated with relevant features of the

Figure 3.1   The relationship between data and phenomena

phenomena being measured, and to measure these as precisely as possible. By "reliably associated" I mean that the observable features of the world being measured by the data track the features of the phenomena they are meant to represent. Essentially, for some feature p of the phenomena, and observable feature q, "when things are arranged in the order of p, under certain specified conditions, they are also arranged in the order of q" (Heidelberger 1993: 146–7, cited in Boumans 2005: 115). Following Boumans, I will call this property the level of "autonomy" of the measurement.

Whether and to what extent our data are autonomous and precise depends, of course, on our data generation procedure. We can think of this procedure as comprising three basic steps. First, we must determine which aspects of the phenomena are relevant with respect to the kinds of puzzles we wish to investigate. Second, we must select observable and quantifiable features of the world that we believe to be associated with the relevant aspects of the phenomena in a stable manner. Third, we must provide a procedure for measuring these observable and quantifiable features (this will include the specification of a measurement apparatus, if such is necessary) and measure them. The relationship between the phenomena of interest, the observable representation of those phenomena and the data (i.e. the numerical representation of the observable representation of the phenomena) is depicted in Figure 3.1. The issue of autonomy is primarily related to the first arrow – i.e., to what extent have we picked out observable features of the world that reliably correspond to the desired features of the phenomena? The issue of precision is primarily related to the second arrow – i.e., given a particular observable feature of the world to measure, does our measurement process deliver consistent measurements across similar situations?

Although precision of measurement is clearly important, and there is much to say about it, I am here primarily concerned with autonomy. As noted above, the extent of autonomy of the data representation depends upon the extent to which the observable features of the world chosen as representations of the relevant features of the phenomena actually do track those features. For ease of exposition, I will call the characterization of the observable features of the world that are meant to represent the phenomena the "intension of the data." Put roughly, the intension of the data is the description one would need to give to someone tasked with gathering those data. The corresponding "extension" of the data would be the matrix of numbers gathered according to those instructions. The relationship between the phenomena and the intension of the data is the one we are concerned with here. We can think of the intension of the data as describing a mapping from the phenomena to the observable world. In order for the mapping to be autonomous (at least to some degree), it is necessary not only that it attach to stable features of the phenomena, but also that the dynamics of the observable features track those of the phenomena. In other words, there must be what Boumans calls a relationship of *homomorphism* between the empirical structure of the phenomena and the numerical structure of the extension of the data (Boumans 2005: 109).[3] Formally, we can express this as follows:

Take a well-defined, non-empty class of extra-mathematical entities Q . . . Let there exist upon that class a set of empirical relations $R = \{R_1, \ldots, R_n\}$. Let us further consider a set of numbers N (in general a subset of the set of real numbers Re) and let there be defined on that set a set of numerical relations $P = \{P_1, \ldots, P_n\}$. Let there exist a mapping M with domain Q and a range in N, $M: Q \rightarrow N$ which is a homomorphism of the empirical relationship system $<Q,R>$ and the numerical relation system $<N,P>$ (Finkelstein 1975: 105, cited in Boumans 2005: 109).

This condition of homomorphism is necessary (though not sufficient) for a measurement to be autonomous for the same reasons that any apt representation requires more than simply representation *simpliciter* (as discussed in Chapter 1). Without this homomorphism, the measurement may cease to track the aspects of the phenomena we wish to capture over some ranges. Note that it is not necessary that the relation between the phenomena *in its entirety* and the intension of the data be homomorphic. We require only that there be a similarity of structure with respect to the aspects of the phenomena that we wish to capture, and the structure relevant to the kinds of puzzles we wish to address through exploration of the data.

---

[3] Note that the numerical structure of the data is determined by the intension of the data. The extension is merely a particular realization of that structure. Thus, another way to put this statement would be to say that the empirical structure of the phenomena must be homomorphic to the empirical structure of the intension of the data.

The requirement of homomorphism between the data and the phenomena under study is exactly parallel to the requirement of essential compatibility between theoretical models and their targets discussed in the previous chapter. And this is no coincidence. As purely quantitative representations of the target objects of study, economic data reside in the world of the model and function as a part of the model in empirical modeling exercises. Inferences about the data are inferences about model objects and are therefore a part of the model narrative. We can validly interpret such inferences about the data as possible inferences about the underlying social phenomena *only* to the extent that we have established the plausibility of a homomorphic relationship between the data and the aspects of the underlying phenomena they are meant to represent. This homomorphism requirement, then, is an extension of the essential compatibility requirement: in empirical modeling exercises, the requirement of essential compatibility between model and target includes a requirement of homomorphism between data and target (because the data are a part of the model).

Econometricians are, of course, well aware of the importance of the relationship between the data and the underlying phenomena of interest. In the literature, this relationship is generally couched in terms of a data-generating process (DGP) – i.e., "the actual, complicated underlying process that generates the data" (Hoover 2005: 19). The DGP is meant to be a highly unrestricted concept. As Kevin Hoover explains, it "need not be simple or stable through time, and it is certainly not observable" (Hoover 2001: 175). If we were to be able to perceive the true DGP in its entirety, we would essentially know the complete underlying structure whose observable precipitates are the data. Our only evidence of the DGP, however, is the data. And it is the goal of econometrics to use the data "to characterize pieces of the data-generating process in meaningful ways" (Hoover 2001: 175).

It is important to note, however, that characterizing pieces of the data-generating process is an intra-model activity. It reveals the possible mathematical structure underlying a matrix of numbers, and it is properly judged according to (and only according to) the relevant rules of mathematics. In contrast, the requirement that a relation of homomorphism exist between the data and the underlying phenomena is concerned with the relationship *between* model and target entities. The extent to which data satisfy this requirement in any given case cannot be determined through econometric analysis, nor does econometric analysis obviate the need to establish that the requirement is met. On the contrary, as discussed above, the results of an econometric analysis of a given data set – i.e. the characterization of a piece of its DGP – can be validly interpreted as providing epistemic access to the target *only if* it is plausible that a relation of homomorphism holds between the data and the aspects of the target they ostensibly represent.

The foregoing discussion suggests that empirical modeling exercises follow essentially the same process and face the same interpretive challenges as theoretical modeling exercises. Both seek to project inferences about a mathematical construct (either a theoretical model or an empirical model (which includes the data being analyzed)) onto a social target in order to gain some kind of epistemic access to the latter. And, for both, essential compatibility between model and target is a necessary condition for the aptness of the model. The similarity in form of empirical modeling exercises to theoretical ones is strongest in cases of what we might call "stand-alone" empirical modeling exercises – i.e. those that are not meant to be explicit tests of theory or of a theoretical model. As with theoretical modeling exercises, stand-alone empirical modeling exercises involve only one set of representational relations – i.e. those between the empirical model (including the data) and the target. As such, the illuminative process follows the same stages as that of theoretical modeling exercises (see Figure 2.1). Juselius and Franchi (2007) is an example of a stand-alone empirical modeling exercise. The authors' empirical analysis is not meant to test the implications/hypotheses of a particular theory or theoretical model, but rather to determine whether a given set of assumptions (taken from Ireland 2004) about data on output, capital, labor hours, and consumption conformed to "economic reality" (Juselius and Franchi 2007: 2).[4]

Empirical modeling exercises that *are* meant to be explicit tests of theory follow the same basic illuminative process, but the involvement of the theoretical model being tested introduces some interpretive complications. For one, there is the issue of the motivating question of such exercises. It may seem obvious that the target under study in an empirical test of a theoretical model is the theoretical model – for example, that our motivating question is something along the lines of: "Is Shapiro–Stiglitz efficiency wage theory supported by the data?" We must recognize, however, that to the extent the theoretical model is a model *of* some aspect of the economy, the ultimate target of our empirical test will necessarily be the social phenomena represented by the theoretical model. That is, the motivating question above should be understood to mean: "Are worker effort, wage and unemployment

---

[4] The role of the Ireland (2004) model in Juselius and Franchi (2007) is that of a foil rather than the object of an empirical test.

(as understood in their social context) related in the manner suggested by Shapiro–Stiglitz efficiency wage theory?"

Second, the involvement of the theoretical model complicates the representational relations at play in the empirical modeling exercise. Whereas in stand-alone empirical modeling exercises we had one set of representational relations, in empirical tests of theoretical models we have several. The empirical model (including the data) is no longer simply representing the social phenomena underlying the data, it is also representing the theoretical model. Inferences drawn from the empirical modeling exercise about the data will be interpreted as informative not only about the underlying social phenomena but also about the merits of the theoretical model. Additionally, we must remain aware that the theoretical model being tested is itself a representation of some social target or set of possible social targets. (Presumably, the social target of the empirical modeling exercise will be included in the set of possible targets of the theoretical model.)

3.2   The analysis extended

Despite the additional interpretive complexities of empirical tests of theoretical models, however, we will find that such exercises ultimately follow essentially the same process as those of theoretical and stand-alone empirical modeling exercises. This is most readily shown through an example. To complement the previous chapter's exploration of Shapiro and Stiglitz (1984), we will use Sushil Wadhwani and Martin Wall's 1991 paper "A Direct Test of the Efficiency Wage Model Using UK Micro-Data" for this purpose.

The stated purpose of Wadhwani and Wall (1991) is "to test the efficiency wage model by examining some of its predictions for the determinants of a firm's productivity" (Wadhwani and Wall 1991: 529). Specifically, the authors aim to "assess the validity" of several theoretical efficiency wage models that "rationalise[ ] ... the relationship between the wage and productivity" differently (Wadhwani and Wall 1991: 530). And they indicate that the source of the data for this assessment will be "the published accounts of 219 UK manufacturing companies over the period 1972–82" (Wadhwani and Wall 1991: 533).

It is in the Denotation phase that we begin to see the representational complexities involved in empirical testing of theoretical models. Like Shapiro and Stiglitz (1984), the authors assign mathematical correspondents to the social phenomena of interest. But whereas this was a one-to-one correspondence in Shapiro and Stiglitz (1984) – i.e. each social phenomenon was assigned one mathematical analogue – each social phenomenon of interest in Wadhwani and Wall (1991) will be assigned at least two, and generally three, mathematical analogues. The two analogues assigned to all of the phenomena of interest are their representations in the empirical model and the data, respectively. A third analogue will be assigned to elements of the DSP that also appear in the theoretical model being tested *if* the empirical analysis is explicitly couched as a test of that theory (as is the case in Wadhwani and Wall 1991).

We can trace the assignment of all of these analogues in Wadhwani and Wall's (1991) treatment of "effort." They begin with a straightforward theoretical representation of effort as a function $e(\cdot)$, which is meant to be analogous to Shapiro and Stiglitz's (1984) "*e*". But because effort is not directly observable – a foundational assumption of efficiency wage theory – such a direct representation can be neither a right-hand-side variable in the econometric specification nor a legitimate data variable. The authors address this by hypothesizing a functional form for effort with the observable arguments "relative wage" and "unemployment"

$$e(\cdot) = -a + b\,(W/W^*)^{\gamma 1} u^{-\gamma 2} \tag{3.1}$$

In their empirical model, the social concept "effort" is represented not by $e(\cdot)$, but rather by the right-hand side of expression (3.1). It is important therefore to note that "$-a + b(W/W^*)^{\gamma 1} u^{-\gamma 2}$" does not *replace* "effort" as an object of interest, but rather *represents* it. We will see this in the Interpretation phase, where the authors draw conclusions about $e(\cdot)$ and effort on the basis of the behavior of "$-a + b(W/W^*)^{\gamma 1} u^{-\gamma 2}$" in the empirical analysis.

What remains in the Denotation phase is to specify the empirical model (including a solution concept) and the data representations of the model objects. The empirical model is designed to perform a specific test of the theoretical model. As such, it need not cover all of the ground of the theoretical model, though it does need to accurately reflect the particular dynamics of the theoretical model that are being tested. In this case, the authors wish to test the implication of the theoretical model that higher relative wages and higher unemployment induce greater effort and, therefore, increase the value added by labor. For this purpose, they utilize a Cobb–Douglas production function in which the effect of the labor input is affected by the function $e(\cdot)$, from expression (3.1) above. Specifically, the authors consider two *e*-augmented functional forms – one in which *e* augments the labor input multiplicatively:

$$Y_{it} = A_i K_{it}^{\alpha} (e(\cdot) L_{it})^{\beta} \exp(\varphi)$$

$$= A_i K_{it}^{\alpha} \left(\left(-a + b \left(\frac{W_{it}}{W_{it}^*} \right)^{\gamma 1} u^{-\gamma 2} \right) L_{it} \right)^{\beta} \exp(\varphi) \qquad (3.2)$$

and one in which e affects the labor elasticity of production (i.e. the exponent on L):

$$Y_{it} = A_i K_{it}^{\alpha} L_{it}^{\beta(e(\cdot))} \exp(\varphi) = A_i K_{it}^{\alpha} L_{it}^{(\beta_0 + \beta_1 \ln(W_{it}/W_{it}^*)^{\gamma 1} \ln u_t^{-\gamma 2})} \exp(\varphi) \qquad (3.3)$$

For their empirical models, the authors use log-linearized forms of these expressions:

$$\ln Y_{it} = \alpha_0 + \alpha_1 \ln K_{it} + \beta_0 \ln L_{it} + \beta_1 \ln \left(\frac{W_{it}}{W_{it}^*} \right) + \beta_2 \ln u_t + \varepsilon_{it} \qquad (3.2')$$

$$\ln Y_{it} = \alpha_2 + \alpha_3 \ln K_{it} + \beta_3 \ln L_{it} + \beta_4 \ln L_{it} \ln \left(\frac{W_{it}}{W_{it}^*} \right)$$

$$+ \beta_5 \ln L_{it} \ln u_t + v_{it} \qquad (3.3')$$

where ε_{it} and v_{it} are error terms. The authors' solution concept for these models is to calculate best-fit parameter values and to produce various test statistics. To accomplish this, they utilize Ordinary Least Squares and Generalized Method of Moments estimation techniques.

Our final element of the Denotation phase is the data representations of the elements of the empirical model. For this example, we will be interested only in the data representations of "W," "W^*" and "u." In order to differentiate clearly between the empirical model variables and their data representations, I will put the latter in curled brackets. The authors utilize UK government data covering the period 1972 to 1982 for all three variables. $\{W\}$ consists of wage data taken from the EXSTAT database; $\{W^*\}$ consists of industry-specific average wage data from the UK Department of Employment *Gazette*; and $\{u\}$ consists of UK male unemployment rate data from the *British Labour Statistics Historical Abstract*, the Department of Employment *Gazette*, and the British Labour Statistics *Year Book*.[5]

---

[5] Wadhwani and Wall reference Layard and Nickell (1986) as the source of their unemployment data. This is the complete explanation of the construction of the unemployment data from the data appendix of Layard and Nickell (1986: S373): "Male unemployment rate. The series used is 'males wholly unemployed as a percentage of the number of employees (employed and unemployed) at the appropriate mid-year, for the UK.' The numbers unemployed exclude 'temporarily stopped' but include

Table 3.1 Selected correspondences of Wadhwani and Wall (1991)

Social phenomena (ordinary language)	Proto-model (mixture of languages, informal statement of formal structure)	Formal model (mathematical language) (T=theoretical model; E=empirical model; DR=data representation)
Relative wage	Amount of money paid per unit time of work to a worker divided by an average of wages paid throughout the relevant industry. Qualitatively identical across all workers in all locations in all time periods.	T and E: W/W^* DR: $\{W\}$: Wage data from EXSTAT $\{W^*\}$: Industry wage data from Department of Employment *Gazette.*
Unemployment	The proportion of individuals in the work force who do not have formal, paid work. Qualitatively identical across all workers in all locations in all time periods.	T and E: u DR: $\{u\}$: Male unemployment rate from *British Labour Statistics Historical Abstract*, Department of Employment *Gazette* and *British Labour Statistics Year Book*
Effort	The worker's sole input into the work process, which s/he dislikes performing. Qualitatively identical across all workers in all locations in all time periods.	T: $e(\cdot)$ E: $-a + b(W/W^*)^{\gamma 1}u^{-\gamma 2}$ DR: $-a + b(\{W/W^*\})^{\gamma 1}\{u\}^{-\gamma 2}$

The three representations of the social phenomenon "effort" can be expressed in a Catalogue of Correspondences as shown in Table 3.1.

Despite the additional complexity of this Catalogue of Correspondences (as compared to that of Shapiro and Stiglitz 1984), the Solution phase remains conceptually straightforward. As with all mathematical modeling exercises, at the end of the Denotation phase we have a mathematical construct and its solution concept. Bringing the construct to its solution involves *only* mathematical reasoning. As long as there have been no mathematical errors in the articulation of the construct and solution concept, these will already embody a solution – all that is left is to trace the path to the

school-leavers. The data are published in [*British Labour Statistics Historical Abstract*], the [British Labour Statistics *Year Book BLSHA*] and finally [Department of Employment *Gazette*]. We consider the male rate to be the most accurate available measure of the aggregate unemployment rate (including unregistered women). The data refer to the pre-1982 definition of the male unemployment rate; more recent data have been appropriately adjusted."

Table 3.2 Parameter estimates from Wadhwani and Wall (1991)

Independent variable	Parameter estimate (t-statistic)
$\ln(\{W\}/\{W^*\})_{it}$	0.39
	(4.89)
$\ln(\{u_t\})$	0.05
	(2.12)

solution (or conclude that there is no solution or that it is impossible to determine whether or not there is a solution) using definitions of the model and the rules of the relevant branch of mathematics.

For Wadhwani and Wall (1991), these solutions consist of parameter estimates and test statistics. I will focus here only on those that are relevant to the representation of "effort," and, for the sake of brevity, will consider the results from only one of their six regressions. For regression equation (3.2′) above, estimated using GMM, the authors report the regression parameters and t-statistics shown in Table 3.2.[6]

As this statement is a part of the Solution phase, the correct standards for assessing it are those of the relevant branch(es) of mathematics and statistics. That is, when we ask whether or not the statement above is correct, we are asking (and *only* asking) whether the statement was arrived at in a manner that did not violate any rules of the relevant mathematics and statistical theory. Just as with *Statement 2.1* from the previous chapter's discussion of Shapiro and Stiglitz (1984), the statement in Table 3.2 is a "natural implication" (to use Shapiro and Stiglitz's term) of regression equation (3.2′) and GMM theory because the mathematical operations performed to arrive at the statement were performed *only* on mathematical objects that were proper inputs into the operations. This is crucial – just as it was, above, in the Shapiro and Stiglitz (1984) example. The operations here were performed on the objects $\ln\{Y_{it}\}$, $\ln(\{W\}/\{W^*\})_{it}$ and $\ln(\{u_t\})$ – among other mathematical objects of the proper form – which are nothing more or less than matrices of numbers. The same can be said about *all* of the results of the Solution phase in Wadhwani and Wall (1991) and, moreover, the results of the Solution phase in *all* mathematical modeling exercises in which no

---

[6] The authors give different names for the independent variables: "(Wage/Ind. Wage)" instead of "{W/W*}" and "Unemployment" instead of "{u}." I have used the curled bracket names for purposes of clarity. Using the ordinary language names in the report of the solution converts the statement into an Interpretation phase statement. I discuss this in more detail below.

mathematical mistakes or violations of the governing mathematics have occurred. Thus, with respect to the Solution phase, there is complete parallelism between empirical and theoretical mathematical modeling exercises.

The additional complexities of empirical mathematical modeling exercises that involve explicit tests of (some aspect of) a theoretical model manifest themselves in the Interpretation phase. As with Shapiro and Stiglitz (1984), the interpretation of results in Wadhwani and Wall (1991) is generally expressed by restating the mathematical solution with the ordinary language names of the delimited social phenomena substituted in for their mathematical analogues. The following statement is typical:

We have found evidence that <u>firm-level productivity</u> increases when either <u>relative wages</u> rise, or the level of <u>unemployment</u> rises. The estimated <u>effort-wage</u> elasticity is about 0.6, while the <u>effort-unemployment</u> elasticity is about 0.05. Moreover there is some support for the idea that a change in the <u>relative wage</u> also increases <u>productivity</u>. Our result that higher <u>relative wages</u> are consistent with higher <u>productivity</u> are consistent with those of Levine (1988), while evidence of a link between <u>unemployment</u> and <u>work intensity</u> has also been reported by Schor (1988). This provides some support for the efficiency wage models. (Wadhwani and Wall 1991: 545, underlining added)

As with *Statement 2.1* from the previous chapter's discussion of Shapiro and Stiglitz (1984), the statement above is a conjecture conflating two claims. The first is the claim that the things said about the underlined terms are true of their data representations, and the second is the claim that these things are true of the ordinary language version of the terms.

But disentangling the claims is more complicated here than was the case with Shapiro and Stiglitz. In the latter, we needed only to consider two versions of the statement: the statement as it was actually written, and its Solution phase version (i.e. the same statements with the mathematical terms put back in, in place of ordinary language terms). This allowed us to see that the truth or falsehood of the Solution phase version had indeed been established through the analysis, but that it had not been established for the statement as written. *Statement 2.1* was simply a re-statement of the relationship between the proto-model elements. The claim of its connection to the delimited social phenomena remained unexplored and, therefore, unsupported.

The direct analogy between the Shapiro and Stiglitz example and the passage above would be to consider the passage as written versus a version in which the underlined terms are understood to be the data representations of the objects in question. Concretely, the first two sentences of the passage would become:

We have found evidence that $\{Y_{it}\}$ increases when either $\{W/W^*\}_{it}$ rise[s], or the level of $\{u\}$ rises. The estimated $\underline{(-a + b(\{W/W^*\}_{it})^{\gamma1}\{u_t\}^{-\gamma2}} \, \text{-} \, \{W/W^*\}_{it}$ elasticity is about 0.6, while the $\underline{(-a + b(\{W/W^*\}_{it})^{\gamma1}\{u_t\}^{-\gamma2}} \, \text{-} \, \{u_t\}$ elasticity is about 0.05

with the rest of the passage being transformed similarly. This statement can be judged entirely under the standards of the relevant mathematics and statistics. As long as none of the rules of these theories was violated in arriving at the parameter estimates, then the statement above is true. To assess the validity of the previous passage – in which the underlined terms were the ordinary language names of the phenomena – we would need to assess the validity of the implicit claim that inferences about the data representations flow all the way through the Catalogue of Correspondences to the social concepts they ostensibly represent. As discussed above, this would require at a minimum establishing that conditions (1*) and (2*) (see Chapter 2) are satisfied.

If, as is the case here, the empirical analysis is also meant to be a test of an underlying theory, we have an extra layer of implication to consider – namely, the implication that flows from the data representations through the empirical model to the theoretical model. On one level, this is straightforward: the claim is that the data represent not only the delimited social phenomena but also the model objects of the empirical model, which, in turn, represent the model objects of the theoretical model. In other words, the claim is that all of these links in the Catalogue of Correspondences are tight.

But what does it mean for these latter links to be tight? The standards of econometrics give considerable guidance regarding the link between the data and the empirical model. The identifying assumptions of the various estimation techniques place restrictions on the distributional properties of the data and the interrelationships between various data elements. For example, Ordinary Least Squares estimation requires, *inter alia*, that error terms be normally distributed with zero (conditional) mean and constant (conditional) variance, and that the independent variables do not exhibit multicollinearity. And this is, of course, just the tip of the iceberg. There is a voluminous and continuously growing literature on the necessary properties of data (as well as tests and remedies for violations) for the myriad special types of estimation that economists confront.

The standards for judging the tightness of the link between theoretical models and empirical models are less well defined. All empirical economists must, of course, obey the relevant rules of mathematics in deriving a testable mathematical model from a given theoretical one. But this still leaves considerable leeway, and, in general, the ability of an economist to produce an effective empirical model is regarded largely as an art. In summary, then, as long as an empirical model faithfully preserves the mathematical properties of interest in a theoretical model, and the data adhere to the strictures of the chosen estimation technique, these latter links are taken to be tight. In such a case, it will be judged that the empirical test is a valid test of at least some aspect of the theory.

Ultimately, however, this judgment cannot be made in isolation from the link to the delimited social phenomena, because all these representations – the theoretical model, the empirical model, and the data representations – are meant to be representations *of* those phenomena. In light of this, the most crucial link in the Catalogue of Correspondences is the left-most link, the one that connects to the delimited social phenomena. If this link is weak, then the tightness of the other links is irrelevant because the ultimate purpose of mathematical economic modeling exercises is to provide insight into these phenomena *in their social context*.

Consider, for example, the claim that the positive, significant values for (a) the "effort-wage" and (b) "effort-unemployment" elasticities and (c) the relationship between "relative wage" and "productivity" are evidence in support of efficiency wage theory. Let us assume, for the sake of argument, that the links between the data representations, the empirical model, and the theoretical model are strong, but that we have not yet assessed the strength of the link to the delimited social phenomena. In such a case, the most that one could legitimately claim is that the analysis can be a test of a theory about the phenomena *only if* those phenomena are so-constituted as to be legitimate inputs into that theory. As discussed in Chapter 2 above (in reference to Shapiro and Stiglitz 1984), the latter characteristic requires that the DSP fulfill conditions (1*) and (2*).

The case of "effort" offers a clear example of the necessity of (1*) and (2*), as its mathematical representations were forced to go through considerable contortions to allow the authors to arrive at the conclusion that their regressions were a test of efficiency wage theory. Interpreting regression equations (3.2′) and (3.3′) as statements expressing a relationship between "effort" and "productivity" requires, among other things, a parsing of "effort" into modular (in this case, additively separable) component parts, treating a certain combination of those parts as identical in meaning to the whole, re-stating the relationship between effort and productivity as a relationship between the component parts of effort and productivity, and then log-linearizing the statement of the relationship.

The left-most link of the Catalogue of Correspondences bears quite a lot of weight here. What does it mean to break the concept of "effort" into its component parts, deploy the parts individually to stand in for the whole, and then log-linearize them? This is a crucial element in the economic explanation of the relationship between "effort" and "productivity," and so we must be able to account for it. As discussed in Chapter 1, economic explanation does not consist merely of the end-result of the analysis – for example, the estimate of the regression coefficients and the corresponding significance tests – it also consists of the dynamics that bring us to that end-result. And anything that cannot plausibly be conceived in terms of such dynamics will not be capable of arriving at the end stage of those dynamics. In other words, if we cannot conceive of "effort" as capable of undergoing the type of manipulation that brought us from $e(\cdot)$ to equations (3.2') and (3.3'), then Wadhwani and Wall's analysis cannot provide insight into "effort" and its role in economic and social life. Consequently, we need a guide to help us understand how these dynamics could be meaningfully projected onto the social world in which "effort" resides. Merely asserting a Catalogue of Correspondences conceals the issue rather than addresses it – and it is a crucial issue.

If we have not established that (1*) and (2*) are satisfied, then the most we could claim is that the analysis could be a test of a theory about the proto-model form of the delimited social phenomena. By definition, proto-model entities possess the characteristics needed to be legitimate inputs into the theoretical model, but as discussed above their connection to the actual DSP is purely conjectural unless the economist explicitly explores whether (1*) and (2*) hold. Put briefly, without establishing that (1*) and (2*) are fulfilled, a mathematical modeling exercise answers only the question of what would be true of the relevant social phenomena if they possessed *only* the same kind of complexity as their mathematical analogues. But, surely, one of the most vexing aspects of social behavior is that we generally do not *know* what kind of complexity underlies it. The question of the stability, modularity, and law-like relations of the social phenomena of interest, then, is lexicographically prior to any questions about the legitimacy of the econometric specification and the appropriateness of the data. Unless and until this prior question is addressed, we can have no idea what the econometric results imply about the social phenomena in which we are interested.

3.3   Empirical modeling exercises using actively generated data

The example just considered – Wadhwani and Wall (1991) – utilized passively observed data taken from a pre-existing data set to draw inferences about the phenomena ostensibly represented by that data. Given the widespread use and growing influence of experimental methods, it is apposite to consider whether the conclusions reached so far about empirical modeling in general also apply to empirical analyses using experimentally generated data. In brief, the answer is yes. In the arguments above, economic data were characterized simply as quantitative representations of social phenomena, without reference to their source. As such, (1*) and (2*) will be necessary conditions for the representational aptness of experimentally generated data for exactly the same reasons as in the case of passively observed data.

It is worthwhile exploring, however, whether experimental methods may be better suited than non-experimental methods to producing models that are essentially compatible with their targets. Put another way: Do experimental methods *per se* allow us to construct quantitative representations that will more reliably (relative to non-experimental methods) correspond to the phenomena under study in the manner discussed above? In this section, I will argue that they do not. We can see why this is the case most clearly by considering laboratory experiments and field experiments separately.

The primary advantage claimed for economic laboratory experiments is the control they afford the economist over the behavioral environment. With skillful experimental design, the economist can eliminate or control for many of the confounding factors that may obscure the manifestation of the phenomena of interest and the causal relations between them in non-experimental settings (see, e.g., Davis and Holt 1993: 16; Guala 2005: 108, 119, 128). One factor that the economist cannot control for in the laboratory, however, is the effect of the laboratory environment itself. And this raises a potential problem for the *external validity* of the experiment (i.e. the applicability of the experimental results to environments different from that of the experiment itself). If one's ultimate targets are social phenomena as they occur outside the laboratory, and if the behavior exhibited in a laboratory experiment is significantly influenced by the fact that it is taking place in a laboratory, then the data are of ambiguous value in drawing inferences about the former. And this is true regardless of how precisely one is measuring whatever it is that is being measured in the lab.

This issue is well known to experimental economists. As early as 1982, Vernon Smith argued that experimental results can be validly applied to environments outside the laboratory only to the extent that the two environments exhibit sufficient "parallelism" – that is, only to the extent that "[p]ropositions about the behavior of individuals and the performance of institutions that have been tested in laboratory microeconomies apply also to non-laboratory microeconomies where similar *ceteris paribus* conditions hold" (Smith 1982: 936). And, as Smith goes on to point out, the extent of parallelism between an experiment and its target phenomena cannot be determined within the laboratory itself, but rather "*can only be determined empirically by comparison studies*" (Smith 1982: 936, emphasis original).

Seen in this light, the requirements for the external validity of an experiment sound remarkably similar to the requirements of apt representation more generally.[7] In both cases, the representation (i.e. model or experiment) and target must be similar enough in relevant respects to support the claim that narratives drawn from the former are interpretable as possible narratives about the latter.[8] One might argue that experimental methods offer a significant advantage in establishing the required similarity because they allow us to construct in the lab the kinds of "real-life" situations we mean to represent. Smith (1976: 275), for example, argues that the laboratory is a place "where real people earn real money for making real decisions about abstract claims that are just as 'real' as a share of General Motors." And Guala (2005: 217) suggests that

[e]xperimental systems are reliable if they are made of the same stuff as real-world economies. No process of abstraction from the material forces at work is needed in order to draw the analogy from the laboratory to the outside world. One may abstract from "negligible" causal factors but not from the basic processes at work. The similarity is not merely formal but holds at the material level as well.

But it is important to recognize that, in the absence of further evidence, the kinds of similarity between laboratory phenomena and "real-world" phenomena that Smith and Guala reference are merely cases of positive analogy rather than something stronger, like homomorphism (or, *a fortiori*,

---

[7] Uskali Mäki (2005) has suggested that the distinction between economic experiments and economic models is thin to the point of vanishing.

[8] Regarding experiments, Francesco Guala writes: "Whatever the real causal process, we can use laboratory tests to study selected aspects of specific real-world economies as long as we are confident that the same (unknown) basic principles of behavior apply in both cases ... The trick is to *make sure* that the target and the experimental system are similar in most relevant respects so as to be able to generalize the observed results from the laboratory to the outside world" (Guala 2005: 216–17).

isomorphism). The fact that real people may earn real money for making real decisions in a laboratory tells us nothing about whether those decisions are sufficiently similar to the specific instance of decision making (or type of decision) in the world outside of the laboratory that is the experiment's intended target. And, just as in the case of models more generally, the experimental exercise itself cannot provide the kind of information we would need to establish that similarity.

The same is true of randomized controlled trials (RCT) conducted in the field. The main attraction of RCT is that it (ostensibly) allows the economist to identify relative treatment effects more cleanly than would generally be possible with non-experimental data. In the latter case, detecting and measuring such effects requires filtering out potential confounding factors through statistical control techniques. The problem with these methods, as Gary Burtless points out, is that "they rest on an ultimately untestable assumption about the distribution of the error term or the specification of the equation representing the decision to participate in a program." Consequently, "if critics of a non-experimental estimator question the reliability of the key assumption, other social scientists (and policymakers) often have no reliable method to decide whether the maintained assumption is a good approximation of reality" (Burtless 1995: 72). RCT, in contrast, allows the economist to control for confounding factors *ex ante* by randomizing assignment of the treatment. If the assignment is truly random and the responses of the treatment group are measured accurately, the thinking goes, then the difference in response of the two groups cleanly identifies the treatment effect.

It is important to recognize, however, that the assumptions of proper randomization and accurate measurement *are* assumptions. One might argue (as, for example, Burtless does) that the RCT assumptions are more straightforward and easily assessed than those of the *ex post* statistical controls required in non-experimental settings. But it is far from clear that this optimism is warranted. As with laboratory economic experiments, RCT studies are generally meant to provide evidence about effects beyond the scope of the experiment itself – whether to different populations or to the same population in the future. And, again, as with laboratory experiments it is not possible to control for the effects of the experimental environment itself. James Heckman and Jeffrey Smith, for example, point to the possibility of what they call "randomization bias," which occurs

when random assignment causes the type of persons participating in a program to differ from the type that would participate in the program as it normally operates.

Randomization bias also results from changes in participant behavior due to the threat of service denial, like reductions in complementary training activities undertaken prior to application to the program. (Heckman and Smith 1995: 99)

This is a troubling prospect for RCT studies because the presence of randomization bias "cannot be confirmed or denied on data from these experiments because there are no non-experimental versions of these programs" (Heckman and Smith 1995: 99).

But the potential for such experimentally undetectable confounding effects is not limited to randomization bias. Consider, for example, the issue of the definition of the treatment itself. Is it merely a particular good or service, or do its effects depend also on the manner in which it is administered and/or by whom it is administered? If the latter, why and how do these things matter to the population? We need to know the answers to such questions to know just what it is that is being tested and what it would mean to deliver "the same" treatment to other populations. In some cases, the economist will be able to address some of these questions through experimental design. Recent studies of the effect of pricing/subsidization on the uptake and use of health-improving technologies in Kenya and Zambia provide a good example.[9] But we cannot presume that all such relevant factors will be addressable experimentally. Moreover, and more importantly, determining which such questions *are* important and why they matter may be best accomplished through less structured and stylized interactions than those of the experimental setting.

The best evidence for this comes from RCT practitioners themselves. In their recent book *Poor Economics: A Radical Rethinking of the Way to Fight Global Poverty*, Esther Duflo and Abhijit Banerjee (2011) argue that RCT has revolutionized development economics by producing actionable on-the-ground knowledge about the realities of the lives of the poor. And they cite an impressive array of recent work to support their claim. What is perhaps most revealing about Duflo and Banerjee's discussion of the accomplishments of RCT, however, is how prominently situation-specific knowledge gleaned in the field (but outside of the experimental setting) figures in the insights generated in crafting their treatments and interpreting their results.[10] The informal ethnographic work through which the authors garnered this information is seldom highlighted as an essential part of the study design, but it is clear from the manner in which the authors appeal to this information to justify their design choices and the interpretation of their results that the information was

---

[9] On the provision of anti-malaria bed netting in Kenya see, e.g., Dupas (2014); Cohen and Dupas (2010). On the provision of water purification systems in Zambia, see Ashraf *et al.* (2010).

[10] See Duflo and Banerjee (2011: 36, 41, 60–1, 86, 192, 197). Reddy (2013) makes a similar point.

both essential and highly unlikely to have been generated through the experimental process itself. What this suggests is that, to the extent these studies have produced unusual insight it is not due to RCT *per se*, but rather to the judicious use of ethnographically obtained information in crafting and interpreting the results of experiments employing RCT.

Conclusion

The above account of empirical mathematical analyses demonstrates that even with the added complexities of empirical testing, the left-most link in the Catalogue of Correspondences remains the most crucial to the ability of any mathematical analysis to fulfill its representational ideal. Moreover, recognizing that the data themselves are models of the delimited social phenomena allows us to see that, when conditions (1*) and (2*) are not satisfied, mathematical empirical analysis is an inadequate tool for assessing the aptness of an economic model. In Chapters 6 and 7, I will expand on this finding to argue that methodological reforms are needed to make economics a more reliable and faithfully empirical science. Before turning to this, however, it is necessary to establish that the findings of the previous two chapters are not dependent upon any particular features of the two papers considered in this and the previous chapter. Toward that end, the next two chapters will apply the findings of Chapters 2 and 3 to two additional cases.

Part II

The critique applied

4 The New, New Institutional Economics[*]

This chapter examines a relatively new offshoot of the institutional economics literature that we can call the New, New Institutional Economics, or "NNIE," to distinguish it from the New Institutional Economics associated with, *inter alia*, Douglass North and Oliver Williamson. NNIE is an ambitious approach to institutional economics that includes important contributions from Daron Acemoglu, James Robinson, Andrei Shleifer, Edward Glaeser, and others. Its practitioners employ highly parsimonious formal models to capture the central role of institutions in the explanation of various grand historical changes in power, politics and long-term economic trends, including, among others, the success and failure of democratization, the rise of the American regulatory state, and the prospects for the realization of Immanuel Kant's state of perpetual peace. The work has appeared in top economics journals and in the books of top university presses, though up to now it has received little attention within the institutional economics literature for its achievements.[1] This lack of recognition should not be interpreted as evidence that the work is not properly categorized as "institutional economics." Its practitioners are using economic methodology to investigate the role of socio-politico-economic institutions in economic activity and thus their work falls, undeniably, on the turf of institutional economics.

This chapter offers an overview and methodological assessment of this work, concluding that although the NNIE has built upon and extended the work of the Old and New Institutional Economics in important ways, it has, at the same time, set back economists' understanding of institutions by overstating the applicability of its formal models. Specifically, it finds that the NNIE has contributed to institutional economics by (1) expanding

---

[*] "This chapter appeared previously, in substantially the same form in the *Journal of Institutional Economics* as Spiegler and Milberg (2009). © The JOIE Foundation 2009. Reprinted with permission. I am grateful to Will Milberg for allowing me to use the material here."

[1] The work is absent, for example, from recent surveys of new developments in economic thought that are otherwise sympathetic to institutionalism. See Colander *et al.* (2004); Colander (2005a); Hodgson (2007); Davis (2007).

the application of economic modeling tools to new areas of inquiry; (2) insisting on parsimonious and rigorous formal models of institutional outcomes; and (3) introducing the role of (political and economic) power to the study of the determination of institutions, thereby allowing for consideration of institutional change that is not Pareto improving. But while NNIE has made these important contributions to positive political economy and institutional economics, its models are arguably too parsimonious to illuminate meaningfully the complex institutions they ostensibly represent. The explanatory power of NNIE analyses ultimately comes not from the pure form of their formal models, but rather from their proto-model analogues – i.e. essentially rough, ordinary language articulations of what the formal model is meant to represent. The formal model and proto-model are meant to be different articulations of the same underlying model, but close examination shows that it is only the proto-model that is used for analysis, interpretation, and testing. Once the formal model is isolated from the proto-model, we can see that the correspondence between the two is loose and that the untethered nature of the proto-model renders it inadequate as a source of rigorous conjecture.

Perhaps most importantly, the claim that the formal models of the NNIE are its true analytic engine leads to unwarranted conclusions about institutions. The formal models represent institutions as mere background conditions to decision making, whose effects on outcomes are determined by exogenously determined parameter values. This representation of institutions amounts not to investigating but to denaturing or taming them. Essentially, it renders institutions susceptible to economic analysis by converting them into something else – something compatible with a conception of the social world as a series of constrained optimization problems. Yet if, as is argued below, the NNIE's formal models do not and *cannot* generate the insight contained in NNIE work, then this treatment of institutions is an unhelpful distraction.

This chapter has three sections. Section 4.1 discusses the theoretical conditions for the emergence of the NNIE, emphasizing the breakdown of general equilibrium economics and the abandonment of the traditional criteria of robustness in the determination of advances in economic knowledge. Section 4.2 assesses the aptness and efficacy of some NNIE modeling exercises using the four-part framework introduced in Chapter 2. Section 4.3 compares the NNIE conception of institutions with that found in the Old and New Institutionalism, showing that the NNIE offers greater precision of modeling but less descriptive power and greater ambiguity in its implied conjectures.

4.1   Introducing NNIE

The 1970s saw the economics profession move away from its longstanding concern with the robustness of its model of a competitive, private enterprise economy. In part, this move was prompted by the inability to prove the uniqueness and stability of general equilibrium (GE). But more than this, the aridity of the GE approach – i.e., its insulation from institutional and historical detail – itself engendered a degree of self-questioning and rethinking. As the limited applicability of GE was becoming more apparent to economists, a small, internal response began to form. A "New Economics" arose in a series of subfields in the profession, including international economics, labor economics, industrial organization, and macroeconomics. These new approaches all sought greater relevance, and had some common features across subfields, including an emphasis on imperfect (rather than perfect) market competition, asymmetric (rather than perfect) information, on increasing (rather than constant) returns-to-scale technology, and on strategic (rather than independent) behavior by firms and governments in relation to their rivals. This greater relevance, however, was bought at the expense of robustness and generality, with New Economics models generating results that were more contingent, explosive, and path dependent than those produced in the era of GE analysis. In fact, some complained that the models were *ad hoc* and could be used to model *any* pre-determined outcome (Solow 1979). Moreover, results were not only not unique – multiple equilibria were now the norm rather than the exception – they were not robust; that is, the results were highly sensitive to the choice of assumptions, parameter values, and functional forms.[2]

In the era of competitive general equilibrium analysis, an economic model was understood to generate new knowledge if it provided a proof of a known result, but required weaker, i.e. more general, assumptions than did existing proofs of the same result. The great strength of this methodology was the clarity of its criterion for establishing the progress of knowledge: that is, the increased mathematical generality, or robustness, of its proofs. In the era of the New Economics, robustness was abandoned as a methodological ideal.[3]

---

[2] The lack of robustness was identified early on in the development of this paradigm, and was used to downplay the significance of its policy implications. See, e.g., Grossman (1986).

[3] In fact, the discussion of robustness has shifted more into the realm of empirics and in particular the support for a particular econometric result under different variable definitions, different choices of instrumental variables, and alternative model specifications. See, e.g., Rodrik *et al.* (2004).

In the context of this New Economics, institutions emerged as a focus of research for at least two reasons. One was that the New Economics' modeling methodology allowed more freedom in taking up a broad set of issues not traditionally considered within the scope of economic inquiry. Second, with the New Economics' lack of consensus over the preferred model and model assumptions, and its abandonment of the traditional criteria (i.e. robustness and generality) for judging the progress of economic knowledge, "institutions" were frequently called upon as the important missing explanatory factor of economic life.

This rediscovery of the importance of institutions is a genuinely significant development of the last thirty years of economic thought, in contrast to many other recent innovations – such as complexity theory, behavioralism, and experimentalism – which are largely technical advances rather than new conceptions of how an economy functions. Today, it is standard practice in the study of economic growth and economic development to cite institutions in the explanation of outcomes (see Barro 1997; Rodrik *et al.* 2004). And with institutions now more squarely within the confines of economics, the scope of inquiry has broadened significantly, to include such issues as culture (Guiso *et al.* 2006), religion (McLeary and Barro 2006), politics (Rodrik *et al.* 2004), and the sociology of business (Langlois 2003). This enhanced view of the importance of institutions in these contexts is recognized by both neoclassical and non-neoclassical economists (see, e.g., Barro 1997; Chang 2006).

Perhaps the most ambitious effort to integrate institutions into contemporary economics is that of the New, New Institutional Economists – a group that has sought, along the lines of much of the New Economics, to provide rational choice foundations for historical and market changes, with institutions as background conditions for rational, strategic decision making.

While the NNIE, like any body of literature, is a varied set, the work shares enough salient characteristics for it to be considered a new form of institutional economics. Specifically, the NNIE is characterized by two constitutive characteristics: (1) a stated concern with explaining the origin, dynamics, and/or economic implications of complex socio-politico-economic institutions; and (2) the use of hyper-reductive mathematical models to represent these institutions as a means of explaining them.[4] The NNIE authors are for the most part concerned with big and/or highly socio-politically embedded

---

[4] All models (mathematical or otherwise) of social phenomena are reductive to some extent. The term "hyper-reductive" is meant to capture the NNIE's explicit goal of pushing the parsimony of these models as far as it can go.

institutions – the kinds of institutions that both the academic insider and the layperson would likely consider "important" and not necessarily the kind of target generally associated with economic analysis. This, in fact, is the allure of this work: it aims to tackle big, important issues. The titles of its papers make a point of advertising this. They are short, ambitious and often sound more like the titles of lengthy political economy treatises than of short economics journal articles: "The Rise of the Regulatory State," "The Dynamics of Political Compromise," "Persuasion in Politics," "Social Culture and Economic Performance," "Accountability in Government," "War and Democracy."[5] There is, also, at least one major book-length contribution to this literature: Daron Acemoglu and James A. Robinson's (2006) *Economic Origins of Dictatorship and Democracy*, which intentionally recalls Barrington Moore's (1966) influential sociological treatise, *Social Origins of Dictatorship and Democracy*.

It is the interaction of the two characteristics, though, that gives rise to both the promise and the peril of the NNIE approach. The prospect of adequately understanding highly complex social phenomena without needing to delve into all of their particularities and context-dependency has been a major (if not *the* major) selling point of economics since the marginalist revolution of the late nineteenth century.[6] The NNIE is perhaps the most audacious example of this approach. We turn now to a detailed examination of the methodology of the NNIE to determine how well it is able to overcome this peril and to deliver on its substantial promise.

4.2   An analysis of NNIE methodology

NNIE analyses seek to explain and understand institutions by representing those institutions with hyper-reductive mathematical models, and positing the dynamics of those models as the underlying dynamics driving the institutions as well. The attraction and promise of this approach is not only that it provides illumination of apparently puzzling and complex institutions, but also does so using models that are parsimonious and formal (and therefore simple and precise). Because of this combination of illumination and parsimony, the NNIE is presented by its practitioners as an advance over previous versions of institutional economics.

---

[5] These titles belong, respectively, to Glaeser and Shleifer (2003), Dixit *et al.* (2000), Murphy and Shleifer (2004), Fang (2001), Maskin and Tirole (2004), and Hess and Orphanides (2001).

[6] For a review of the nature and significance of the marginalist revolution, see Black *et al.* (1973).

Although straightforward in conception, the precise workings of this explanatory methodology are complicated. In order to critically assess the methodology, we must first explicate it clearly. To do so, we will use the four-part framework introduced in Chapter 2 to analyze three leading examples of NNIE work. We will focus primarily on Daron Acemoglu and James A. Robinson's book *Economic Origins of Dictatorship and Democracy* (2006), and secondarily on Edward L. Glaeser and Andrei Shleifer's "The Rise of the Regulatory State" (2003), and Eric Maskin and Jean Tirole's (2004) "The Politician and the Judge: Accountability in Government."

4.2.1 Delimitation

The Delimitation phase of Acemoglu and Robinson (2006) includes statements in ordinary language about the authors' target subject matter and the particular puzzles they will seek to illuminate. As is typical of NNIE work, their research questions are broad and ambitious: "Why is it that some countries are democracies, where there are regular and free elections and politicians are accountable to citizens, whereas other countries are not?" (Acemoglu and Robinson 2006: xi). Specific questions that the authors see as falling under this general rubric include: "What determines whether a country is a democracy? Which factors can explain the patterns of democratization we observe? Why did the United States attain universal male suffrage more than a century before many Latin American countries? Why, once created, did democracy persist and consolidate in some countries, such as Britain, Sweden, and the United States, and collapse in others, such as Argentina, Brazil, and Chile?" (Acemoglu and Robinson 2006: xii). Again, these questions are phrased in ordinary language, and are meant to bring to mind the delimited social phenomena – countries, democracy, elections, citizens, etc. – as we actually encounter them, embedded in their social context.

We also find Delimitation phase statements targeting large, complex institutions in ordinary language in Glaeser and Shleifer (2003) and Maskin and Tirole (2004). Glaeser and Shleifer (2003) delimit the set of phenomena associated with the various regulatory regimes and corporate liability laws before and during the Progressive Era in America as their target phenomena. Articulating the main aim of their paper, they state: "we attempt to understand why these changes occurred in the United States between 1887 and 1917" (Glaeser and Shleifer 2003: 401). Maskin and Tirole (2004) delimit the set of phenomena associated with accountability in representative democratic government. "The premise behind democracy," they write, "is that public decisions should reflect the will of the people. But in most democracies, comparatively few decisions are made *directly* by the public. More often, the power to decide is delegated to *representatives* ... But if representatives decide for the public, what induces them to act in the public interest?" (Maskin and Tirole 2004: 1034–5).

4.2.2   Denotation

The Denotation phase of NNIE analysis involves connecting the delimited social phenomena to a formal model. This typically involves at least two stages. First, the structure of the model is described informally using the ordinary language names of the phenomena under study. The following passage from Acemoglu and Robinson (2006) is an example of this stage:

> To starkly illustrate our framework, consider a society in which there are two groups: an elite and the citizens. Nondemocracy is rule by the elite; democracy is rule by the more numerous groups who constitute the majority – in this case the citizens. In nondemocracy, the elite get [*sic*] the policies it wants; in democracy, the citizens have more power to get what they want. Because the elite loses under democracy, it naturally has an incentive to oppose or subvert it; yet, most democracies arise when they are created by the elite. (Acemoglu and Robinson 2006: xii)

This statement combines elements of the formal model and the socially understood phenomena under study. The authors use terms that invoke social experience – for example, society, democracy, non-democracy, elite, citizens, policies, power, etc. – but they also gesture toward a structure that belongs to the world of the formal model they will later introduce. Significantly, although the authors will ultimately want to claim that this structure also represents the causal dynamics underlying the delimited social phenomena, that claim is still conjectural in statements like the one quoted above. Put succinctly: presentations of the structure of the model using ordinary language terms are necessarily conjectures unless and until an argument is made establishing the truth value of the conjecture.

We see such informal, ordinary language descriptions of model structure in Glaeser and Shleifer (2003) and Maskin and Tirole (2004) as well. Glaeser and Shleifer (2003) offer the following description:

> we develop a theory of law enforcement in which private litigation, government regulation, a combination of the two, and doing nothing are considered as alternative institutional arrangements to secure property rights. In our theory, whatever law

enforcement strategy the society chooses, private individuals will seek to subvert its workings to benefit themselves. The efficiency of alternative institutional arrangements depends in part on their vulnerability to such subversion. (Glaeser and Shleifer 2003: 401)

And Maskin and Tirole (2004) offer the following informal description of (a portion of) their model's structure:

we set out a two-period model with a homogeneous electorate. In each period, there is a decision to be made between two possible actions. One action is "popular" in the sense that the electorate believes it to be optimal with better than fair odds. The electorate will either decide for itself (direct democracy) or delegate the decision to an official, who knows which action is optimal. Each official is either congruent (i.e., she has the same preferences as the electorate) or noncongruent with society, although *ex ante* the electorate does not know which case holds. She also places some weight on holding office for its own sake. (Maskin and Tirole 2004: 1036)

As with the similar statement from Acemoglu and Robinson (2006) above, both of these statements are meant to (a) introduce the structure of the model, but (b) in a way that is intended to get the reader used to the idea that that structure is also a possible structure for the social phenomena described in the Delimitation phase, while (c) not yet submitting that conjecture to a test in order to support its validity.

In the second stage of the Denotation phase, the structure of the model is formalized. Specifically, during this phase the authors provide mathematical analogues of the phenomena under study, formal definitions of these mathematical analogues, and a solution concept for the model described by this collection of new mathematical objects and rules. The full version of the model ultimately used in Acemoglu and Robinson (2006) has many parts – too many to present in full here. We can, though, provide a few illustrative elements of the model and the authors' presentation of these elements as formal analogues of various elements of the delimited social phenomena. The following passage provides mathematical analogues to the social concepts of income, distribution, distributional conflict, and inequality:

Consider … a society consisting of two types of individuals: the rich with fixed income y^r and the poor with income $y^p < y^r$. To economize on notation, total population is normalized to 1; a fraction $1 - \delta > 1/2$ of the agents is poor, with income y^p; and the remaining fraction δ is rich with income y^r. Mean income is denoted by $\bar{y}$. Our focus is on distributional conflict, so it is important to parameterize inequality. To do so, we introduce the notation θ as the share of income accruing to the rich; hence, we have:

$$y^p = \frac{(1-\theta)\bar{y}}{(1-\delta)} \text{ and } y^r = \frac{\theta\bar{y}}{\delta}$$

Notice that an increase in θ represents an increase in inequality. Of course, we need $y^p < \bar{y} < y^r$, which requires that: $\frac{(1-\theta)\bar{y}}{(1-\delta)} < \frac{\theta\bar{y}}{\delta}$ or $\theta > \delta$. (Acemoglu and Robinson 2006: 104)

By the end of the Denotation phase, then, we have the three articulations of the phenomena under study introduced in Chapter 2: (1) *The ordinary language articulation:* an articulation in ordinary language, whose referents are the phenomena of interest in their socially embedded context; (2) *The formal model:* an articulation in mathematical language, whose referents are mathematical objects whose nature and dynamics are formally defined (and therefore complete and unambiguous) – the claim that this articulation is a representation of the phenomena of interest is still a conjecture at this point; and (3) a hybrid articulation, *The proto-model,* that expresses the structure of the model informally, using the ordinary language names of the phenomena of interest. This articulation is an embodiment of the conjecture that the model represents the phenomena of interest, as it places those phenomena within the model structure. The referents of the proto-model are ambiguous, with authors implying sometimes that its terms refer to the socially embedded phenomena and sometimes to the mathematical analogues. Table 4.1 summarizes the Denotation phase elements of the statement

Table 4.1 Catalogue of selected correspondences of Acemoglu and Robinson (2006)

Social phenomena (ordinary language)	Proto-model (*mixture of languages, informal statement of formal structure*)	Formal model (*mathematical language*)
poverty	The state of being in the majority, possessing income lower than that of an individual belonging to the minority, and being identical to all others in this state.	$y_i = y^p = \frac{(1-\theta)\bar{y}}{(1-\delta)}$
wealthiness	The state of being in the minority, possessing income higher than that of an individual belonging to the majority, and being identical to all others in this state.	$y_i = y^r = \frac{\theta\bar{y}}{\delta}$
inequality	A state of affairs in a populace with two types of citizens (with total intra-group homogeneity) in which the minority group earns an income which, in terms of percentage of the mean income, is greater than their share of the population.	$\theta > \delta$

quoted above in a "Catalog of Correspondences" between the social phenomena and the formal model.

This is just an example of a part of the Catalog of Correspondences. The full version of the Catalog of Correspondences would also include the rules and relations that compose the solution concept. In this case, the model is solved using game theory, and the solution concept is Nash equilibrium (specifically, either subgame perfect Nash equilibrium or Markov perfect equilibrium, depending upon the version of the model). Appendix 4.1 depicts the simplest version of Acemoglu and Robinson's (2006) formal model of democratization.

Glaeser and Shleifer (2003) and Maskin and Tirole (2004) also introduce the formal version of their model in the manner reviewed above. For the sake of brevity, we will include here just a summary version of portions of their Catalogs of Correspondences (see Table 4.2).

Table 4.2 Catalogue of selected correspondences of Glaeser and Shleifer (2003) and Maskin and Tirole (2004)

Social phenomena (*ordinary language*)	Proto-model (*mixture of languages, informal statement of formal structure*)	Formal model (*mathematical language*)
Glaeser and Shleifer (2003)		
Firms	There are only two possible (mutually exclusive) types of firms in the economy	$\{\alpha, \beta\}$
All-things-considered cost to society of any kind of industrial accident	Social cost per unit of economic activity	$D \in \mathbb{R}_+$
Level of "law and order" in a society	Level of payment required to avoid a fine or liability payment for an accident – which the authors also describe as corresponding to "the maximum fine that can be enforced by either regulators or courts without subversion." (410)	$X \in \mathbb{R}_+$
Optimal regulatory policy	Policy which achieves the "first-best," which is interpreted as inducing precautionary effort only in firms whose accident probability is affected by their level of precaution.	$Q = \begin{cases} Q_2 > 0 \text{ if type} = \alpha \\ Q_1 = 0 \text{ if type} = \beta \end{cases}$

Table 4.2 (cont.)

Social phenomena (*ordinary language*)	Proto-model (*mixture of languages, informal statement of formal structure*)	Formal model (*mathematical language*)
Maskin and Tirole (2004)		
Public policy	There are only two possible (discrete, independent) actions for government in any given period.	$\{a, b\}$
Level of political knowledge of the citizenry	The probability that the electorate prefers the public policy that is actually optimal for them.	$p \in [0,1]$
A political official's personal benefit from holding office	Utility derived from "perks, prestige, etc." (1039)	$R \in \mathbb{R}$
Society ruled by judicial power	Society with any form of government in which officials cannot be removed from office by a vote of the citizenry, and therefore where officials choose actions according only to their own preferences.	Solution concept: Agent 1 solves $$\underset{\substack{x_1 \in \{a,b\} \\ x_2 \in \{a,b\}}}{\text{Max }} U_{\text{Agent1}}(x_1, x_2)$$

4.2.3   Solution

As is generally the case with mathematical modeling exercises, the Solution phase is the most straightforward of the phases as it resides purely in the mathematical realm and involves only the working out of the mathematical model according to the formal definitions and solution concept specified in the Denotation phase. As long as the model has been appropriately articulated, mathematically speaking, then either a solution (or solutions) exists, a solution does not exist, or it is not possible to determine whether or not a solution exists. In the case of Acemoglu and Robinson (2006), the Solution phase consists of articulating subgame perfect Nash or Markov perfect equilibria for their extensive form game. For both Glaeser and Shleifer (2003) and Maskin and Tirole (2004), it involves solving objective maximization problems under different parameter values, and ranking the desirability of each of these solutions according to formally defined criteria.

Rather than simply reporting the solution in purely mathematical terms – i.e. as a set of statements that is immediately either true, false, or undecidable depending entirely and only on the formal definitions given in the paper and the relevant rules of mathematics – the solutions in these NNIE works are often reported with ordinary language names substituted for the mathematical names of the objects. As was the case with the efficiency wage theory examples in Chapters 2 and 3, this is a conflation of the Solution phase and the Interpretation phase. It amounts to reporting as a *solution* something that is a *conjecture* (i.e. the conjecture that the solution to the mathematical model also represents a solution to the social puzzle articulated in the Delimitation phase) rather than a true (i.e. internally consistent) mathematical statement.

Proposition 6.1 (from Acemoglu and Robinson 2006) is an example of such a hybrid form of solution presentation. Boldface has been added to the ordinary language terms to emphasize this. (Note that μ is a parameter meant to measure "the material cost of revolution," and that θ is the share of income going to the "rich"):[7]

PROPOSITION 6.1

There is a unique subgame perfect equilibrium $\{\tilde{\sigma}^r, \tilde{\sigma}^p\}$ in the game described in [Appendix 4.1], and it is such that:

- *If $\theta \leq \mu$, then the **revolution** constraint does not bind and **the elites** can **stay in power** without **democratizing** or **redistributing income**.*
- *If $\theta > \mu$, then the **revolution** constraint binds. In addition, let μ^* be defined by [equation (6.6) in Appendix 4.2]. Then:*
  - *(a) If $\mu \geq \mu^*$, the **elites** do not **democratize** and set the **tax rate** $\hat{\tau}$ to **redistribute enough** income to avoid a **revolution**.*
  - *(b) If $\mu < \mu^*$ and [equation (6.7) in Appendix 4.2] holds, **concessions** are insufficient to avoid a **revolution** and the **elites democratize**.*
  - *(c) If $\mu < \mu^*$ and [equation (6.7) in Appendix 4.2] does not hold, there is a **revolution**.*

(Acemoglu and Robinson 2006: 185, emphasis added)

As noted above, this way of presenting the solution involves both mathematical and ordinary language terms. A purely mathematical presentation of the solution would look like this:

---

[7] The game in Appendix 4.1 substitutes purely mathematical language for many of the ordinary language terms used by Acemoglu and Robinson (2006). For purposes of translation: "The elites" are Agent 1, "the citizens" are Agent 2, A and B represent "democratizing" and "not-democratizing," respectively, and α and β represent "revolution" and "no revolution," respectively. Note also that Proposition 6.1 contains some elements that we have not defined above. The necessary supplemental information is provided in Appendix 4.2.

PROPOSITION 6.1'

There is a unique subgame perfect equilibrium $\{\tilde{\sigma}^r, \tilde{\sigma}^p\}$ in the game described in [Appendix 4.1], and it is such that:

- *If $\theta \leq \mu$, then the actions of Agent 1 include $\tau_{1,1} = \tau_{1,2} = 0$; $\phi = B$*
- *If $\theta > \mu$, then, with μ^* defined by [equation (6.6)]:*
  - (a) *If $\mu \geq \mu^*$, then the actions of Agent 1 include $\phi = B$, $\tau_{1,1} = \hat{\tau}$. The actions of Agent 2 include $\rho = \beta$.*
  - (b) *If $\mu < \mu^*$ and [equation (6.7)] holds, the actions of Agent 1 include $\phi = A$.*
  - (c) *If $\mu < \mu^*$ and [equation (6.7)] does not hold, the actions of Agent 2 include $\rho = \alpha$.*

Proposition 6.1', which does *not* appear in Acemoglu and Robinson (2006), can be assessed solely against the definitions of the model and the relevant rules of mathematics. On this basis, it is a true (i.e. internally consistent) statement, and one that has no necessary connection to the phenomena under study. Unlike Proposition 6.1, it is not a conjecture.[8]

Glaeser and Shleifer (2003) also present their results in hybrid form. The following is an excerpt from their Solution phase (with emphasis added to ordinary language terms) demonstrating this hybrid form (supplementary definitions are provided in Appendix 4.2):

PROPOSITION 1.

If $P_a < P_1$, then:

- (f) *for $\frac{X}{S} < \frac{C}{P}$ the only feasible option is **laissez faire**;*
- (g) *for $\frac{C}{P} < \frac{X}{S} < \frac{C}{P}$ **regulation** dominates **laissez faire** if $D > \frac{C}{(1-\pi_a)(P_1-P_2)}$, and vice versa if this condition does not hold;*
- (h) *for $\frac{C}{P} < \frac{X}{S} < \frac{C}{P_1-P_2}$ **negligence** achieves first-best; and*
- (i) *for $\frac{X}{S} > \frac{C}{P_1-P_2}$ both **negligence** and **strict liability** achieve first-best.*

    (Glaeser and Shleifer 2003: 410)

This is a hybrid statement because it reports a mathematical result using the ordinary language terms "laissez faire," "regulation," "negligence," and "strict liability" – terms that refer to actual social institutional arrangements, but also have mathematical representations in the paper (Glaeser and Shleifer

---

[8] For a different version of the model later in the book, Acemoglu and Robinson (2006: 149) themselves present two different versions of the subgame perfect Nash equilibrium as we do here. They do not, however, discuss the conceptual difference between the two. Rather, the conjectural version (which they refer to simply as an "alternative, more intuitive form") of the solution is presented as an unproblematic elaboration of the Formal Model solution.

2003: 409–10). The statement above would be unobjectionably true (i.e. internally consistent) if it referred only to the purely mathematical elements of the Catalog of Correspondences. As it is written, however, Proposition 1 (like Acemoglu and Robinson's (2006): Proposition 6.1) is a conjecture whose truth value has not yet been established or even probed.[9]

4.2.4 Interpretation

The Interpretation phase of NNIE analysis involves interpreting the solution of the model as a solution to the puzzle articulated in the Delimitation phase, and, if there is an empirical element to the paper, providing empirical support for this interpretation. The interpretation is generally presented through hybrid statements that are very close to the explicit expression of the formal model solution – i.e. by articulating the solution to the formal model with ordinary language terms substituted for their mathematical counterparts. For example, Acemoglu and Robinson's (2006) Proposition 6.1 above – which replaces some of the formal model's mathematical names with ordinary language ones – is really a part of the Interpretation phase, whereas Proposition 6.1' is the Solution phase statement underlying it.

The justification for the interpretation is generally offered in one or both of two ways: (1) by comparing proto-model statements to historical experience – i.e. by re-describing an episode of current or historical experience as conforming roughly to the structure of the model, and/or (2) through quantitative/graphical presentation of statistical relationships that, it is claimed, were predicted by the model.[10] It is in this stage that the problems inherent in NNIE methodology become apparent. As implemented in current NNIE work, neither of these two strategies provides adequate justification for the claim that the parsimonious formal models employed to explain complex institutional dynamics actually do so. In the remainder of this section, we will explain why the problems with these justificatory strategies undermine the claims of NNIE regarding the efficacy and power of its methods.

The central problem with the first strategy is that, whereas historical experience is matched with *some* version of the model, it is not matched with the version of the model that is presented as the analytical engine of the work. Specifically, it is the proto-model against which the experience is

---

[9] Similar hybrid Solution phase statements are found in Maskin and Tirole (2004: 1040–9). I omit discussion of these passages here purely for the sake of brevity.

[10] Some NNIE work pursues this strategy through formal econometric testing. See, for example, Rodrik (1999), Blomberg and Harrington (2000), Burton *et al.* (2002), Botticini and Siow (2003), and Hanssen (2004).

assessed rather than the formal model. As such, the most that this strategy can do is provide support for the claim that the proto-model – a vague and informal statement of the structure of the formal model – is not inconsistent with historical experience. This may be helpful, but it falls short of the heroic claims of NNIE practitioners.[11] Moreover, NNIE proto-models are, in general, incapable of generating falsifiable hypotheses. As such, work that depends on "tests" of these hypotheses for justification of the formal model cannot satisfy the representational ideal of mathematical modeling exercises, and therefore cannot even be considered a legitimate candidate for generating scientific knowledge.

This problem generally manifests itself in NNIE work through the adducing of evidence in a manner that is too nuanced, vague, or imprecise to correspond to the formal model (but that is well suited to correspond to the proto-model). A good example of this problem can be found in Acemoglu and Robinson's (2006) testing of their model's ability to explain the process of democratization in Britain in the nineteenth and twentieth centuries. A portion of the claim being tested is that their model explains the relationship between democratization and the cost of revolution. Specifically, the authors claim that the relationship between the parameter μ and the equilibrium strategy of "elites" (i.e. Agent 1 in the game in Appendix 4.1) matches the relationship between the cost of revolution and democratization in British history.[12] The following passage is presented as empirical evidence in favor of their model:

Beginning in 1832, the British political elites made a series of strategic concessions aimed at incorporating the previously disenfranchised into politics because the alternative was seen to be social unrest, chaos, and possibly revolution. The concessions were gradual because in 1832 social peace could be purchased by buying off the middle class ... Later, as the working classes reorganized through the Chartist movement and subsequently through trade unions, further concessions had to be made. The Great War and its fallout sealed the final offer of full democracy. (Acemoglu and Robinson 2006: 350–1)

The implication is that this series of events corresponds to the value of μ beginning low, and then rising in a manner that changes the equilibrium

---

[11] Indeed, it is a standard feature of NNIE work to emphasize the Formal Model's role as the insight-generating engine of the analysis as the work's central distinguishing factor. For example, see Acemoglu and Robinson (2006: xiv).

[12] In Acemoglu and Robinson (2006), μ is a catch-all index of the ease and attractiveness of mounting a revolution. They define it differently in different contexts. See p. 121 for μ as the cost of revolution in terms of destroyed assets, and p. 125 for μ as the magnitude of the collective-action problem of getting poor people to join the revolution.

strategies of the players: As the value of μ increases, Agent 1's equilibrium strategy changes to include the action $\phi = A$;[13] and similarly, as circumstances in England changed to make mass organization less costly, the elite ultimately realized that their best choice was to offer democratizing reforms.

But the claim that this match between the historical fact pattern and the structure of the model constitutes a test of the formal model is not borne out. In fact, under closer scrutiny, one finds that the formal model is not involved in any important way in this test. While it may be true that the historical fact pattern shares with the formal model the one descriptive characteristic mentioned above (i.e. an increase in μ correlates with $\phi = A$ becoming part of an equilibrium strategy, just as an increase in the "cost of revolution" correlates with democratization), there are many other characteristics of the formal model – not mentioned in this passage – that are *not* shared by the historical experience and that *are* necessary parts of the formal model. For example, consider μ. In addition to having the feature that its level affects equilibrium strategies, it also has the following characteristics (among others): (1) it is one-dimensional; (2) its meaning is unambiguous and constant throughout the model; (3) it affects equilibrium strategies only in formally defined, determinate ways; (4) it is (and must be) capable of being held constant while the values of other elements of the model vary, and is (and must be) capable of varying while the values of other elements of the model are held constant. Not all of these characteristics are constitutive of μ. For example, μ could be multi-dimensional. But characteristics (2), (3), and (4) *are* constitutive. The model would not be capable of the necessary manipulations if μ (and other elements) did not have these characteristics. In addition, all of the precision of the conclusions drawn from the model depend on elements like these. Yet none of these characteristics is shared by the elements of Britain's history that are meant to be analogous to μ. More importantly, it is difficult even to meaningfully conceive of many of these historical elements as possessing such characteristics. As such, the historical fact pattern referenced above cannot be considered to be data for a test of the formal model as a representation of political dynamics. This is why the comparison is done not with the actual elements of the formal model but rather with more nuanced and ambiguous versions of them, i.e. the proto-model.

The same critique applies to Glaeser and Shleifer (2003). They also employ the first justificatory strategy in support of the insight-generating power of their formal model. The following statement is indicative:

---

[13] See Appendix 4.1.

We can use [our model] to understand the rise of regulation in the United States at the end of the nineteenth and the beginning of the twentieth centuries. Our interpretation is that "S" – the scale of economic activity – rose dramatically over the nineteenth century. During the industrial revolution, firms grew sharply in size. The social costs of harm grew roughly proportionately, but the costs of subverting justice did not. As a result, a legal system that may have operated well during the agrarian period failed when faced with entities that had huge incentives to subvert it both legally and illegally. Because higher levels of S lead to subversion of both strict liability and negligence, adding regulation was the efficient response. (Glaeser and Shleifer 2003: 413)

The implication is that the growth of the scale of firms throughout the nineteenth century in the United States and the contemporaneous growth of industrial regulation correspond to the diminution of the statistic $\frac{X}{S}$ that occurs when S increases while all else (except D) is held equal. More generally, the authors suggest that the fact pattern of American regulatory history in the nineteenth and early twentieth centuries matches the relationship between the variables X, S, D, and the formal definitions of "laissez faire," "strict liability," "negligence," and "regulation." They further suggest that this matching counts as support for the aptness of the model and its ability to illuminate the actual causal mechanisms underlying US regulatory history of this period.

But this claim is unsupported, for precisely the same reason that the similar claim from Acemoglu and Robinson (2006) reviewed above was ultimately unsupported. Specifically, although the fact pattern of American regulatory history in this period can be re-described in a manner that highlights certain characteristics and dynamics that are also among the characteristics and dynamics of the formal model, it is also true that the formal model contains many constitutive characteristics that are not and cannot be shared by the elements of historical experience adduced as empirical evidence. Again, as with Acemoglu and Robinson (2006), this is precisely why the authors actually deploy *not* the formal model but rather the proto-model in their comparisons with historical experience. And while it may be true that the proto-model matches well with historical experience, this falls short of what Glaeser and Shleifer (2003) claim.

One might argue that the foregoing critique of the first justificatory method rests on an overly rigid interpretation of the requirements of a "test" of the formal model. But we would argue that, on the contrary, it is the NNIE's formal models themselves that are overly rigid. Both Acemoglu and Robinson (2006) and Glaeser and Shleifer (2003), in the end, abandon the formal model for precisely this reason, and test an informal version of it that is a much more plausible representation of the phenomena under study.

Specifically, in the case of Acemoglu and Robinson (2006), what their test ultimately amounts to is a judgment regarding whether or not a decrease in the "cost of revolution"/"difficulty of overcoming the collective action problem" has been followed in historical experience by moves toward democratization. But these categories are miles away from the precise, formally defined μ and $\phi = A$ of the formal model. To test the predictive power of a model with such precise categories, we would need, at the very least, to construct an equally precise, numerical index of the social phenomena ostensibly being represented: a real-number-valued variable representing the "cost of revolution"/"difficulty of overcoming the collective action problem" and a real-number-valued variable representing the level of democratization.[14] Instead, the authors engage in an ordinary language discussion of their judgments and interpretations of the relationship between the cost of revolution and level of democratization. The result is not a "test" in the Popperian sense – i.e. a moment of truth, in which falsification is possible – but rather merely a re-description of events in a new vocabulary.[15]

The second justificatory strategy – i.e. the quantitative/graphical presentation of statistical relationships that, it is claimed, were predicted by the model – encounters similar difficulties. Put briefly, the problem is that the relationship between the formal model's elements and the statistics that supposedly represent them in the quantitative/graphical representations is generally at least tenuous and at most implausible. For example, Acemoglu and Robinson (2006) offer the following connection between the predictions of their model and a scatter diagram (Figure 3.13 in their text) of an index of level of democracy in various countries versus the labor share of income in these countries:

[O]ur approach to democracy emphasizes the role of social conflict, especially between different groups. One implication of this approach is that inter-group inequality should have an effect on the equilibrium of political institutions and thus on the likelihood that a society ends up as a democracy. The problem, however, is that the relevant notion of inter-group inequality is often difficult to measure (e.g., when it is between two different ethnic groups). Nevertheless, when the major conflict is between the rich and the poor, one variable that captures inter-group inequality is the share of labor income in GDP.

---

[14] Of course, it is possible to construct precise indices of the social phenomena under study, and the authors do so in the course of pursuing the second justificatory method mentioned above. But there are problems inherent in this practice as well, which we discuss below.

[15] I invoke Popper's vocabulary, here, because it is consonant with the representational ideal of mathematical modeling exercises in economics. The question of the legitimacy of Popper's demarcation criterion is a separate matter that is taken up indirectly in Chapter 7's discussion of the implications of the findings of the critique for current economic methodology.

... Figure[] 3.13 ... show[s] the relationship between the labor share in the 1990s and the relevant democracy indexes ... [Figure 13.3] show[s] a positive association between the labor share and democracy. (Acemoglu and Robinson 2006: 58–9)

The authors take pains to suggest that the representations of the level of democracy they use in Figure 3.13 actually are appropriate and meaningful measures of the level of democracy experienced in the countries in question (Acemoglu and Robinson 2006: 48–51). But even if we assume that these measures are appropriate and meaningful, the relevant question for the purposes of Acemoglu and Robinson's analysis is whether these measures correspond to the representation of democracy in their formal model. But again, the answer is that these measures correspond not to the formal model, but rather to the proto-model. The formal model version of democracy corresponds to a value of the variable τ (tax rate) being chosen automatically (according to the Median Voter Theorem), with the outcome (calculated using an exogenously defined objective function for a group of identical representative agents) depending on various exogenously defined parameters and the objective function of a second agent. While it would not be wrong to claim that some of the characteristics of that formal model are also characteristics *in some sense* of the version of democracy represented by the democracy indices used by Acemoglu and Robinson's (2006), it is also true that the model includes many constitutive characteristics that are not and could not be shared by that version of democracy, and vice versa. To give just one example, the Freedom House political rights index – which is one of several indices of democracy used by Acemoglu and Robinson (2006) – takes into account (among other things) whether there are free and fair elections in a country and whether there are competitive parties. These elements are not expressible within the conceptual vocabulary of the Median Voter Theorem, and yet Acemoglu and Robinson's (2006) formal model rests on the foundations of that theorem and all its attendant assumptions.

This critique also applies to NNIE work that uses more rigorous empirical methods, such as those cited in footnote 10 above. In short, (a) the theoretical relationships between various conceptual categories of the formal model are rigorously established (according to the standards of relevant mathematical practice), (b) the statistical relationships discovered between various data categories are rigorously established (according to the standards of econometric practice), but the connection between the referents of the categories in (a) and (b) remains purely conjectural, in the form of the assertion of the Catalog of Correspondences.

The issues reviewed above are not limited to Acemoglu and Robinson (2006), Glaeser and Shleifer (2003), and Maskin and Tirole (2004) but are rather inherent in NNIE methodology. By highlighting these issues, we are not claiming that NNIE work is *a priori* invalid. It is certainly possible for such work to generate insight into its subject matter. We do claim, however, that the role played by the NNIE's hyper-reductive formal models in this insight-generation needs to be examined very carefully, in the manner exemplified above, before we accept the claim that these models are actually doing the heavy-lifting they are said to be capable of.

4.3   NNIE and the denaturing of institutions

For the Old Institutional Economics (OIE), institutions provided the social context in which individual actions occur and in which economic developments take place. Thorstein Veblen (1919: 239), for example, defined institutions as "settled habits of thought common to the generality of men." This definition of institutions was premised on an understanding of individual behavior as endogenous to the set of social institutions, which themselves are molded by cultural and technological forces. Thus from the OIE perspective, institutions are embedded processes that result from technological and other social forces, and economic thought is concerned with both the formation of institutions and, especially, the role of institutions in the endogenous formation of preferences and technology and their consequences. From its inception, the OIE focused both on the forces that molded institutions and on the nature of the economy and economic change that result from having certain traditions and customs in place. Take, for example, Veblen's writings on conspicuous consumption and on the theory of industrial change (Veblen 1912; 1915), or John R. Commons' writings on the evolution and consequences of property law (Commons 1924; 1934). Recent OIE writers continue to seek to explain institutions and their consequences. Hodgson, for example, notes that it is the appreciation of the role of "tradition, custom or legal constraint" that gives institutionalist thought its capacity to understand social organization and its durable, routinized patterns of behavior. "It is this very durability and routinization, in a highly complex and sometimes volatile world," he writes, "which makes social science with any practical application possible at all" (Hodgson 1988: 10).

The New Institutional Economics, exemplified by North's (1990, 1991) writings on economic history and developed with respect to transaction costs and the theory of the firm by Williamson (1975, 1985), takes institutions to be non-market entities that emerge as the efficient and thus rational solution to problems arising in purely market-driven systems: individuals create institutions such as firms and hierarchies when these are more efficient than markets. In this traditional NIE view, institutions do not play a role in the genesis of individual behavior, but instead are the result of that behavior, and ultimately place a constraint on it.

The NIE conception of institutions thus broke from the OIE conception in at least two fundamental ways. First, in the NIE, institutions are endogenous to an economic cost-benefit calculus, with preferences and technologies treated as exogenous determinants of institutional forms. Second, since institutional formations are rooted in the logic of individual rational choice, they are understood to bring Pareto improvements at the level of society. In both these ways, the NIE was fairly comfortably connected to the mainstream of marginalist economics, while the OIE had always seen itself as an alternative to – and a thorn in the side of – the marginalist approach. This was already evident in Veblen's famous 1919 essay "Why is Economics Not an Evolutionary Science?"

We should note that NIE economists, and especially Douglass North, have expanded their notion of institutions, allowing for a greater interaction between culture (ideology, beliefs) and individual identity. In this context, institutions both order the external environment and are formed by it, the result being "a widening discussion of the role of ideology in determining individual behavior" and a deeper consideration of the relevance of "inefficient institutions."[16]

The *New*, New Institutional Economics identifies itself as falling squarely within the neoclassical tradition of the NIE. Acemoglu (2005: 9) cites North (1990: 3) in his definition of institutions as "the rules of the game in a society or, more formally … the humanly devised constraints that shape human interaction." But while the NNIE identifies in some respects with the NIE, it also seeks to extend the NIE in at least two respects. The first is the effort to go beyond traditional NIE concerns with economic institutions – for example, those of property rights protection and contract enforcement – and to extend the analysis to political institutions, including "form of government,

---

[16] See Hodgson (1999). For further development of this point, see Dequech (2002) and Groenewegen *et al.* (1995). In this vein, there is a growing body of work in evolutionary institutional economics which seeks to provide formal mathematical foundations for the origin and development of social norms and institutions (see, e.g., Sethi, 1996; Gintis, 2006). In general, this work is distinct from NNIE work in that while the evolutionary work attempts to model the *origin, nature, and development* of norms and institutions, NNIE work attempts to model the *role* of institutions in socio-economic activity by representing institutions as background conditions to individual or group optimization.

constraints on politicians and elites, separation of powers, etc." – institutions that "shape political incentives and the distribution of political power" (Acemoglu 2005: 10). This introduction of power is important in itself, and allows for the possibility of non-Pareto-improving moves in the formation of institutions, since "institutions are not typically chosen for the good of society, but imposed by groups with political power for their economic consequences" (Acemoglu 2005: 2). This possibility was not addressed in the NIE, as Williamson himself admitted, writing that, in NIE work, "efficiency arguments have mainly prevailed over power interpretations because the latter are tautological, but power issues refuse to go away" (Williamson 2000: 611).

The other contribution of the NNIE is the modeling of social institutions as sets of parameterized cost-benefit problems, and this has been the main focus of the methodological analysis here. As argued above, the explanatory power of the NNIE hinges on the development of a "proto-model" which often corresponds only loosely to the rigorous formal model that gives NNIE work its professional distinction. The proto-model – articulated in a mix of ordinary and formal language, whose ultimate referents are the phenomena of interest in their socially embedded context – is meant to imbue highly abstract but crucial model parameters with actual historical meaning in an effort to give the formal model relevance that it does not carry on its own. But, as we have argued above, the proto-model ends up effectively replacing the formal model as the insight-generating engine of the analysis, rather than improving it. Consequently, the great promise of the NNIE approach – the ability to represent complex institutional dynamics with hyper-reductive models – never gets off the ground.

Conclusion

If the OIE saw institutions as the all-important backdrop to social inquiry, it also placed the emphasis on understanding their function rather than on a full-fledged explanation of their particular form. The NIE, on the other hand, emphasized the rational choice foundation of institutional formation. The NNIE theory of institutions ostensibly adds precision to the analysis of institutions, but at the same time abandons the attempt to understand the nature and dynamics of institutions, representing them as merely a set of exogenous background conditions to cost-benefit analyses in which parameter values trivially lead to various institutional formations. In NNIE analyses, the formal model structure and taxonomy of institutional parameters are difficult to link to actual historical experience and thus are translated into a proto-model that is subjected to casual verifications. In the end, what is accomplished is not illumination of the institutions in question, but rather a forceful fitting of those institutions into familiar optimization methodology. Even the innovative introduction of power into the consideration of institutional formation is lessened by the thinness with which the concept is formulated in the models.[17] In sum, the taming of institutions that is the major accomplishment of the NNIE has come at great cost to the theory of institutions and to the ability to link the theory of institutions to an empirical analysis of economics and history.

Appendix 4.1 The formal model of Acemoglu and Robinson (2006)

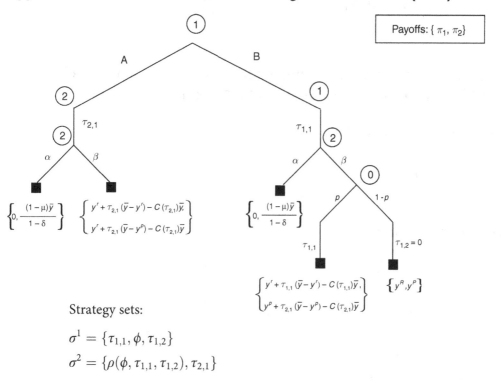

Strategy sets:

$$\sigma^1 = \{\tau_{1,1}, \phi, \tau_{1,2}\}$$
$$\sigma^2 = \{\rho(\phi, \tau_{1,1}, \tau_{1,2}), \tau_{2,1}\}$$

---

[17] In Acemoglu and Robinson (2006), for example, power is expressed in two ways: (1) in the exogenously determined rules of their extensive-form game governing the sequence of moves; and (2) in the exogenously determined parameters (typically one-dimensional, real-valued elements of [0,1]) that alter cost-benefit calculations. For example, the parameter μ (discussed in detail above) is meant to express the costs of mounting a revolution. The lower the value of μ, the more power the "poor" have.

Parameters: $\theta, \delta, \mu, p \in [0, 1]$
Choice variables:
Player 1: $\tau, \phi \in \{A, B\}$; Player 2: $\tau, \rho \in \{\alpha, \beta\}$
Other elements:

$$y^p = \frac{(1 - \theta)\bar{y}}{(1 - \delta)}$$

$$y^r = \frac{\theta\bar{y}}{\delta}$$

$$\tau_{1,1} = \left\{ \underset{\tau \in [0,1]}{\operatorname{argmax}} \, y^i + \tau(\bar{y} - y^i) - C(\tau)\bar{y} \right\}$$

$$\text{where } y^i = \operatorname{med}[Y]; \, Y = \{y^1, \ldots, y^n\}$$

$$\tau_{2,1} \in [0, 1]$$

Appendix 4.2 Supplementary information for solution phase statements of Acemoglu and Robinson (2006) and Glaeser and Shleifer (2003)

Acemoglu and Robinson (2006)

$$\mu* = \theta - p(\tau^p(\theta - \delta) - (1 - \delta)C(\tau^p)) \tag{6.6}$$

$$\mu \geq \theta - (\tau^p(\theta - \delta) - (1 - \delta)C(\tau^p)) \tag{6.7}$$

Glaeser and Shleifer (2003)

C = per unit cost of precautionary action
S = scale of the firm
P_α = probability of an accident occurring, for type αs
P_1 = probability of an accident occurring for type βs when precaution is taken
P_2 = probability of an accident occurring for type βs when no precaution is taken
π_α = proportion of population that is type α

5 The financial crisis and economics

One of the central implications of the critique presented in Chapters 2 and 3 is that mathematical modeling, even at its best, is an inherently incomplete means of investigating social phenomena. Mathematical models (both theoretical and empirical) must presume that certain mathematical properties can inhere in the particular target system under study. But the plausibility of this presumption can only be evaluated in a non-question-begging way using methods that do not themselves rely on the presumption – it cannot be evaluated by mathematical methods alone. Failure to perform such an evaluation (or, worse, failure even to recognize the need for it) leaves one susceptible to the possibility that one's model is incapable of functioning as an apt representation of the target regardless of how well it may perform in mathematical analyses. Put another way, mathematical modeling on its own leaves us blind to the possibility that the target is organized in ways, and is subject to dynamics, that are *essentially* different from what the modeling exercise requires. In order to guard against this possibility, we need to supplement mathematical models with methods of investigation of the target that cast a wider net – specifically, methods that allow us to be sensitive to information that would indicate such essentially different configurational and dynamic possibilities.

In this chapter, I will apply these insights of the critique to the case of economic research in the years surrounding the financial crisis. In particular, I will argue that the kind of built-in blindness to relevant information discussed in Chapters 2 and 3 played a crucial role in the failure of economists to foresee the crisis, and that the post-crisis debate within the discipline about the implications of the crisis suggests that only minimal methodological reform is likely to take place. The chapter will proceed as follows. Section 5.1 will explore recent criticisms of the performance of Dynamic Stochastic General Equilibrium modeling in the lead-up to the crisis. Section 5.2 will examine the pre-crisis mainstream economics literature more broadly as well as the coverage of the precursors to the crisis in the financial press. Section 5.3 will examine the post-crisis debate.

5.1 Macroeconomics, dynamic stochastic general equilibrium models, and the financial crisis

On September 2, 2009 the *New York Times Magazine* published a now famous article by Paul Krugman exploring the question "How Did Economists Get it So Wrong?" Although the title suggests a general indictment of economists, the primary focus of the article is macroeconomic methodology and, in particular, Dynamic Stochastic General Equilibrium (DSGE) modeling based on real business cycle and New Keynesian theory.

Krugman's article is not idiosyncratic in this respect. By a wide margin, DSGE modeling has borne the brunt of post-crisis criticism of the pre-crisis literature. And there are good *prima facie* reasons for this focus – three in particular. First, the financial crisis was a systemic crisis – initially involving two important sectors (housing and finance) and then spreading through the entire economy – and the systemic level is the bailiwick of macroeconomics. Second, by the dawning of the crisis DSGE methodology had become the *lingua franca* of macroeconomics. In testimony before Congress in 2010 (on which, more below) V. V. Chari put the point pithily: "A useful aphorism in macroeconomics is: 'If you have an interesting and coherent story to tell, you can tell it in a DSGE model. If you cannot, your story is incoherent'" (Chari 2010: 35). Finally, up to the very eve of the crisis DSGE methodology was being lauded for its success. For example, writing on August 12, 2008, about a month before the collapse of Lehman Brothers, Olivier Blanchard wrote:

For a long while after the explosion of macroeconomics in the 1970s, the field looked like a battlefield. Over time, however, largely because facts do not go away, a largely shared vision both of fluctuations and of methodology has emerged. Not everything is fine. Like all revolutions, this one has come with the destruction of some knowledge, and suffers from extremism and herding. None of this is deadly, however. The state of macro is good. (Blanchard 2008)

Just a year later, circumstances had changed so drastically in the economies of the industrialized world that another prominent macroeconomist, Willem Buiter, would write about the need for a "new paradigm":

Standard macroeconomic theory did not help foresee the crisis, nor has it helped understand it or craft solutions ... [B]oth the New Classical and New Keynesian complete markets macroeconomic theories not only did not allow the key questions about insolvency and illiquidity to be answered. They did not allow such questions to be asked. A new paradigm is needed. (Buiter 2009: 1)

Buiter was one of the first economists to publicly attack economic orthodoxy in the wake of the crash. But his intervention became part of a massive wave of articles, essays, letters, and blog posts seeking to explain the reason that the much-lauded consensus approach to pre-crisis macroeconomics gave no hint of a coming economic collapse.

The primary theme of this critical post-crisis literature was that the DSGE approach had failed because it rested on assumptions that were not only highly unrealistic, but, moreover, were unrealistic in ways that rendered DSGE models irrelevant to the actual economy. It is this latter point that I would like to focus on in this section. As discussed above, lack of realism *per se* is not a *problem* in modeling, it is an essential *aspect* of modeling. But we have also seen, in Chapters 2 and 3, that not all unrealisms are created equal. Negative analogies between model and target with respect to *essential* properties *are* problematic – potentially fatally so.

I will suggest in this section that one way of reading the post-crisis critiques of DSGE modeling is as a claim that DSGE models failed because they violated the "no essential negative analogy" condition. To be clear about what such a reading would mean, we need to recall that the "no essential negative analogy" condition is not simply about the dyadic relationship between model and target, but also incorporates the modeler's purpose P and the relevant disciplinary norms N – specifically, P and N help to define what will count as an "essential" property in a given modeling exercise. As such, my reading of the post-crisis critical literature on DSGE is that its main thrust is that (at least some of) the underlying assumptions of DSGE modeling made it inherently unsuitable for the purposes to which it was ostensibly put, as judged by the relevant norms governing such analyses.

This reading will be helpful in two ways. First, it will help us to assess the meaning and merits of a persistent counter-argument to the DSGE critics – namely, that the failure to predict the crisis was not actually an indication of problems with the DSGE methodology because it was never the purpose of DSGE models to predict crises. Second, it will help us to see that the central conclusions of the critical DSGE literature fail to adequately comprehend the implications of the problems it brings to light.

It will be helpful to begin by briefly characterizing the nature and aims of DSGE modeling and some of its central assumptions. DSGE models are, by their nature, quite complex. Their aim is not only to represent the macro-economy in a highly parsimonious manner, but also to do so in a way that expresses the microeconomic foundations of macroeconomic dynamics, that can incorporate uncertainty, and that depicts the behavior of the macro-economy over time rather than simply statically. Meeting all of these desiderata in a closed form mathematical model – as Finn Kydland and Edward Prescott (1982) famously did in their seminal DSGE model in 1982 – required suppressing many of the sources and types of complexity that seem to be regular features of actual economies.

Three types of simplification are particularly important both to the structure and functioning of DSGE models and to the post-crisis criticisms of them. The first is the representation of aggregate economic activity as being generated by the optimizing behavior of "representative" agents – generally a single household and a single firm.[1] The second is the assumption that financial markets are efficient, in the sense that "asset prices aggregate and fully reflect all relevant fundamental information, and thus provide the proper signals for resource allocation" (Buiter 2009). The third simplification is the expression of the macroeconomy as a linear (usually log-linear) system. The real business cycle and New Keynesian theories that form the basis of DSGE models generally involve (or, at least, can involve) significant non-linearities. To make the DSGE model tractable, it is generally linearized around a steady state of the system.

For DSGE practitioners, these simplifications were necessary means to the worthwhile end of embedding macroeconomic theory (in particular, real business cycle and New Keynesian theory) in a fully general framework. Significantly, the simplifications were not seen as significant obstacles to the practical applicability of DSGE methodology. This was not because of a lack of recognition that the simplifications were "unrealistic," but rather because the focus was on the other side of the ledger – i.e. the unified, general framework. The latter was presented as an important practical advance, as it provided a check on the plausibility of theories that partial equilibrium approaches could not provide.[2] To the extent that the unrealisticness of the

---

[1] The development of DSGE methodology included the introduction of many variations on the general themes established by Kydland and Prescott (1982). This includes the introduction of some heterogeneity among households and firms, and some types of credit and/or insurance market imperfections. See, e.g., Aiyagari (1994), Krusell and Smith (1998), Kehoe and Levine (2001), Kiyotaki and Moore (1997). For a helpful review of the heterogeneous agent literature, see Krusell and Smith (2006).

[2] Since the macroeconomy is a complex, integrated system, the story went, partial equilibrium models will always be incomplete, by their very construction. Generality is a disciplining mechanism. This is the sentiment behind Chari's macroeconomics aphorism, quoted above.

assumptions was addressed in the DSGE literature, it was generally in the context of introducing incremental changes to reduce the degree of specific simplifications rather than to explore the implications of the simplifications for the applicability of the model. Questions of the practical merits of the DSGE approach were referred to the data, and its proponents read the empirical results as confirming its practical relevance, and spectacularly so. The models were credited not only with fitting the historical macro data extremely well, but also with providing the basis for sound macroeconomic policymaking. In a 2006 article on the state of macroeconomics in the *Journal of Economic Perspectives*, for example, V. V. Chari and Patrick Kehoe wrote

Over the last three decades, macroeconomic theory and the practice of macroeconomics by economists have changed significantly – for the better. Macroeconomics is now firmly grounded in the principles of economic theory. These advances have not been restricted to the ivory tower. Over the last several decades, the United States and other countries have undertaken a variety of policy changes that are precisely what macroeconomic theory of the last 30 years suggests. (Chari and Kehoe 2006: 1)

... macroeconomic theory has had a profound and far-reaching effect on the institutions and practices governing monetary policy and is beginning to have a similar effect on fiscal policy. The marginal social product of macroeconomic science is surely large and growing rapidly. (Chari and Kehoe 2006: 26)

Robert Lucas (2003) and Ben Bernanke (2004) offered laudatory assessments in the same vein.

In the wake of the financial crisis, these laudatory assessments have been called into question. Many critics have interpreted the general failure of macroeconomists to anticipate the crisis as a clear indication that DSGE models had been misleading rather than successful.[3] The apparent empirical success of DSGE models, these critics contend, was not evidence of the models' aptness as a guide to the functioning of the economy for two reasons: first, because the models' underlying assumptions were unrealistic in a way that made it invalid to interpret them as being *about* an actual macroeconomy; and second, because the methods used to empirically estimate DSGE models rested on (and therefore could not assess the validity of) the assumption that the data were generated by the kind of process represented in the model.[4] The result was that, despite its pretensions to empirical and policy

---

[3] See, e.g., Caballero (2010), Krugman (2009), Mirowski (2013), and Smith (2011).

[4] Put another way, empirical DSGE analyses answer the question: "Assuming the economy is structured like a DSGE system, what are the values of the parameters?"

relevance, DSGE modeling (both theoretical and empirical) amounted to little more than elaborate exploration of objects whose relationship to the economy was at best unclear.

What made the simplifying assumptions of DSGE so problematic was that they rendered invisible (and, therefore, unaddressable) many of the things that make the macroeconomy a puzzle and an object of interest in the first place. Note that this is different from the general issue of information loss due to abstraction. All simplifying assumptions of models result in the suppression of some aspect(s) of the target. The particular complaint of critics of DSGE is that some of its simplifications suppressed aspects of the target that were integral to the inquiry – that is, they were aspects that need to be explored (or at least explorable) in order to fulfill the purpose of the modeling exercise. As Ricardo Caballero put the point in his 2010 critical review of DSGE methodology: "It is fine to be as 'goofy' as needed to make things simpler along inessential dimensions, but it is important not to sound 'funny' on the specific issue that is to be addressed" (Caballero 2010: 90).

The representative agent assumption is a clear example of this latter point. To paraphrase Alan Coddington (1975), its contribution to our understanding of the macroeconomy is like "the contribution of flatness to mountaineering."[5] If economies exhibited no complexities beyond those which inhere in isolated individual behavior (whatever that might mean), this would indeed make social inquiry simpler – just as mountaineering would be simpler if mountains were plains instead of mountains. But if we want to entertain the possibility that this might not be the case, we cannot do so with a representative agent model. In fact, we cannot even articulate what we would mean by such a thing. The flip side of this is that if we decide we want to stick with the representative agent model come what may, then anything we observe that seems to be the result of other-than-individual decision making must be ascribed to something else. Robert Solow put the point colorfully in written testimony to a congressional hearing on DSGE modeling in 2010. The DSGE approach, he wrote,

always treats the whole economy as if it were like a person, trying consciously and rationally to do the best it can on behalf of the representative agent, given its circumstances. This can not be an adequate description of a national economy, which is pretty conspicuously *not* pursuing a consistent goal. A thoughtful person, faced with the thought that economic policy was being pursued on this basis, might reasonably wonder what planet he or she is on. (Solow 2010: 14)

---

[5] Coddington was referring specifically to the empirical applicability of general equilibrium theory.

The same can be said of the efficient markets and linearity assumptions. The problem is not simply that they are unrealistic, but further that they preclude consideration of dynamics that are incompatible with the assumptions. Seeing the world through a model containing these assumptions means seeing a world in which the only kinds of economic problems that can arise are those with linear dynamics that would arise in a world of efficient markets. Truly disruptive or chaotic dynamics are both inconceivable and inexpressible with the conceptual vocabulary of DSGE. In his 2009 *New York Times Magazine* piece, Paul Krugman identified the kind of tunnel vision this engenders as a major factor in the failure of DSGE macroeconomics to anticipate the crisis:

this romanticized and sanitized vision of the economy led most economists to ignore all the things that can go wrong. They turned a blind eye to the limitations of human rationality that often lead to bubbles and busts; to the problems of institutions that run amok; to the imperfections of markets – especially financial markets – that can cause the economy's operating system to undergo sudden, unpredictable crashes; and to the dangers created when regulators don't believe in regulation. (Krugman 2009)

Put in terms of the vocabulary introduced in Chapters 2 and 3, the point being made here is that the simplifying assumptions were a source of essential negative analogies (i.e. negative analogies with respect to essential properties) between model and target. The assumptions related to essential properties of both model and target in that (1) they were necessary features of the model – without them the model could not be dynamic, stochastic, general, *and* tractable in the required manner;[6] and (2) the ostensible target-system correspondents of the model-system elements restricted by these assumptions were central to the motivating questions of many DSGE exercises. To put this second point another way, the model assumptions of DSGE restricted *a priori* the set of conceivable target-system dynamics even though the question of what kinds of dynamics could be driving the behavior of the variables of interest was often itself precisely the question at issue. The financial crisis revealed that there had been negative analogies among the essential properties related to these simplifying assumptions – specifically, that economic processes that were inexpressible (indeed, inconceivable) in the model were important drivers of the behavior of the target with respect to

---

[6] Of course, one can explore ways of relaxing the simplifying assumptions to make them less restrictive. And, indeed, this has been one of the central strategies for developing and improving DSGE models (see Cochrane 2011). But as I discuss below, this strategy cannot address the root of the essential negative analogy problem.

precisely the kinds of questions/puzzles under study. As such, DSGE models not only failed to anticipate the crisis, they had been inherently incapable of doing so.

Framing the issue in this way is helpful in understanding the debate over the implications of DSGE's perceived failings for macroeconomic methodology. Detecting the presence of essential negative analogies between a model and its target requires us to access information about the target through means other than the model because it requires us to explore the possibility that the target possesses properties not expressible in the terms of the model.[7] This implies both a retrospective and a prospective duty for the modeler. Prospectively: before/during the model-building stage, the modeler should seek out information about the target in a broad manner (i.e. in a way that does not presumptively prohibit any particular mode of access to the target) for the purpose of avoiding essential negative analogies. Retrospectively, once the modeler has built and deployed a model, she must be sensitive to information from the target system that would indicate the presence of an essential negative analogy with respect to that particular model and modeling exercise.

The complaints against pre-crisis DSGE modeling discussed above clearly imply at least some level of dereliction on both fronts. On the retrospective front, as we have seen, critics charged that the central simplifying assumptions of DSGE models rendered them inherently insensitive to the kinds of processes and dynamics that *seem to have been* important drivers of the crisis (I will elaborate on the phrase "seem to have been" below). And they charged that DSGE practitioners' high level of confidence in the efficacy of the approach meant that they did not seek out information outside of the model's conceptual map. But because DSGE models are insensitive to such a wide range of conceivable economic processes, the charge of dereliction of the retrospective duty in itself does not provide much prescriptive guidance. What it implies depends upon what one takes to have been relevant information.

We get a better indication of what the critics have in mind prescriptively from the charge of dereliction of the prospective duty. To the extent that "ought" implies "can," such a charge would imply that the prospective duty could have been fulfilled in a meaningful way – specifically, that sufficient information was available in the pre-crisis period to make it clear that DSGE

---

[7] As discussed in Chapters 2 and 3, this is true for both theoretical and empirical modeling exercises, and so applies to theoretical models, empirical models, and data.

modeling exercises violated the no essential negative analogies condition. And we do see this charge from the critics, often as an elaboration of the retrospective charge. Buiter (2009), for example, follows his criticism of the linearity assumption with the following reflection on well-known non-linear dynamics in financial markets:

Those of us who have marvelled at the non-linear feedback loops between asset prices in illiquid markets and the funding illiquidity of financial institutions exposed to these asset prices through mark-to-market accounting, margin requirements, calls for additional collateral etc. will appreciate what is lost by this castration of the macroeconomic models. Threshold effects, critical mass, tipping points, non-linear accelerators – they are all out of the window.

The implication of Buiter's comment is that in order to be policy-relevant (as many DSGE modeling exercises were meant to be) a model of the current macroeconomy must at least be sensitive to the possibility of such dynamics, and that this was well-understood before the crisis.

But this raises the question of what kind of information *was* relevant and how it could have been known to be relevant at the time. With the benefit of hindsight, we can give concrete answers to these questions. The record shows that relevant information about the underlying problems of the housing and financial sectors was available in the several years before the crisis, but that much of this information manifested itself in ways and through sources not generally recognized as legitimate data sources by economists. Thus, while it was indeed the case that the simplifying assumptions of DSGE modeling created blind spots that rendered the evidence of the gathering storm invisible, it was also the case that other approaches within mainstream economics did not fare better. The problem was not merely insensitivity to relevant information, but also a failure to cast a wide enough information-gathering net to know what we needed to be sensitive *to*.

5.2   The financial crisis: What was known? What was knowable?[8]

As we now know, the central cause of the 2008–9 financial crisis was the concentration of investment in the US housing market, particularly via derivative securities (e.g., credit default swaps and various forms of collateralized debt obligations and mortgage backed securities). The massive inflow

---

[8] Much of this section is drawn from an article published in *The Journal of Economic Methodology* (Spiegler 2012), accessible online: http://www.tandfonline.com/10.1080/1350178x.2012.714149.

of investment during the late 1990s and throughout most of the 2000s inflated a bubble in US (and, eventually non-US) housing and related assets that unraveled and burst when, in 2007, housing prices began to level off and mortgage defaults began to rise. When the bubble had burst and losses began to be realized, it became clear that the use of opaque derivatives on a massive scale to take and hedge positions in the mortgage-related asset market had intertwined the fate of a large portion of the international financial industry.

What has also become clear is that this was no simple speculative bubble. Rather, it was a product of a peculiar political, regulatory, and commercial (hereinafter "PRC") environment created by, *inter alia*, private financial institutions, legislators, the Federal Reserve, and the Treasury department. Among the primary elements of this environment were regulatory decisions that had allowed over-the-counter derivatives markets such as those for credit default swaps to remain non-standardized and opaque; a problematic framework for relations between credit rating agencies and their clients that encouraged misleading ratings of complex mortgage derivative products; severe moral hazard problems on the part of mortgage originators caused by massive demand for securitization of mortgages; and the spread of accounting and compensation practices that encouraged short-term thinking and high degrees of leverage in the creation and marketing of highly complex structured financial products. Although presumably it was not the intent of the agents involved in creating this environment to cause a financial crisis, there *was* a clear intent to remove barriers to highly leveraged investment strategies utilizing lightly regulated and unregulated derivatives.[9] One result of this was that the US housing and mortgage markets in the late 1990s and 2000s were not simply standard asset markets. They were crucial points in a larger capital and risk allocation mechanism that had grown out of the peculiar PRC environment of the time.

Reporting in the financial press gives a window into how much of this was perceivable in real time. Gillian Tett of the *Financial Times* began reporting on the growing size and importance of markets in privately traded credit derivatives (including collateralized debt obligations (CDOs) and credit default swaps (CDSs)) in the Spring of 2005. Already in these early stories we find some of the most important features of the PRC environment coming into focus. Tett recounted concerns on the part of financial regulators and market

---

[9] This story has been covered in many venues. The most comprehensive account is that of the US Senate Committee on Homeland Security and Governmental Affairs, which is available at http://www.hsgac. senate.gov/imo/media/doc/Financial_Crisis/FinancialCrisisReport.pdf. For a good overview with historical perspective, see Johnson and Kwak (2010).

professionals about the complexity of the securities and the opacity of the markets. In particular, there were concerns that many purchasers of the securities seemed not to be sophisticated enough to understand what they were buying, and more generally that the prodigious and continuing growth of the markets might be based in part on excessive optimism about their ability to withstand a change in the credit environment (Tett 2005a). Tett also reported on concerns about credit rating agencies' ability to accurately assess the risk of the securities, and about investors' heavy reliance on those ratings due to the complexity of the securities. Relatedly, Tett reported in July of 2005 that derivatives ratings had become the agencies' most lucrative business (Beales and Tett 2005). By October, she was able to offer the following assessment of the risk implications of the developments in the credit derivatives markets:

while shifting credit risk might improve the health of the visible, regulated banking sector, it also pushes more risk into the unregulated world. At present almost all trading in loans and credit derivatives takes place in private deals, not on regulated exchanges ... That makes it much harder for regulators to monitor these flows, let alone control them in a crisis. In essence, the financial system looks increasingly like a giant version of Enron: what is happening on the balance sheet of public [i.e. publicly traded] entities provides less and less of a guide to the distribution of risks. (Tett 2005b)

In the ensuing years, through the lead-up to the crisis, Tett's reporting chronicled the continuing growth of the credit derivatives markets – and the increasing proportion of these derivatives that were tied to mortgages – as well as concerns of regulators about their opacity. In late 2006 and early 2007, financial journalists in the US began reporting on the impending collapse of the subprime mortgage market, and the connection of its rise and fall to a combination of political, regulatory, and commercial factors.[10] Gretchen Morgenson's reporting in *The New York Times* in March of 2007, in particular, drew out the connections between the problems in the subprime market, on the one hand, and lax regulation, the rise of enormous and opaque credit derivatives markets, and the perverse incentives that these engendered in the mortgage backed securities and mortgage origination markets, on the other.

For our purposes, there are two important things about this reporting. The first is that the contours of the PRC environment that fueled the financial crisis were perceivable by 2005. Although many of the finer details of the environment began to emerge only after the collapse of Lehman Brothers and

[10] See, e.g., Morgenson (2007) and Bajaj (2006).

the ensuing scrutiny of its books, Tett's reporting shows that it was apparent in 2005 that the credit derivatives market was shifting the landscape of credit risk and that it was rapidly growing, relatively poorly understood, and almost completely opaque to regulators. And Morgenson's reporting shows that the linkages between these opaque credit derivatives markets and the US housing and mortgage markets were clear by early 2007. Second, and more importantly, it is clear that these facts were not only perceivable but also actually widely *perceived* by financial regulators and market participants. The facts of Tett's (2005a and b) stories are supported by and related through statements by a wide array of regulators (including Alan Greenspan, Timothy Geithner, then President of the New York Fed, and John Tiner, then Chief Executive of the UK Financial Services Authority) and market professionals from a range of financial institutions (including major investment and commercial banks, hedge funds, brokerages, law firms, and financial consultancies). In other reporting, we hear the same concerns echoed throughout this period by officials at the US Securities and Exchange Commission, the Bank of International Settlements, the European Central Bank, the International Monetary Fund, and the French Autorité des Marchés Financiers, as well as from an array of market participants ranging from small niche brokerages to the bulge bracket banks. The main features of the PRC environment underlying the financial crisis, then, were a matter of clear, ongoing, and public concern to a broad community within the financial sector from the Spring of 2005 at the latest.

The unprecedented rise in US housing prices in the 2000s was apparent to economists concerned with such issues, and not surprisingly many papers were written on the subject. What is surprising is the almost complete lack of connection in the mainstream academic economic literature between the dynamics of the housing market, the activity in the related securities markets, and the nexus of PRC factors that was fueling the interplay between the two. A review of six of the discipline's top generalist journals and three specialist journals related to housing, banking and finance from 2003 to 2008 turns up no papers that explicitly explored these connections.[11,12] Faccio *et al.* (2006) and Schneider and Tornell (2004), two papers that explore the link between political connections and bank bailouts, are possible exceptions,

---

[11] The journals in question are *The American Economic Review, The Journal of Economic Literature, The Journal of Economic Perspectives, The Journal of Finance, The Journal of Housing Economics, The Journal of Money, Credit and Banking, The Journal of Political Economy, The Quarterly Journal of Economics,* and *The Review of Economic Studies.*

[12] In what follows, I will take the contributions to these journals between 2003 and 2008 to be a proxy for the mainstream of academic economic work in the lead-up to the crisis.

though their focus is largely non-US and they do not address the specific dynamics of the PRC environment (in the US or elsewhere).

In general, what we find in the mainstream literature, in the lead-up to the crisis, are analyses of the housing market and its attendant financial markets from within the perspective of existing economic models. As such, there is an implicit presumption that the particular objects and relations under study were not substantially qualitatively different from the markets, institutions, and behaviors that had been the subject of similar models. For example, with respect to the behavior of housing prices, we generally see papers examining the impact on prices of specific individual factors in isolation from broader consideration of the PCR environment. Several papers addressed the narrow question of whether or not there was a bubble in housing prices by regressing prices against "fundamental" factors and exploring the extent to which the residual contained a substantial amount of the variation (and also, in some cases, gauging the psychology of home buyer expectations through surveys).[13] Other papers examined the role of land use and construction regulation on home prices.[14] Many papers explored the question of house price dynamics in the abstract by developing general models. Some of these did integrate financial and policy factors – for example, collateral requirements, borrowing constraints, the secondary mortgage market, monetary policy – but none made specific reference to the peculiar PRC environment of the late 1990s–2000s market in particular.[15] Another group of papers examined the risk in the financial system in general, with several focusing on the role of liquidity in banking crises and others focusing on other issues in bank risk.[16] But, again, none of these incorporated the wider PRC environmental factors.[17]

We see in the broader mainstream literature of the pre-crisis period, then, the same susceptibility to blind spots that we saw in the DSGE literature. And just as with the DSGE literature, the fact that the analyses reviewed in this

---

[13] See, e.g., Case and Shiller (2003), Shiller (2007), Goodman and Thibodeau (2008), Himmelberg et al. (2005) and Smith and Smith (2006). There are also several papers examining the phenomenon of bubbles in general, either through historical review (e.g., LeRoy 2004) or through the construction of a theoretical model of bubbles (e.g., Scheinkman and Xiong 2003).

[14] See, e.g., Glaeser et al. (2005) and Quigley and Rafael (2005).

[15] See, e.g., Peek and Wilcox (2006), Iacoviello (2005), Ortalo-Magné and Rady (2006).

[16] In the former group, see, e.g., Diamond and Rajan (2005), Ericsson and Renault (2006), and Gorton and Huang (2004). In the latter group, see, e.g., Morrison and White (2005), Dell'Ariccia and Marquez (2006), Krishnan et al. (2005), and Van Order (2006).

[17] For the sake of brevity, I do not discuss here the mainstream literature on the macroeconomy in general. The general tenor of this literature was quite upbeat during the 2000s (see, e.g., Chari and Kehoe 2006), though the excessive abstraction of Dynamic Stochastic General Equilibrium modeling during this time has subsequently come in for significant criticism (see, e.g., Colander et al. 2008 and Colander et al. 2009).

section were deemed to have been empirically adequate under the discipline's assessment standards suggests not simply that relevant information was missed, but further, that this information was not recognized to have been relevant in the first place. Note that this is quite different from pointing out that economists in general failed to *predict* the crisis. This is also true, but it is a red herring. Accurate prediction of the timing of the crisis is an improper metric for assessing the merits of pre-crisis analyses. What is much more important is whether these analyses give us an adequate picture of the fault lines in the economy and the important sources of pressure on those fault lines. It is on *this* measure that mainstream economics failed, and it is crucially important that we recognize this so that we may properly diagnose the causes of the failure and consider what methodological reforms may be necessary.

The discussion above suggests that one of the important lessons to be drawn from economics' pre-crisis performance is that our assumptions about what constitutes relevant information and valid information sources were inappropriately narrow. In Chapters 6 and 7, I will argue that addressing this shortcoming requires going outside of the current toolkit of economics and developing/adapting qualitative and interpretive methods for economic use. Before doing so, however, it will be helpful to consider some of the suggestions for reform that have arisen within the discipline in the aftermath of the crisis.

5.3   The post-crisis reform debate[18]

The period from 2008 to 2010 witnessed an extensive and widely ranging debate among economists about the implications of the financial crisis for economic methodology. Although there is considerable diversity among the many contributions to the debate, one can nevertheless place most of the responses into one of four categories, which I will call: (1) "Do Nothing," (2) "Model Finance," (3) "Add Complexity and Institutions," and (4) "Reconsider Formalism." I will discuss each of these categories below. Before doing so, however, it will be helpful as a starting point to describe a newly emerging consensus view within the mainstream of the discipline.

---

[18] This section draws substantially from an article published in the *Forum for Social Economics* (Spiegler and Milberg 2013), accessible online: http://www.tandfonline.com/10.1080/07360932.2013.814089. I am grateful to Will Milberg for allowing me to use the material here.

5.3.1   The emerging consensus view

Organizing the current debate into four categories is intended not only to bring some structure to the analysis of the reform of economics today, but also to give a sense of the variety of responses. This variety has not, in general, been reflected in the consensus view that has recently begun to emerge – essentially, the view that although the discipline did not perform optimally, the remedies for any shortcomings are to be found within existing economic methodology. All that is needed in response to the crisis, on this view, is a more robust application of certain aspects of the incumbent methodology – a kind of methodological "doubling down." This view has been articulated more or less explicitly in several "blue ribbon" venues, including: two letters from the British Academy to Queen Elizabeth in response to her question of why no one had predicted the financial crisis, two panels organized by the Allied Social Sciences Association at its 2009 and 2010 annual conferences, testimony before Congress by several leading economists, and a keynote address by Lawrence Summers to the 2011 Institute for New Economic Thinking conference at Bretton Woods.[19]

Although there is some diversity among these four sets of contributions, there is virtual unanimity (with one exception, discussed below) in the view that there is no need to look outside of economics' current toolbox for answers. The British Academy letters take the position that there was not enough of a culture of questioning within British academic and government economic circles, and that this needs to change in order to let the (essentially correct) incumbent methodology do its work. The ASSA panels and the congressional testimony essentially take the position that, to the extent anything ought to be done differently, economists should add new mathematical components to their models to capture currently under-modeled complexities in the world; for example: including the explicit modeling of deleveraging cycles and other feedback effects of bursting asset bubbles, and the intensification of the use of behavioral economics. Significantly, however, the suggestion is that the discipline need not consider new methods for incorporating the under-modeled complexity.[20] Summers echoes these

---

[19] For the British Academy letters, see Besley and Hennessy (2009; 2010); for the ASSA panels, see Allied Social Sciences Association (2009; 2010); for David Colander's testimony, see Colander (2009); for Summers' remarks, see Summers (2011).

[20] The one possible exception to this is the plea by Colander (2010) and Page (2010) for agent-based computer simulation, and the former's additional plea for a bifurcation of the discipline into mathematical analytic and interpretive branches, with more attention given in the future to training individuals in the latter group. These suggestions constitute searching outside of the current toolbox only to the extent that one considers the kind of mathematical modeling involved with agent-based

views in his INET keynote address. While he explicitly criticizes real business cycle and DSGE approaches to macroeconomics and praises the nuanced crisis theories of John Maynard Keynes, Hyman Minsky and Charles Kindleberger, his recommendation is to pursue such insights using the existing mathematical toolbox of mainstream (including behavioral) economics.

When one looks carefully into the collection of individual responses to the crisis from the wider community of economists, however, one finds significantly more diversity than is suggested by the blue ribbon consensus. These voices are organized below into the four broad categories mentioned above, according to the extent of their call for change. The first two categories – "Do Nothing" and "Model Finance" – generally recapitulate the spirit of the blue ribbon consensus in counseling either no change or only minor methodological change. The other two categories – "Add Complexity and Institutions" and "Reconsider Formalism" – go a bit farther, with some voices in the latter group even calling for profound reconsideration of current practice.

5.3.2 Do nothing

The "Do Nothing" view has been articulated largely in recent interviews with prominent economists, including Thomas Sargent (2010), Eugene Fama (Cassidy 2010a), and John Cochrane (Cassidy 2010b). For this group, the macroeconomic paradigm dominant in the pre-crisis years proved perfectly adequate for predicting and explaining the recent global recession. Contrary to the view that unexpected financial collapse caused the recession, these economists point to natural frictions in the economy and market distortions caused by public policy. Cochrane, for example, comments that "[r]ight now ten percent of people are unemployed. Many of them could find a job tomorrow at Wal-Mart but it is not the right job for them ... [S]ome component of unemployment is people searching for better fits after shifts that have to happen. The baseline shouldn't be that unemployment is always constant ... " (Cassidy 2010b). And Casey Mulligan (2009), Cochrane's colleague at the University of Chicago Graduate School of Business, argues

simulations to be different in type from mathematical modeling (including computational simulation) methods that are already within the toolkit of mainstream economics. One possible way to evaluate this claim would be to consider whether the methodology of agent-based simulation *per se* (e.g., leaving aside the question of the quality of the argument and the status of the author) would make a paper's publication in one of the discipline's top generalist journals less likely. This is an empirical question, and one that we do not attempt to answer here. (For a judgment on this matter from within the mainstream, consider the comments of V. V. Chari at a recent congressional hearing on the crisis, expressing the opinion that agent-based modeling is perfectly compatible with DSGE methodology (Chari 2010: 58).) In any event, its answer does not affect the main themes or arguments of this chapter.

that the real business cycle model was highly successful in identifying the underlying causes of the current downturn. He writes:

When it came to this recession, the neoclassical decomposition quickly led me to look further at public policies – absent from some of the other recessions – that might have caused the supply of labor to shift relative to its demand. Like others, I noticed that the federal minimum wage was hiked three consecutive times. I also turned up a major policy (the Treasury and FDIC plans for modifying mortgages) that creates marginal income tax rates in excess of 100 percent. Much research remains to be done, and undoubtedly other users of the neoclassical growth model will make convincing cases for the roles of monetary and other factors. Paul Krugman's scorn is all we have to suggest that marginal tax rates in excess of 100 percent are not worthy of attention, and that today's low employment is not even partly a consequence of public policy.

For these economists, the role of the financial crisis has been overplayed relative to other factors that are well understood by current models.

But these economists do not simply ignore the financial crisis or claim that it was unimportant. On the contrary, they recognize its importance and argue that while the leading pre-crisis models may not have performed particularly well in predicting the crisis, this cannot be seen as an indictment because the models were never meant to predict such things. Sargent, for example, argues that:

[t]he criticism of real business cycle models and their close cousins, the so-called New Keynesian models, is misdirected and reflects a misunderstanding of the purpose for which those models were devised. These models were designed to describe aggregate economic fluctuations during normal times when markets can bring borrowers and lenders together in orderly ways, not during financial crises and market breakdowns. (Sargent 2010)

But, according to the proponents of the Do Nothing view, that does not mean that mainstream economics lacks models for the world as we actually encounter it. In fact, they contend, mainstream economics is replete with such models. "Pretty much all [macroeconomists] have been doing for 30 years," Cochrane (2009) writes, "is introducing flaws, frictions and new behaviors, especially new models of attitudes to risk, and comparing the resulting models, quantitatively, to data." What is needed for an adequate understanding of the macroeconomy, on the Do Nothing view, is not new methods, but rather the skills and the fortitude to continue pushing the mathematical complexity that is necessary to refine the existing models. Replying specifically to Paul Krugman's charge (Krugman 2009) that economics' overemphasis on mathematical modeling was a major factor in its recent failure, Cochrane asserts that

[t]he problem is that we don't have *enough* math. Math in economics serves to keep the logic straight, to make sure that the "then" really does follow the "if," which it so frequently does not if you just write prose. The challenge is how hard it is to write down explicit artificial economies with these ingredients, actually solve them, in order to see what makes them tick. Frictions are just bloody hard with the mathematical tools we have now. (Cochrane 2011)

Thus, although the Do Nothing view acknowledges that economists can do better at predicting and understanding financial crises and recessions, the proposed remedy is a more intensive application of existing methodology rather than methodological reform.

5.3.3   Model finance

Contrary to proponents of the Do Nothing view, a substantial group of mainstream economists believe that the recent crisis has revealed inadequacies in existing methodology – most notably, the failure to adequately incorporate the financial sector into our macroeconomic models. Paul Krugman, for example, has recently argued that "[u]ntil now the impact of dysfunctional finance hasn't been at the core even of Keynesian economics. Clearly, that has to change ... [Economists] have to do their best to incorporate the realities of finance into macroeconomics" (Krugman 2009). How precisely to do this is a matter of some controversy. But the general sentiment that economic theory needs to incorporate the financial sector more effectively *somehow* is widespread. We refer to this position as the "Model Finance" view.

A relatively tame version of this position advocates using mainstream methodology in new ways. For example, one could retain the existing framework of Dynamic Stochastic General Equilibrium (DSGE) models, but simply make certain important aspects of the financial sector endogenous. This is the possible near-future of macroeconomics envisioned by James Morley (2010) in a recent posting on J. Bradford DeLong's *Grasping Reality* blog: "it is a safe bet," Morley writes, "that future versions of DSGE models will incorporate more complicated financial sectors and allow for different types of fiscal policies. And guess what? The new-and-improved DSGE models will turn out to imply (ex post) that the Great Recession was actually due to serially-correlated financial intermediation shocks and suboptimal fiscal policy."[21] Daron Acemoglu (2009) proposes something along the lines envisioned in Morley's comment. He has argued that the overvaluation of the "reputation capital" of firms has led to an inability of economic models to detect overly risky behavior by firms – in particular, financial firms. His proposed remedy is to simply incorporate a mathematical representation of reputation capital into our models, with the attendant concepts of investment-in and returns-to that capital allowing us to judge when reputation capital is being valued efficiently by market participants. Along similar lines, Ben Bernanke (2010) has argued that the core methodology of macroeconomics is sound, but that "understanding the relationship between financial and economic stability in a macroeconomic context is a critical unfinished task for researchers." To accomplish this, he counsels building on existing work using the current methodological toolkit.

A stronger version of the "Model Finance" view calls not only for incorporation of the financial sector into macroeconomic models, but also for a reform of the manner in which we model finance. Some of the economists espousing this approach focus specifically on the efficient market hypothesis – the model of financial markets adopted by most mainstream macro models – with a subset of this group explicitly arguing that the abandonment of this hypothesis is crucial to the reform of economics. The Post-Keynesian movement, in particular, has been associated with this position. In assessing the Post-Keynesian contributions to the debate, however, it is important to distinguish between the different strains of this work. Some of these contributions have counseled only modest reform, insisting mainly on the need to add "financialization" into otherwise relatively standard Post-Keynesian and Kaleckian modeling (for a review of the flurry of literature, see Stockhammer and Onaran 2012). This is true even of many of the contributions promoting Minsky's notion of financial fragility, because the main prescription of these proposals is that we understand finance as an endogenous driver of cycles, which does not in itself require a fundamental rethinking of the way economics is done or that economic actors are understood to behave.

In contrast, others falling within the "Model Finance" category have promoted a revival of some of the key concepts of traditional Keynesianism – most prominently that of the importance of fundamental uncertainty in macroeconomic dynamics. These contributions have come mostly in the

---

[21] Morley sees this as an undesirable outcome. He concludes his statement ruefully: "Alas, these conclusions will be driven much more by the DSGE framework than by the data."

form of new books on Keynes (e.g., Taylor 2010, Davidson 2009, Skidelsky 2009, and Eatwell and Milgate 2011). George Akerlof and Robert Shiller (2009) also hearken back to Keynes in emphasizing that irrationality (they adopt Keynes' term "animal spirits") rather than rationality may drive the psychology of markets, including financial markets, and that economics must integrate this insight into its models.

The "Model Finance" position has been quite prominent in the current debate and is likely to remain so, primarily for two reasons. First, it is championed by a number of high profile economists, including Nobel laureates and other scholars holding prestigious positions inside and outside of academia. Second, at least with respect to some of the more prominent contributions, it dovetails nicely with reforms already underway within economics – most notably the rise of behavioral finance. As such, it does not necessarily require substantial deviation from trends in current practice.

5.3.4   Add complexity and institutions

In addition to the voices counseling no change or only minor change, there are a number of calls for a more thorough reform of economic methodology. Such appeals often focus on the issue of the complexity of existing models, and the urgent need to reconstitute our methods to accommodate such complexity. Caballero (2010), for example, argues that current macro models are not nuanced enough to comprehend the web of interdependencies that transform individual actions into aggregate economic activity. "One of the core weaknesses of the core [mainstream macro models]," he writes,

stems from going too directly from statements about individuals to statements about the aggregate, where the main difference between the two comes from stylized aggregate constraints and trivial interactions, rather than from the richness and unpredictability of the linkages among the parts.

Caballero counsels that we should create formal representations of this additional complexity and incorporate it into our models: "We need to spend much more time," he writes, "modeling and understanding the topology of linkages among agents, markets, institutions, and countries" (Caballero 2010: 9).

Other calls for the recognition of greater complexity suggest that adequately representing this complexity will require the use of alternative mathematical modeling techniques. The body of literature promoting agent-based computational economic (ACE) modeling is one example. This approach eschews both the representative-agent and equilibrium aspects of DSGE modeling in favor of a computational approach that defines characteristics of various types of agents and simulates the dynamics of their interactions under various conditions. It takes its inspiration not from economic modeling, but from recent developments in physics and biology (see, e.g., LeBaron and Tesfatsion 2008; Colander *et al.* 2008; Gallegati and Richiardi 2011). Agent-based models are complex mathematical models – often with hundreds of differential equations. In fact, the models' primary distinctive feature is that they cannot be solved but can only be simulated in an effort to understand their properties. Heterogeneous individual agents are not assumed to behave optimally. Instead, agents may behave according to specified rules, and these may be connected to both the behavior of other agents and to macro trends that emerge out of the behavior of all agents.[22]

It is important to note that while proponents of ACE do argue that equilibrium and representative-agent-based mathematical modeling fails to capture certain types of social complexity, they do not believe that this complexity can have other-than-mathematical structure. Colander (2009), for example, counsels a mathematical doubling-down in the face of this currently untheorized complexity. "Inevitably," he writes,

complex systems exhibit path dependence, nested systems, multiple speed variables, sensitive dependence on initial conditions, and other non-linear dynamical properties. This means that at any moment in time, right when you thought you had a result, all hell can break loose. Formally studying complex systems requires rigorous training in the cutting edge of mathematics and statistics. It's not for neophytes. (Colander 2009)[23]

In contrast, some scholars calling for the incorporation of increased complexity have argued that the discipline's commitment to formal methodology itself should also be up for reconsideration.[24] It is to this final group that we now turn.

---

[22] See Farmer and Foley (2009) for a discussion of the relevance of agent-based models to the post-crisis world.

[23] This statement is from Colander's written testimony before Congress, to which the paper Colander *et al.* (2009) was appended.

[24] Colander *et al.* (2009) assert that the kind of mathematical modeling they have in mind (e.g., ACE) need not be highly formal in nature. But such a view seems to conflate the nature of mathematical models with their use. Mathematics may be *used* informally – e.g., if it is used merely as a heuristic device, or if its terms are used loosely to motivate a relatively unconstrained thought experiment. However, mathematical objects *qua* mathematical objects are inherently formal. This is as true of Arrow and Debreu's topology as it is of, say, the extensive-form games of Acemoglu and Robinson (2006), even though the latter is *used* in a more informal way – i.e. to make broad, sometimes vague claims about actual polities. As such, it seems more proper to view ACE as a formal analytic

5.3.5 Reconsider formalism

From the diverse perspectives of old-style institutionalism, critical realism, and some Post-Keynesianism, a small group of economists has argued not only that rigid adherence to orthodoxy in the lead-up to the crisis masked deeper complexities but, further, that it is incumbent upon us at least to consider that an *a priori* commitment to methodological individualism and mathematical modeling may be more an obstacle than a conduit to empirical understanding. As with Caballero (2010) and Colander *et al.* (2009), these voices indict rigid adherence to orthodox models as dangerous and untenable. Hodgson (2009), for example, suggests that the dogmatic adherence to belief in the efficiency of markets led economists to ignore warnings of a coming crisis: "When economists believe in the informational efficiency of markets and their self-correcting capacity, then warnings of collapse are disregarded because they go against the conventional wisdom." And Leijonhufvud (2009) notes that "the repeated occurrence of financial crashes or crises hardly seems consistent with intertemporal equilibrium theory."

Unlike Caballero (2010) and Colander *et al.* (2009), however, these economists urge us to consider letting our choice of methodologies be guided by a nuanced understanding of empirical reality, regardless of what methodologies are best suited to this. Hodgson (2009: 1218) sees the unseating of mathematics as the prime concern in moving to "a discipline more oriented to understanding real-world institutions and actors." To achieve this, he argues, "[t]here must be an end to the use of mathematics as 'an end in itself' and to dogmatic teaching styles that leave no place for critical and reflective thought." Elsewhere, he writes that "[t]he pressing question now is whether the financial crisis of 2008, which is the most severe crisis since the Great Depression, will reverse this fascination with mathematical technique over real-world substance" (Hodgson 2008: 276). He further adds that

[o]ne likely reaction to the current downturn is that we should try harder to develop better models. Perhaps we should. But we must also learn the vital lesson that models on their own are never enough. Economists need to appreciate the limitations of modeling. These limitations are generic and result from the intractabilities of uncertainty, complexity and system openness in the real world.

Tony Lawson has been equally outspoken on this issue. In Lawson (2009), he argues that the problem "is not so much the use of specific inappropriate

methodology, though one that uses a different formal approach from current mainstream economic modeling methods like DSGE. See also Lawson (2009).

models, but the emphasis on mathematical deductivist modeling per se. Such models can provide limited insight at best into the workings of the economy (or any other part of social reality). Indeed, I will suggest that the formalistic modeling endeavor mostly gets in the way of understanding" (Lawson 2009: 760). Lawson's opposition to mathematical formalization is rooted in his particular version of realism – namely, that mathematics imposes a closed-system ontology that does not reflect the reality of economic life, since "the nature and conditions of social reality are such that the forms of mathematical deductivist reasoning favoured by economists are almost entirely inadequate as tools of insightful social analysis." He calls for a "more grounded framework" to better understand this "open, structured, totality in motion" (Lawson 2009: 763).

The calls for reconsidering the discipline's commitment to formal methodology have generally come from outside of the mainstream, but there have been a small number of similar pleas from inside it as well. Two of the most notable examples are George Akerlof's recent appeal for more "fine-grained" (read: qualitative/interpretive) methods in economics (Akerlof 2011) – to ensure that our models are actually capable of representing the phenomena we claim to explain – and Paul Krugman's (2009) recent criticism of economics' *a priori* commitment to mathematical modeling. Such contributions from inside the mainstream, however, are exceptional. Judging by their absence in the various articulations of the Blue Ribbon consensus, it is apparent that they are currently only fringe contributions.

Conclusion

The financial crisis of 2008–09 was largely unanticipated by economists. This chapter reviewed the pre-crisis literature to consider the possible causes of this failure and its implications for economic methodology. The review suggested that the analytic methods employed in the mainstream of the discipline in the lead-up to the crisis failed to recognize the importance of the peculiar political, regulatory, and commercial environment of the late 1990s and 2000s. A review of the post-crisis debates over the implications of the crisis for economic methodology suggests that the discipline's response to the crisis will be a re-commitment to mathematical modeling with greater emphasis on behavioral models, explicit modeling of dysfunctional finance, and (to a lesser extent) agent-based computational economic models.

Part III

A reform proposal

6 | Why reform?

Chapters 2 and 3 identified shortcomings inherent in mathematical economic modeling methodology that render contemporary economics blind to certain kinds of explanatory failure. In Part III, we turn to the question of how to move beyond recognizing the problem to actually addressing it. In rough terms, this task corresponds to answering two questions: *So what?* and *What should be done about it?*

The current chapter addresses the first of these questions, arguing that the problems identified in Parts I and II cannot be safely ignored because they can pass undetected through economics' current assessment methods even when they have serious empirical consequences. I demonstrate this by first providing more detail on precisely what kind of information economists would need to detect these problems, and then arguing that our current methodology is both ill-suited to gathering and processing such information and blind to the need to do so. These arguments set the stage for the presentation of a reform proposal, in Chapter 7, that addresses both of these shortcomings.

6.1 The problem

As was argued in Part I above, the use of a mathematical model implies a commitment to the view that the subject matter under investigation can aptly be represented mathematically. Specifically, mathematical modeling presupposes that the objects under investigation are plausibly *stable, modular*, and *quantitative*, with no qualitative differences among instantiations of each type, and that the relations between them are *fixed* and *law-like* throughout the context under study in the modeling exercise. But the validity of this presupposition can be demonstrated neither by the mathematical model itself nor by any inferences drawn from it. It can be secured only by *independent* evidence that the subject matter under investigation conforms to that description. The question to be explored, then, is how to secure this evidence. What should we be looking for in the target subject matter and how should we go about looking for it?

To fix terms, and for the sake of expositional simplicity, in what follows I will refer to phenomena possessing the properties cited above as "modular-stable." The term is meant to capture all of the elements of (1^*) and (2^*) (see Chapter 2), and so determining that the target objects and relations identified in the Delimitation phase are suitably modular-stable amounts to a determination that the necessary conditions for essential compatibility between model and target can be met. For example, with respect to Wadhwani and Wall (1991), if we were to establish that "unemployment" and "effort on the job" were modular-stable with respect to labor relations in the UK between 1972 and 1982, this would provide partial support for the claim that the necessary conditions were met within the relevant context.

Modular-stable is a vague term at this point, and although I will make it more precise in what follows, a certain amount of vagueness will necessarily remain. Since the phenomena we will be concerned with are social phenomena, their meanings will be at least to some extent fluid, evolving, and imprecise. This is necessarily so, because their meanings are formed dialectically – i.e. by agents acting within norms and conventions which are in turn shaped by those individual actions. As such, we cannot hope to establish that a given set of social phenomena *are*, objectively speaking, modular-stable. The necessary conditions for essential compatibility derived in Chapter 2 are phrased to reflect this: it is necessary only that the objects and relations under study be *plausibly understood* as modular-stable. Consequently, these necessary conditions do not generate a requirement that we rigorously "test" the social phenomena under study according to an objective standard. Rather, they require that we assess the social phenomena against standards of plausibility generated from within our discipline – i.e. against *intersubjective* standards.

One element of vagueness in the notion of stability that must be addressed up front, however, is the vagueness surrounding its proper context: that is, with respect to *what*, precisely, must a set of social phenomena be modular-stable in order for a mathematical modeling exercise to be coherent? There are several possible relevant contexts. For example, I could be claiming that the relevant social phenomena must be modular-stable *for the people involved in the social interactions under study*. With respect to Wadhwani and Wall (1991), this would mean that assessing whether or not the necessary conditions were met would involve getting direct testimony from UK workers about their experience from 1972 to 1982 (or utilizing direct testimony taken by others). This is obviously problematic, for all of the reasons that individuals' accounts of their actions, beliefs, and intentions may be unreliable – from simple carelessness or lack of careful self-analysis to full blown false consciousness.

On the other end of the spectrum, I could be claiming that the relevant categories must be modular-stable *according to some general theory of the structure of the phenomena under study*. Under this view, we need not look to the subjective assessments of the individuals involved in the social interactions. Rather, we would focus on the categories posited by our theory of social structure – not as proxies for individuals' self-assessment but rather as the true drivers of social phenomena. For example, taking a broadly Marxian approach to understanding social behavior, one would be less concerned with individuals' self-assessments of their actions than with the realities of class interests (because individual self-assessment would be merely epiphenomenal). As such, in the context of a mathematical modeling exercise, one would be concerned with the stability of the posited social categories with respect to class interests rather than with respect to individual self-reports. This approach is also problematic in the context of mathematical modeling exercises, however, as there is no way to assess independently the aptness of the underlying theory of social structure. The econometric tests of Wadhwani and Wall (1991), for example, can tell us nothing about the aptness of a Marxian view of labor relations unless such a view would generate a particular (and unique) econometric specification of efficiency wage theory. And even in this case, our test would be difficult to interpret with respect to the aptness of the Marxian view for the standard Duhem–Quine reasons,[1] we would be testing the joint hypothesis of the aptness of a Marxian description of social life along with (*inter alia*) the particular specification we derived.

Each of these approaches to assessing the modularity-stability of social phenomena – i.e. with respect to individual self-assessment and with respect to general social theory – suffers from an unwarranted emphasis on single aspects of social meaning taken in isolation. A more fruitful approach – the "hermeneutic" or "interpretive" approach – combines these two extreme stances: it seeks to uncover the meaning of social actions from the point of view of the agent, but remains cognizant of the inherently social nature of the norms and conventions that give those individual actions meaning (and also of the fact that the individual actions themselves shape the norms and conventions that give them meaning). The approach is "hermeneutic" in the

---

[1] See the discussion of the Duhem–Quine thesis in Chapter 1 above.

sense that it involves deriving meaning through *interpretation* rather than through (objective) discovery or mere subjective reporting.

This interpretation necessarily involves two highly inter-related activities: determining the appropriate interpretive framework to apply to the phenomena under study, and determining the meaning of those phenomena in the light of that framework. The two elements inform each other dialectically: the practitioner may begin with an idea of the social categories and interpretive framework that are relevant to the phenomena under study, and will interpret the actions of the agents involved accordingly; but the practitioner must be prepared to revise his/her categories and interpretive framework when confronted with experience.[2,3] This provides a rich sense of the meaning of social actions. Rather than interpreting social phenomena with respect to an objectively imposed criterion (e.g., defining change in test scores per dollar spent as "educational productivity"; consumption as "welfare"; or GDP per capita as "well-being" or "development"), the hermeneutic approach offers insight into what Charles Taylor calls "experiential meaning": i.e. meaning *for* someone *of* something *in relation to* the meanings of other things in the subject's experience (Taylor 1985: 21–3).

It is this notion of meaning that is relevant to the necessary conditions adumbrated in Chapter 2. That is, in order for mathematical economic modeling exercises to be coherent, the objects under study (and the relations between those objects) must be shown to be suitably modular-stable in the interpretive sense just discussed. If they cannot be plausibly so-described, the practitioner must determine what *are* modular-stable objects and relations within the phenomena under study and reform her model to reflect this new understanding. Using the vocabulary developed in Chapter 2, this means that the left-hand-side elements of the catalog of correspondences (which are social phenomena) must be shown to be suitably modular-stable to be represented by the right-hand-side elements (which are mathematical objects and relations). If they cannot be plausibly so-described, then there will be a disconnect between the question posed in the Delimitation phase and the analytics being deployed to address it, and the practitioner must reform her model accordingly.

---

[2] This interdependency of meaning and interpretive framework is often referred to as the "hermeneutic circle." See, e.g., Gadamer (1987: 87, 127; 1989: 265–7) and Taylor (1985: 18).

[3] This dialectic process of meaning-generation bears some resemblance to the Bayesian recursive meaning-generation process. Both processes involve the incorporation of new information to update one's understanding of a set of phenomena. There is a major difference between the two processes, however: whereas the Bayesian updating process involves interpreting empirical phenomena from within a probabilistic framework, it is constitutive of the hermeneutic updating process that the interpreter attempt to extract from the phenomena themselves the proper framework for their interpretation.

6.2 Why reform is necessary

Although the process I have just described – assessing the aptness of an economic model by comparing it to empirical evidence – will sound very familiar to economists, one of the central claims of this book is that the requirements of essential compatibility and the challenges they raise are *unfamiliar* to economists and that their remedy requires the development of new methods. Before sketching out a proposal for a new field to develop such methods, then, it will be necessary first to explain clearly why reform is necessary in the first place. That is, I must explain why the requirements of essential compatibility and the challenges they raise cannot be treated like other methodological difficulties that are well-understood by and addressable with the current toolkit of economics.

Toward that end, I will consider three possible interpretations of the essential compatibility requirement that would render it relatively unproblematic. The first such interpretation is that the essential compatibility requirement is merely a species of modeling challenge, akin to, for example, the challenge of finding a suitable specification of the utility function in models of consumption behavior. Under this interpretation, the essential compatibility requirement is not at all a new type of challenge (let alone one that would require methodological reform) but rather a challenge that the discipline currently comprehends, and one that can be (and regularly is) addressed using the discipline's current toolkit.

The second interpretation (which is related to but distinct from the first) is that (a) the essential compatibility requirement is important if and only if it has empirical implications, and (b) that if it does have empirical implications they can be assessed using econometric techniques. Under this interpretation, we do not need to be especially worried about the essential compatibility requirement because we will be able to determine when it is an important (i.e. empirically consequential) problem and can then deal with it by suitably respecifying the offending model. This interpretation also implies that there is no need to develop new methods to address the essential compatibility requirement.

The third interpretation (which, again, is related to but distinct from the aforementioned interpretations) is what I will call the "As-If" or "Black Box" interpretation, which takes models to be merely black boxes that convert inputs (initial conditions and/or data) into outputs (hypotheses). If the outputs correlate closely with observed phenomena, then the model is a good one. As we saw in Chapter 1, this is essentially the view expressed by Milton Friedman in his 1953 essay "The Methodology of Positive Economics," in which he argued that economic models do not need to represent the *actual* mechanisms generating observed behavior, but rather need only represent *some* mechanism for generating that behavior. The model generates hypothetical states of the world that would result from people acting *as if* they were motivated by the dynamics of the model. If the hypotheses of the model are not falsified, we have reason (albeit provisionally, and always with a readiness to change our judgment in the face of a future falsification) to believe that the theory underlying the model is a good predictor of behavior even though it is not necessarily an accurate representation of the mechanism *actually* generating that behavior.[4] So the proper response to the essential compatibility requirement is: *So what? We never claimed that the model represented actual motivations. If the model generates non-falsified hypotheses it is a good model, full stop.*

I will answer each of these interpretations in turn, using examples of empirical analyses of Shapiro–Stiglitz efficiency wage theory as illustrations.

Interpretation #1: Failure to establish essential compatibility is just a species of bad modeling

Response: While it is true that an economic model whose elements represent social categories that turn out not to be plausibly modular-stable *is* an example of a bad model, the badness of modeling is different in type from standard badness of modeling (standard, that is, with respect to the standards of current mainstream economics). It is different in type because it involves potential incoherence rather than just ineffectiveness.

Recall the example of the chess master's relationship advice from Chapter 2. In that case, the chess master's story was shown to be incoherent as an explanation of her friends' relationship difficulties because it could not have been *about* their relationship. It operated on a conceptual map some of whose essential properties could not possibly have been shared by the phenomena they were meant to represent. Similarly, economic modeling exercises whose models are bad because they represent with mathematical language social phenomena that are not plausibly modular-stable are not merely ineffective, they are incoherent. Specifically: they posit the solution of the mathematical model as an answer to the question posed in the Delimitation phase when that solution process is not capable of representing the possible dynamics of the

---

[4] The connection between a model and the theory underlying it is complex, as discussed in Chapter 1. Friedman (1953) elides these complexities, and so my description of his position does so as well.

social phenomena under study. Note that, as with the example above, this does not mean that such a model could not make a correct prediction, only that it would only be capable of doing so accidentally.

We can also illustrate the problem by returning to Wadhwani and Wall (1991). In that paper, the authors claim that the results of their analysis constitute evidence in support of two predictions of efficiency wage theory: that "changes in unemployment will increase a firm's productivity" and that "a high relative wage [paid by a particular firm] will make it more productive than its counterparts" (Wadhwani and Wall 1991: 529). In Chapter 3, I argued that this claim was not well-founded because it rested upon the assumption that the categories of social life represented by the authors' mathematical model were modular-stable, and that the authors had not provided any evidence to support this assumption.

According to the interpretation of the essential compatibility requirement I am considering here, one could offer the following objection: *Your criticism amounts to a claim that the paper has a weak link in its inferential chain; specifically, that the authors' chosen representation of "effort" may be too indirect to be convincing. But addressing this sort of concern is indeed part of the regular business of current economics. And if a particular modeling exercise suffers from it, then this is an indictment of that modeling exercise and not an example of potential problems in economics as a whole. It is an issue not of the root of economics but, rather, of one of its buds.*

If this is a proper interpretation of my criticism, then it should be possible in principle to construct an empirical analysis of efficiency wage theory that addresses the inadequacy of Wadhwani and Wall's representation of "effort" in a manner that (a) uses only mathematical modeling methods and (b) moots the essential compatibility requirement problem. But I will argue that this is not the case.

To see why, it will be helpful to examine, briefly, another empirical M-M efficiency wage paper – Cappelli and Chauvin (1991) – that is preferable to Wadhwani and Wall (1991) with respect to the treatment of "effort," but that is not capable of addressing the essential compatibility requirement problems I raise. Cappelli and Chauvin (1991) has a slightly different focus from that of Wadhwani and Wall (1991), as its goal is to examine the relationship between effort and relative wage, rather than the relationship between effort and productivity. Despite this difference, however, the two papers both concern themselves with the relationship between effort and relative wage, whether as an intermediate or terminal question. The important difference between the two papers for my purposes is that Cappelli and

Chauvin (1991) employs two non-interpretive strategies that provide some support (albeit incidental and indirect) for the modularity-stability of the social categories represented by their model. As such, Cappelli and Chauvin (1991) embodies the point of the objection raised above. As I will argue below, however, the paper still falls short of the standards of this book's critique and requires additional support from interpretive strategies for establishing the modularity-stability of the social categories represented by their model. Moreover, the reasons why it falls short are not peculiar to the authors' approach, but rather inhere in economic modeling methodology.

The first non-interpretive strategy employed by Cappelli and Chauvin is the shortening of the inferential chain. Unlike Wadhwani and Wall (1991) which examines effort indirectly, Cappelli and Chauvin (1991) utilizes a direct measure of "effort" – or, rather, the lack of effort, which they call "shirking" – whose meaning within the context studied is stabilized to some extent by its definition. Specifically, they equate the level of shirking with "the rate at which workers were dismissed at each plant for disciplinary reasons." After a brief discussion of the shortcomings of alternative measures of shirking employed by other researchers, the authors offer non-interpretive evidence in support of the appropriateness of their measure:

The costs associated with dismissals are exactly the mechanism behind the shirking model of efficiency wages. Further, we can be reasonably certain that these disciplinary actions in fact result from poor performance and productivity, broadly defined (e.g., low performance levels, tardiness, absenteeism, breaking safety procedures, bad relations with supervisors or fellow workers, etc.). The United Auto Workers' contract with the employer limits management's ability to discipline employees to such performance-related issues, and as enforced by a strong union and grievance procedures, these restrictions effectively eliminate arbitrary and capricious actions. (Cappelli and Chauvin 1991: 776)

This lends some support to the assumption of category modularity-stability, but the support is necessarily indirect because it relies on an inference about experience from an objective rule definition. Specifically, while the authors purport to examine shirking *per se*, they really are examining *actions whose occurrence may signal the presence of shirking*. And while this seems like a more direct link to shirking/effort than was found in Wadhwani and Wall (1991), we are still several steps removed from shirking *per se*: (1) actual shirking, (2) definition of a certain type of action as evidence of shirking, (3) actual occurrence of that action, (4) quantitative representation of that occurrence. We cannot know to what extent workers' and managers' actual experience of shirking, discipline, dismissal, etc., match up to the given definition, or to what extent actual occurrences of disciplinary firing fit the given definition, without interpretive investigation.

The second strategy is the use of control variables specifically in order to avoid mistaking non-shirking behavior for actual shirking. The authors conjecture that some of the disciplinary issues they want to identify as "shirking" might actually be workers' expression of grievances. To the extent that the workers' sense of "voice" (in Hirschman's (1970) sense of the term) is low, they may need to act out to express themselves. In recognition of this, the authors include in their regressions a variable representing corporate-level managers' assessment of the quality of the problem-solving ability of local unions and management at each of the company's plants (on a scale from 1 to 10 where 1 = confrontational relations and 10 = cooperative, problem-solving relations). Again, this provides some indirect support for the plausibility of the stability of the category "shirking." To the extent that the statistical controlling strategy is legitimate, it will lend credence to the idea that the authors' direct measure of "shirking" is modular-stable throughout the context under study. Specifically, the controlling strategy lends support to the idea that at least one source of possible variation in the meaning of "the rate at which workers were dismissed at each plant for disciplinary reasons" has been ruled out.

This support is undermined, however, by the circularity of its logic: it would be necessary first to establish the modularity-stability of the categories represented by the model before having confidence that the dynamics of statistical control are projectible onto the delimited social phenomena. The circularity arises because statistical control in an econometric specification is a species of mathematical modeling, as discussed in Chapter 3. As such, while it is certainly not an inherently unhelpful exercise, it is not capable of providing support for the modularity-stability of the categories of social life represented in the model because it pre-supposes such modularity-stability.

Concretely, the problem with using statistical control techniques to establish the modularity-stability of social categories is that such techniques can only be helpful with respect to right-hand-side links in the catalog of correspondences, and not the far left-hand-side link which is the primary site of essential compatibility requirement-related difficulties. I will elaborate on this in my response to Interpretation #2 below, but will offer a brief sketch of my point here. As discussed in Chapter 3, the catalog of correspondences of an empirical analysis contains at least one more layer than a purely theoretical model. For example, whereas in Shapiro and Stiglitz (1984) the entry for "effort" was "effort − e," in Wadhwani and Wall (1991), the entry for "effort" is effort – $e(\cdot)$ – $(-a + b(W/W^\star)^{\gamma 1} u^{-\gamma 2})$ – quantitative representation of $(-a + b(W/W^\star)^{\gamma 1} u^{-\gamma 2})$ (i.e. the data), and in Cappelli and Chauvin (1991), the entry for effort was shirking – the rate at which workers were dismissed at each plant for disciplinary reasons – DISL (variable name for the quantitative representation of this phenomenon) (i.e. the data).

As discussed in Chapter 2, the primary site of essential compatibility requirement-related problems will be the left-most link in the chain of a catalog of correspondence entry. This is the site of the problem of category non-modularity-instability. In theoretical M-M analyses, this is often the only link (as with the Shapiro and Stiglitz (1984) entry for "effort" above). In empirical modeling exercises, it generally is not the only link (as with the examples above). The reason this is the most problematic link for the purposes of our discussion is that it is the bridge from ordinary language to mathematical language, and from social concepts to mathematical ones. Evidence that the far left-hand-side element of the catalog entry is plausibly modular-stable enough to support its end of the bridge to the mathematical realm *must* have roots in the social world. Techniques of statistical control may seem like they are rooted in social experience – because they deal with "data" – but as we can see from the entries in the catalog, they are not. Rather, they are quantitative representations of a theorized representation of social phenomena, as discussed in Chapter 3. The questions that are asked and ostensibly answered in empirical analyses are questions and answers about the far left-hand-side elements of the catalog.[5] But the control technique utilized by Cappelli and Chauvin (1991) sought only to provide evidence for the precision of meaning of the far right-hand-side element. Since the site of essential compatibility requirement-related problems is the far left-hand-side link, techniques addressing the far right-hand-side can only be seen as addressing essential compatibility requirement-related problems to the extent that all of the links in the chain are presumed to be strong; i.e.,

---

[5] See Chapter 3 for relevant excerpts of such questions and answers from Wadhwani and Wall (1991). Comparable statements from Cappelli and Chauvin (1991) are as follows. *Question/Puzzle*: "Efficiency wage models are based on the notion that there is a relationship between relative wage levels and worker productivity, broadly defined, which in turn explains a variety of otherwise puzzling behavior such as the presence of involuntary unemployment. Perhaps the most popular of these arguments have been those suggesting that wage premiums and the threat of losing them create incentives for workers to reduce unproductive behavior or 'shirking.' . . . This paper provides a direct test of the main implications of the shirking efficiency wage model using plant-level data from the auto industry" (p. 769). *Answer/Conclusion*: "The wage premium appears to provide incentives to avoid dismissal rather than leading to the selection of workers less inclined to shirk. . . . It is difficult to identify the value of reduction of shirking associated with a given wage premium, but it does seem that there could be nontrivial returns associated with a wage premium" (p. 785).

evidence that the values of the variable DISL really are just measuring one thing very precisely and in a constant manner across the data set can be considered evidence that the social behavior category "shirking" is stable across the social context under study *only if* DISL is presumed to be meaning-homomorphic with the social concept "shirking". But this is question-begging.

Thus, although the methodology of Cappelli and Chauvin (1991) is an improvement over that of Wadhwani and Wall (1991) with respect to the issues raised in Part I, it still suffers from a lack of interpretive evidence regarding the plausibility of category modularity-stability. The non-interpretive strategies utilized to tighten the inferential chain that leads from the econometric results to conclusions about social phenomena do indeed tighten the chain, but they do not address and cannot address the strength of the left-most link. This is a major problem and one that is not peculiar to Wadhwani and Wall (1991) or Cappelli and Chauvin (1991). It is a characteristic of economic modeling exercises in general. I do not mean to suggest that there are *no* economic modeling exercises that employ inter-pretive techniques in building their inferential chains. Indeed, in the next Chapter I will provide examples of economic analyses that do *also* employ interpretive techniques. The point is that such techniques are inherently outside the toolkit of mathematical economic modeling, and their use is currently considered optional or even irrelevant. My contention is that, because non-interpretive techniques cannot address the problems associated with the essential compatibility requirement, interpretive techniques must be a standard part of the economist's toolkit.

Interpretation #2:   Lack of essential compatibility is a problem if and only if it has empirical consequences, and this can be assessed using econometric techniques, so we do not need new methods to detect and assess the implications of a lack of essential compatibility.

Response: This interpretation involves a conflation of two distinct but related claims. The first is that lack of essential compatibility between a model and its target would be a problem if and only if it had empirical consequences. I will call this the "Empirical Consequences Claim." The second is that, since problems with empirical consequences are always in principle detectable (and their impact measurable) using econometric tech-niques, we do not need new methods to detect the presence or assess the implications of a lack of essential compatibility between a model and its target. I will call this the "Econometrics Sufficiency Claim."

It is the Econometrics Sufficiency Claim that is problematic. The Empirical Consequences Claim is a disciplinary judgment. It falls within the realm of issues that can (and must) be decided by a scientific discipline in the course of defining itself. In this case, we have a judgment that economics should adhere to a strict epistemological empiricism – i.e. that things that do not manifest themselves empirically have no knowledge content. One can argue about whether or not this is an appropriate position for economics to espouse, but there is nothing inherently out of bounds about the position.

The Econometrics Sufficiency Claim is a different matter. Whether or not econometric analysis is a sufficient detector of all empirical manifestations in the economy is itself an empirical matter. If we take the Empirical Consequences Claim seriously, then, we must insist upon some standard outside of econometrics to assess the Econometrics Sufficiency Claim – econometric methods alone cannot determine their own scope and suitability. In particular, we would need such a standard to assess whether or not a lack of modularity-stability in one's subject matter can have empirical consequences *even if it has no econometric consequences*.

The argument of Parts I and II suggest that such problems can indeed arise. As discussed in Chapter 3, econometric analysis operates entirely to the right of the left-most link in the catalog of correspondences. It deals only with the ostensible mathematical correspondents of the social phenomena under study. The question of whether these mathematical objects are capable of representing their ostensible social correspondents is outside the scope of econometrics. From a purely quantitative standpoint, the results of econometrics analyses are *entirely unaffected by* this question. With respect to interpreting the meaning of econometric results, however, the resolution of this representational question is crucially important. In fact, it has lexicographic priority: the quantitative results can legitimately be interpreted as addressing the social question under study *only if* the mathematical objects that produced that result are capable of representing their ostensible social correspondents.

For example, consider, once again, Wadhwani and Wall (1991). As noted above, the "effort" entry in the catalog of correspondences of this paper is effort – $e(\cdot)$ – $(-a + b(W/W^*)^{\gamma 1}u^{-\gamma 2})$ – quantitative representation of $(-a + b(W/W^*)^{\gamma 1}u^{-\gamma 2})$ (i.e. the data). Imagine that it is implausible that the category "effort on the job" was modular-stable within the context of the experience of work in the UK between 1972 and 1982 – for example, because an increase in antagonism between the working class and capitalist class midway through this period sharply eroded workers' sense that effort on the job was owed to their employer. What would this imply for the econometric results of Wadhwani and Wall (1991)? The answer is that it would not necessarily imply anything, quantitatively speaking, since the estimation of their regression parameters utilized a quantitative representation of $(-a + b(W/W^*)^{\gamma 1} u^{-\gamma 2})$ in place of "effort."[6] But it would have serious consequences for the interpretation of the parameter estimates as an answer to the puzzle identified in the Delimitation phase, for reasons discussed at length above.

But even if one concedes the point I have made above, one could still argue that I have not identified anything new. For example, it could be argued that empirical economic analyses are always subject to the criticism that their data do not match the concept they are meant to represent. To take an absurd example, imagine that Wadhwani and Wall (1991) had used "height" data for their "effort on the job" variable. This may (or may not) result in unbiased estimators, but it certainly would not pass muster as a test of Shapiro-Stiglitz efficiency wage theory.

This objection is partly valid. It is true that a bad choice of data to represent social phenomena is a problem very much akin to the problem of lack of plausible modularity-stability. They are akin in that they both affect the extent to which one may validly interpret the results of one's econometric analysis as an answer to a question about the social phenomena identified in the Delimitation phase. But it is not the case that the concerns raised in Part 1 are nothing new. What is new in this account is the identification of a specific type of mismatch problem (from within the larger set of mismatch problems that also includes the "height" for "effort" example above) the distinctness of which is not currently recognized within mainstream economics and remedies for which are not currently a part of the economist's toolkit.

Interpretation #3   (The "As-If" or "Black Box" interpretation): The realisticness of an economic theory or model is not relevant to its aptness. The only relevant standard against which to judge a theory or model is its ability to generate hypotheses that are not falsified by empirical observation.

Response: This interpretation suffers from two problems. First, it is based upon an instrumental-positive approach to science which faces insurmountable difficulties of its own. Second, even notwithstanding these difficulties,

---

[6] Note that claiming that $(-a + b(W/W^*)^{\gamma 1} u^{-\gamma 2})$ *is* effort does not help matters; first, because it is literally false, and, second, because it begs the question of whether or not Shapiro–Stiglitz efficiency wage theory does in fact hold.

the interpretation fails to adequately address the challenges associated with the essential compatibility requirement.

The As-If/Black Box interpretation rests upon an instrumental-positive approach to science of the type articulated by Karl Popper (1989) in *The Logic of Scientific Discovery*; namely "falsificationism," which is roughly the view that "*the criterion of the scientific status of a theory is its falsifiability, or refutability or testability*" when confronted with empirical data.[7] This is also the approach to science underlying Milton Friedman's "Methodology of Positive Economics." But there are well-known problems with this philosophy of science that severely undermine the As-If/Black Box interpretation's usefulness as an argument against the importance of the essential compatibility requirement. As we saw in Chapter 1, the underdetermination of hypothesis tests and the theory-ladenness of empirical observation render the standards of falsificationism unattainable. A second difficulty with the falsificationist approach is that it leaves one with no way to justify the generalization of one's results; i.e. it leaves one with no way to ground induction. According to the tenets of falsificationism, a theory can never be *verified* through testing, no matter how many times its attendant hypotheses have avoided falsification because it may always be falsified by its next encounter with data. As such, no amount of testing *on its own* can justify confidence in the prediction that the next encounter will also result in non-falsification. "[T]he attempt to base the principle of induction on experience breaks down," Popper wrote, "since it must lead to infinite regress" (Popper 1968: 29).

Further, it is not at all clear that one may even use instances of non-falsification as grounds for probabilities. That is, whereas it may be tempting to assert, for example, that *since* the sun has risen every day of my life I can at least be *fairly* certain it will rise tomorrow morning, this is an invalid inductive inference. It is invalid because past experience on its own can tell us nothing about what will happen the next time the hypothesis encounters empirical reality.[8] Our confidence in such probability statements must come from somewhere else, and typically it comes from *some kind of* realist theory. For example, to the extent we have confidence that the sun will rise tomorrow, it cannot be *merely* as a result of the past correlation between morning hours and sunlight. Rather, our confidence derives from a confidence in a theory of actual celestial mechanics. The only kind of confidence

---

[7] Popper (1969: 37). Italics in original.
[8] For Popper's comments on this point, see Popper (1968: 254–65).

that could be derived merely from non-falsification would be superstition of the type associated with "cargo cults."[9] Having confidence that, for example, "productivity will probably rise when relative wages rise *simply because* this hypothesis has not yet been falsified and we may therefore operate under the belief that the labor market works *as if* obeying Shapiro–Stiglitz theory" is not in principle different from believing that "supplies will probably arrive on one's island if one builds an airstrip on the grounds that this hypothesis has not yet been falsified and we may therefore legitimately operate under the belief that the world works as if a God of Supplies demands the building of airstrip-shaped tributes." All of this weakens the argument that essential compatibility requirement-related problems are non-problems *on the grounds that* scientific theories should be understood as As-If theories and therefore need not correspond to actual behavior-generating mechanisms.

A third difficulty with the As-If/Black Box view of science – and one that is closely related to the aforementioned problems of hypothesis testing and induction – is that it is question-begging with respect to the proper categorization of the phenomena under study. The notion that empirical testing of statistical regularities is the sole determinant of a theory's goodness presumes that the statistical categories whose correlations are being tested adequately represent what they ostensibly represent. If this is not the case, then the relationship between these categories cannot be interpreted as a test of the theory. For example, Wadhwani and Wall (1991) purports to test Shapiro–Stiglitz efficiency wage theory by testing the relationship between productivity and relative wage. But if it were the case that workers did not actually care about the ratio of their wage to the industry average (even if they had been aware of the value of this ratio), then it would be wrong to interpret the econometric analysis in Wadhwani and Wall (1991) as a test of Shapiro–Stiglitz efficiency wage theory. It *could* still be interpreted merely as the comparison of a prediction about the value of certain statistics to the realized values of those statistics – in much the same way that a comparison of the realized values of some statistic and predictions about that statistic generated by astrology or augury could be "tested." But without some account of how the posited categories actually represent elements of the phenomena under study, the Wadhwani and Wall (1991) test is no more a test of efficiency wage

---

[9] The term "cargo-cult" refers to the practice observed among certain pre-industrial societies, in the wake of contact with industrial societies, of engaging in ritualistic behavior in an attempt to call forth the various kinds of supplies that had regularly arrived in their midst in the course of their contact with the industrialized people. The most salient modern examples are the cargo cults of Melanesian islanders in the years following the use of their home islands as bases during World War II. See, e.g., Worsley (1968). These cults are often used as examples of behavior guided by a conflation of correlation with causation.

theory than a comparison of an ancient Roman augur's predictions about the fate of a dynasty to its actual fate are a test of the plausibility of Roman mythology.[10]

Alasdair MacIntyre (1978) explores the implications of these issues in the context of political science in his essay "Is a Science of Comparative Politics Possible?" MacIntyre considers what would be necessary to meaningfully compare political experience across contexts, and he questions the notion that positive social science methods can establish the existence of generic categories of political action (i.e. categories that are modular-stable across contexts). His skepticism is based in large part on the circularity of the process of establishing and testing such categories in positive social science. One must first posit categories, then decide what aspects of the phenomena under study correspond to the chosen categorization, then posit a theory using those categories (under the assumption that the categorization is apt), then test the theory against data which consist of empirical reality organized according to the posited categories. The circularity becomes apparent when we consider how we would assess the aptness of the initial categorization scheme (which is, after all, an integral part of the theory). The results of our test cannot help us here, as the test presumes the aptness of the categorization.

MacIntyre illustrates these difficulties via an example drawn from Gabriel Almond and Sidney Verba's *The Civic Culture* (1963). In that work, Almond and Verba undertake a comparative analysis of European citizens' commitment to and identification with their governments. They "argue that Italians are less committed to and identified with the actions of their government than are Germans or Englishmen, offering as evidence the fact that the Italian respondents, as compared with the English and German respondents to their survey, placed such actions very low on a list of items to which they had been asked to give a rank order in terms of the amount of pride they took in them" (MacIntyre 1978: 262). But MacIntyre finds fault with this argument, noting that it would be problematic to interpret statistical analysis of such data as a test of the differential identification of citizens with their governments because the concept of "pride" differed markedly across the cultures under study. The problem here is not with the statistical analysis *per se* of these data,

---

[10] I do not mean to suggest that we *could not* interpret a successful prediction of the augur as provisional evidence in favor of the mythology underlying that prediction. Indeed, a strict falsificationist would have to interpret it in that way. Rather, I mean to suggest that, under the As-If/Black Box view of science, there is no difference in principle between interpreting a comparison of the augur's predictions against empirical reality as a "test" of Roman mythology, and interpreting Wadhwani and Wall's (1991) econometric analysis as a "test" of Shapiro–Stiglitz efficiency wage theory.

but rather with the particular categories posited as proper targets of such analysis. It is Almond and Verba's mistake on *this* level that invalidates their findings, according to MacIntyre, regardless of whether or not they follow proper positive science procedure in their analysis. The inputs into that analysis are ill-formed and therefore so will be the outputs. MacIntyre summarizes the danger, in general, for positive social science as follows:

[I]f we identify behavior except in terms of the intentions and therefore of the beliefs of the agents we shall risk describing what they are doing as what we would be doing if we went through that series of movements or something like it rather than what they are actually doing. Nor do we avoid this difficulty merely by finding *some* description of the behavior in question which both the agents themselves and the political scientist would accept. (MacIntyre 1978: 264)

The necessary groundwork of any comparative social science analysis, then, is "to find identifiable units in different societies and cultures about which we may construct true causal generalizations" (MacIntyre 1978: 263). And this cannot be done with positive social science methods alone because these methods presume rather than provide an account of the plausibility of the modularity-stability of the categories they posit. Providing such an account, MacIntyre suggests, requires supplementing positive science methods with "the writing of a series of comparative histories" of the concepts that we wish to posit as stable categories of political life (MacIntyre 1978: 262).

The foregoing three problems – i.e. the problems of hypothesis testing, induction, and stable categorization – undermine the As-If/Black Box interpretation of the critique contained in Part I above. In fact, far from providing a counterargument to that critique, the As-If/Black Box interpretation actually provides support for it. As we have seen above, the As-If/Black Box view of social science requires an appeal to realism that is consonant with (though not identical to) the essential compatibility requirement in order to ground induction and justify the categorizations that underlie its analyses. That is, if the realm under study in a given economic modeling exercise were in fact to conform to (1*) and (2*) (see Chapter 2) and the categories of that analysis were in fact modular-stable, then this would be grounds for having confidence in inductive inferences drawn from the analysis in question. But, of course, one cannot simply assume that (1*) and (2*) hold, and economic modeling methodology itself lacks the tools to justify these assumptions. As such, the essential compatibility requirement-related issues I raise above, and the remedies for such issues I discuss below, are highly relevant to the As-If/Black Box interpretation and are certainly not obviated by it.

The second response to Interpretation #3 is that, even if falsificationism did not suffer from the issues raised immediately above, the essential compatibility requirement would still be potentially problematic, and, further, these potential problems would not necessarily be detectable by positivist scientific methods. As established above in the response to Interpretation #2, essential compatibility requirement-related issues are potentially problematic primarily with respect to the valid interpretation of the results of empirical modeling exercises. These issues *may or may not* affect the results of empirical tests – for example, they may or may not result in detectable specification errors – but irrespective of whether or not they have such an effect, they still can carry significant implications for the proper interpretation of the results of empirical tests.

To clarify precisely how this relates to the As-If interpretation, it is helpful to consider how Friedman himself responded in his 1953 essay to research aimed at investigating actual economic experience. In that essay, Friedman cites the questionnaire method utilized by Henderson (1938) and Meade and Andrews (1938) as an example of irrelevant concern with realism. In order to investigate the effect of changes in the interest rate on various types of business decisions, Henderson (1938) and Meade and Andrews (1938) sent questionnaires to 37 businessmen on the subject.[11] The decision to use questionnaires, moreover, was motivated in part by a belief that information on the actual realities of economic life was relevant to economic analysis. Henderson explains:

The minds of many economics students have been feeling their way in recent years towards the tentative conclusions which have been set out above [i.e. that it is not obvious precisely how changes in the interest rate should affect economic activity, and furthermore that the conventional wisdom may overestimate the impact of changes in the interest rate on several kinds of activity.] But it has seemed desirable to some of us at Oxford that a more systematic effort should be made than hitherto to ascertain whether these conclusions, positive and negative alike, are well founded. There has been in existence for some years among the tutors engaged in teaching economics at Oxford a research group which has been investigating the factors affecting the course of economic activity. These investigations cover a considerable range of problems, and the methods include both statistical analysis and interviews and discussions with business men. (Henderson 1938: 8–9)

Friedman (1953) dismisses the practices and results of Henderson (1938) and Meade and Andrews (1938) on the grounds that questionnaires of

---

[11] Henderson (1938: 9); Meade and Andrews (1938: 14).

businessmen cannot be used as data to test hypotheses. He acknowledges that such questionnaires may have "suggestive" value "in suggesting leads to follow in accounting for divergencies between predicted and observed results," but asserts that they are "almost entirely useless as a means of *testing* the validity of economic hypotheses" (Friedman 1953: 212 n. 22).

Seen in the light of the critique mounted in Part I, Friedman's response misses the point that economic analyses must grapple not only with problems related to the testing of hypotheses, but also with the valid interpretation of the results of those tests. The interviews detailed in Meade and Andrews (1938) could serve to provide a grounding for the interpretation of economic analyses of the impact of changes in the interest rate on business activity.[12] Note that this is different from the point that the interviews could be used as a creative source for the construction of additional hypotheses – a point that Friedman himself makes. While this point is correct, it is not much of a concession. For Friedman, the process of hypothesis construction is unrestricted. The economist may draw on any inspiration, scientific or otherwise.[13] Granting that questionnaires could be used to suggest hypotheses, then, is very faint praise. From the Friedmanite perspective, one could say the same of séances. The crucial point is that Friedman denies even the possibility that questionnaires could be useful in the testing of hypotheses – and in this process of testing we must include interpretation of results, because it is this interpretation that allows us to judge whether or not a test has supported or falsified a hypothesis. My critique suggests, on the contrary, that questionnaires, if done well, could play an important role in this process.

Conclusion

The valid use of mathematical modeling methods in economic analysis requires that the subject matter under study conforms to conditions (1*) and (2*) – i.e. that they be plausibly describable as modular-stable. Since mathematical economic modeling methodology presumes modular-stable subject matter, economists must use different methods to explore whether or not this is actually the case. The appropriate methods for doing so will necessarily

[12] Meade and Andrews' work does have its problems. One could reasonably criticize the authors on some points of their questionnaire technique. For example, the sample size was very small and there is little discussion of criteria for selection of participants. But these are not the grounds on which Friedman objected to their work. He objected to the use of questionnaires *per se* in testing (and interpreting) hypotheses.

[13] See Friedman (1953: 208).

be "hermeneutic" or "interpretive," as what is required is an exploration of the dialectical construction of meanings by agents who simultaneously create the norms of social meaning and operate within them. The kinds of problems that can arise when modularity-stability of the subject matter is not established are not necessarily detectable using the current model assessment methods of economics, as those methods are themselves outside the toolkit of mathematical economic modeling methodology. Because general, discipline-wide standards for using interpretive methods in this way do not currently exist in economics, it will be necessary to build this capacity into the discipline. The next chapter provides a concrete reform proposal for doing so, as well as several examples of what the work of this reformed economics would look like.

7 A reform proposal

In the previous chapter, I argued that the presumption of modularity-stability of the target subject matter implied by mathematical metaphorical modeling requires that those who seek to model social phenomena mathematically offer an account of the plausibility of this presumption. I argued further that this requirement differs significantly from other methodological issues that are well understood by economists, and I suggested the need for new research methods to address the requirement adequately.

This chapter expands on that suggestion by describing the kind of auxiliary work that must be done in economics in order for us to be confident that the kind of mathematical modeling commonly practiced in the discipline is relevant to the social phenomena it seeks to represent. Centrally, I propose the development of a new field within the discipline, the primary task of which would be to develop methods and standards for assessing the essential compatibility (or lack thereof) between economic models and their target subjects. We may call this field "interpretative economics." Work in this area has already begun: giving it a distinct name only serves to concretize the crucial contribution that the field ought to make. Yet the name is incidental in a way the task is not. Without undertaking serious interpretative work to underpin economics as currently practiced, the suggestion that the kind of modeling pursued by economists has the capacity to illuminate human social action and interaction will remain a wish or fervent hope rather than a plausible claim. It would indicate the continued neglect of the testimony of the people who, in the words of Truman Bewley, actually "make economic decisions and observe and participate in economic life." And that, in turn, would make economics "a religion rather than a responsible analysis of experience" (Bewley 1999: 14).

7.1 Hermeneutics and social categories of meaning

The main requirement of M-M mathematical economic modeling exercises in light of my critique, practically speaking, is that they include an account of the modularity-stability of the social objects and relations ostensibly represented by their mathematical models. In the previous chapter, I argued that determining the proper context within which to gauge the modularity-stability of social entities is complicated by the fact that social meanings are constructed dialectically, through the interplay of individual actions and the social norms and interpretive frameworks that give those actions meaning. The additional task I am prescribing to the economist, then, involves two interrelated steps: (a) determining how to properly assess the meaning of the concepts under study, and (b) interpreting the meaningfulness and modularity-stability of the posited categories within that context. This is precisely the process of hermeneutic investigation – the attempt to come to an understanding of a text by interpreting it according to the interpretive framework appropriate to it, which must be determined by the content and form of the text itself. This type of investigation is in contrast with, for example, positive scientific investigation, which presupposes a particular structure of meaning in its objects of study.[1]

Let me illustrate what I mean with an example, from the work of Michael Piore, that nicely contrasts the hermeneutic and positive approaches. In his article, "Qualitative Research Techniques in Economics," Piore recounts a research experience involving the collection and processing of data on "the effect of automation upon the skill composition of manufacturing jobs" (Piore 1979: 560). Through the course of his research, Piore discovered that the commonly held interpretation of the relationship between automation and skill composition of manufacturing jobs differed sharply from the actual experience of these phenomena that he encountered while gathering data in two manufacturing plants. His response was to let go of the understanding of the phenomena with which he had entered into the process, and

---

[1] I do not mean to suggest that hermeneutic investigation requires that the investigator come to the phenomena under study without any pre-suppositions about how those phenomena are organized and/or in what way facts about those phenomena will present themselves. We always bring to any study our own pre-conceptions. But for the hermeneutic investigator, these pre-conceptions are the starting point of a dialectical process of discovery: they are considered to be provisional understandings that will be altered by contact with the phenomena themselves, and then this new hybrid understanding will be a new starting point, also subject to revision, and so on until a stable understanding is reached (which, of course, will also be subject to revision). The key to the success of this project is the self-awareness of the investigator with respect to his/her pre-conceptions.

to try to find a way to allow the experience itself to suggest the appropriate categories and interrelationships. As Piore's experience offers a very good example of the type of category-stability-assessment process I am proposing economists undertake, and because the details are important, I will quote his article at length.

Piore came to his research with a background understanding informed by prior work by others in his field, and by the guidance of his adviser:

At the time, there was considerable controversy about whether technological change was increasing or decreasing the skill requirements of jobs. An important group of analysts in the debates about national economic policy were arguing that skill requirements were increasing, leaving a residue of workers who had, or might have, been employed by the old techniques but who were unqualified for the new jobs. This growing residue was supposed to be a barrier to reductions in the level of unemployment

John Dunlop, my thesis advisor, proposed investigating this question by comparing two factories using old and new techniques. The idea was to find a series of cases where an old factory ... was being torn down or abandoned, to be replaced by a totally new facility, producing the same product. Engineering designs for the two factories would show the various work stations and the jobs associated with them. A comparison of these manning tables, as they were called, would provide the maximum contrast between old and new technologies and thus would indicate the direction of change of the economy as a whole. (Piore 1979: 560)

Due to various practical exigencies, Piore had to spend more time than he had expected in close communication with individuals involved in many different parts of the manufacturing process – "a variety of different company and factory officials." In preparation for his interviews with these individuals, Piore had "developed an elaborate list of questions" based on his fore-understanding of the phenomena under study – by "fore-understanding" I mean, roughly, the models (formal and informal) of the phenomena he had formed before encountering them. But despite this careful preparation, Piore found that "the questions had very little to do with the success or failure of the interview ... [M]ost people had a story to tell. The interviewees used my questions as an excuse for telling their stories" (Piore 1979: 560).

Significantly, Piore decided to allow the interviews to proceed in this unstructured way, primarily because he wanted to develop a good rapport with the interviewees as he would be asking them for a great deal of help and co-operation during the course of his research. Initially, then, Piore saw the interviewees' narratives as instrumentally useful but not necessarily good data for his study. Later in his research, he wished to re-introduce structure into the interviews – forcing respondents "to treat the questions seriously and to give . . . a codable response" – but the interviewees were resistant and would often respond to this approach by "provid[ing] misinformation in order to avoid an anticipated follow-up question." Piore decided to allow the interviews to proceed with the looser, narrative structure (Piore 1979: 561).

Eventually, Piore began to realize that these loose, narrative interviews were yielding precisely the information he needed, although it was different from what he had anticipated. His description of this process of realization and his response to it is highly illuminating:

As this process continued, I became increasingly interested in the stories I was being told in the interviews. The stories revealed that the processes of technological change and labor allocation, indeed the basic process of business management, were totally different from the ways in which the original project had been conceived. The manning tables which I had set out to collect were only tangentially related to the manning structure of the plant and the skill composition of jobs – a consequence of the process diverging so radically from what I had envisioned. *I would never have understood this if I had focused only on the manning tables; what I would have understood was that there was an "error" between the tables and the data I wanted, and I would have looked for, and found, a correction factor.*

Finally, however, the interviews seemed to reveal what the actual process was . . . The actual process was one in which there was no clear distinction between jobs or workers of varying skills. The manning tables were used only as a rough guide to factory layout and cost. The actual manning was arrived at experimentally and evolved over time, through adjustments in which work was first done by design engineers and then gradually transferred to craftsmen who, in turn, taught operators. It was indicative of an informal process of skill development on the job in the process of production or, in the case of new technologies, in the process of technological change. When this process worked well the "skilled" work force was trained without cost by participating in the installation and start-up of the new equipment. *Bottlenecks of the kind envisaged in theories of structural unemployment were created by failures of this informal on-the-job training. Such failures were most often social, rather than economic, and were generated by racial or class distinctions which inhibited the necessary contacts between the skilled and unskilled employees.* (Piore 1979: 561, emphasis added)

The process of methodological adaptation Piore describes is hermeneutic in nature, and not simply a standard example of an economist adapting his/her model in light of new information. The central difference between these two types of adaptation lies in the different methods for effecting the adaptation and the standards for assessing the goodness of the adaptation. In normal economic practice, proper model-building and adaptation of models can occur at a higher level of abstraction than is permitted for the hermeneutic practitioner. In light of new information, the economic practitioner can suggest new mathematical specifications of his/her model according to a vague standard of reasonableness – for example, whether or not certain salient characteristics of the variables and correspondences of the model are consonant with stylized facts found in the data. The proposed adaptation can be constructed according to vague standards of matching with empirical reality because the *ex ante* match with empirical reality is not the relevant measure of a good model. The true test of the goodness of the adaptation will be its performance in formal statistical analyses. Contrarily, the hermeneutic practitioner's adaptation must match very closely the information gleaned from the phenomena under study, with the standard of good matching coming from the phenomena themselves rather than from econometric practice. Put another way, the hermeneutic practitioner does not presume the structure of the phenomena under study *ex ante*. Piore ultimately builds a formal model of technological change in the workplace, but the adaptations he makes to his initial model are made according to standards that are different from those of normal economics and, more importantly, that would not be recognized as *necessary* standards in normal economics.

The Piore anecdote captures several important points about the potential for hermeneutic investigative techniques in empirical social science. First, it demonstrates concretely the manner in which hermeneutic techniques can lead to more illuminating economic analysis. Piore discovered that the fore-understanding he had brought to his research had been mistaken in ways that he would not have discovered if he had proceeded along standard lines. Put into the vocabulary of my critique, we could say that Piore's fore-understanding of the phenomena was based on categories without modular-stable meaning with respect to the formal categories they were meant to correspond to. That is, the formal representations of the phenomena and their interrelations that he believed were meaningful turned out not to correspond to actual meanings and interrelations in the subject matter under study. The left-most link in the catalog of correspondences was weak. By observing the phenomena in an unstructured way, he was able to extract categories of meaning that were more plausibly modular-stable in the context under study. Moreover, proceeding as he did provided him with evidence to construct a concrete argument for the plausibility of the modularity-stability of the categories in his account.

Second, it is significant that Piore only arrived at this understanding accidentally rather than through standard economic techniques. He admits that if he had not had the benefit of the information he gleaned from his open-ended interviews, he would have interpreted the mismatch between his model and his observations as an "error" and found a correction factor. The point is not whether or not he actually would have found a valid correction factor, but rather that he would have been following standard operating procedure in responding to the mismatch by searching for one. More importantly, it is not at all certain that he would even have been aware of the disconnect between his fore-understanding and the actual experience of the manufacturing process without having discovered the stable categories of meaning through direct and open-ended contact with those involved in the experience.

But even if the mismatch could have been identified as a problem using standard methods, how could it have been dealt with within the M-M framework? The standard approach would be to re-assess one's model and return to the phenomena with a different set of coded questions and possibly a different econometric specification.

One might reasonably object, here, that I have mistaken bad execution for faulty methodology. *Piore had come with one particular set of coded questions,* it might be argued, *but perhaps those were just badly chosen. Why is it necessary to take a hermeneutic approach to extracting modular-stable categories from the phenomena? And how would we **know** whether the categories we extract in this manner are in fact meaningful and modular-stable?*

The answer to the first of these questions is that the hermeneutic approach allows us to access a different, and necessary, type of knowledge about the phenomena under study, and one that cannot be gained by mathematical modeling techniques; namely, knowledge about the experience of the social phenomena under study which provides a legitimate basis for building the left-most link in a catalog of correspondences. Piore's open-ended conversations accomplished just that. The information he gathered allowed him to identify modular-stable categories within the phenomena under study and construct a plausible left-most link, on which he could then more confidently build a mathematical construct if he desired. For reasons discussed above, mathematical modeling techniques alone could not have accomplished this.

With regard to the second question, we cannot "know" that a hermeneutic interpretation of social phenomena is correct in the same way that we "know" that a regression coefficient is significant and unbiased – although the former type of knowledge is not necessarily any less secure or legitimate than the latter. The two types of knowledge are assessed under different standards.

Standards for correctness of interpretation (in the hermeneutic sense) of the proper categorization of a set of social phenomena cannot be gauged with the results of statistical tests of any hypotheses it may generate, for reasons discussed above. Rather, its correctness must be judged against *some other standard of plausibility.*

Such standards for assessing the goodness of interpretive practice do exist and are in regular use in other disciplines – the most notable example among the social sciences is anthropology. These standards do not currently exist in economics, and developing such standards (and/or tailoring existing anthropological standards to the particularities of economic practice) would be an integral part of any attempt to introduce hermeneutic methods into economics. I will discuss the development of such standards in more detail in the next section. For now, it suffices to note that the standards will deal with assessing both the content of a practitioner's interpretation and the process by which he/she comes to that interpretation. This latter point is crucial, as one of the most salient aspects of hermeneutic investigation is an openness to revising one's fore-understanding of (or "prejudice" or "bias" about) the phenomena in the face of conflicting evidence.[2] It is this element of hermeneutic investigation that makes it more than a subjective and idiosyncratic process.

Of course, Piore's experience is just a single example, and one would need to be careful about drawing general conclusions from it if it were indeed an isolated and idiosyncratic instance of the application of hermeneutic methods. Fortunately, this is not the case. Investigations of social life that utilize direct and open-ended contact with individuals involved with the phenomena under study, and that utilize interpretive techniques to understand those phenomena, are the rule in anthropological research, and also are not absent from other social science disciplines, including economics. Below, I will touch on some of the specific interpretive methods currently in use, and will then sketch out how these methods could be (and in some cases already are) deployed in economics to address the essential compatibility requirement-related issues detailed in Part 1.

Although there are many ways to undertake interpretive investigations of social life, the single unifying element of all of these is the focus on actual

---

[2] This is precisely what Piore did, which counts in favor of his account. Of course, it could be argued that he was not sufficiently open, that he developed new biases that he did not open to revision, etc. These would be valid points and if true would count against Piore's account. These are examples of the kinds of considerations that compose the standards of good hermeneutic practice. I discuss this in more detail in the next section.

lived experience and the desire to understand that lived experience on its own terms. These investigations will necessarily involve three related steps: (1) choosing or constructing a fore-understanding of the phenomena to be studied; (2a) refining this fore-understanding dialectically through contact with the actual phenomena that is open-ended enough to allow the phenomena to speak for themselves;[3] and (2b) interpreting the phenomena under study utilizing the understanding of their context gained from (1) and (2a). (This is the process followed by Piore in the example above (though step (2a) was accidental in his case.) I have grouped the last two steps together to indicate their highly interrelated nature.

Step (1), the forming of a fore-understanding is the least structured of the steps, and could consist of a wide range of activities. At one extreme, it could consist of the practitioner's (critical or uncritical) application of his/her discipline's conventional wisdom regarding the modular-stable categories and dynamics of a particular set of phenomena. For example, the practitioner could use neo-classical economic theory as a fore-understanding – that is, as a starting point for hermeneutic investigation of a particular set of social phenomena. Michael Piore utilized the then-regnant economic theory of technological change in the workplace as a fore-understanding in the example above. He ultimately deployed the theory not according to standard usage – i.e. gathering data according to the categories posited by the theory and utilizing econometric techniques to assess the degree to which the data conform to the predictions of the theory – but rather as a starting point for hermeneutic investigation of the phenomena under study.

At another extreme, the forming of a fore-understanding could consist of an elaborate critical analysis of an accepted understanding of a particular set of social phenomena in order to develop a new fore-understanding. Examples of the latter type of work include Richard Tuck's (1979) reconsideration of the notion of "rights," aimed at clarifying what had become an increasingly vexing category of social discourse, Amartya Sen's (1999) reconsideration of the proper understanding of development and human flourishing, and Stephen Marglin's (1974; 1975) reconsideration of the categories of labor relations.

Steps (2a) and (2b) comprise the main work of what is broadly referred to as "ethnography." Under this broad umbrella, I would like to distinguish

---

[3] Gadamer (1989) offers a nice description of this element of the process: "The important thing is to be aware of one's own bias, so that the text can present itself in all its otherness and thus assert its own truth against one's own fore-meanings" (p. 269).

between two types of interpretive method. The first, "participant observation," involves immersion of the practitioner in the culture under study.[4] With participant observation, the practitioner collects information both through communication with the individuals involved in the particular context under study, as well as through personal direct experience of that context. This practice is widespread in anthropology but not in other social sciences. Famous examples of such work include Margaret Mead's (1953) work in Samoa and Clifford Geertz's (1973, Chapters 14–15) studies of Balinese culture.

The second type of interpretive method, "interpretive interview techniques," involves collecting information from individuals involved in the context under study, but does not involve the practitioner's actually participating in that culture.[5] Interpretive interview techniques will involve some element of open-ended questioning, in order to allow for the possibility of gleaning information that the interviewer did not or could not have anticipated. At the other extreme of this type of method would be a survey with completely coded responses and no opportunity for free response. The research of Michael Piore referred to above began as a relatively strictly coded survey, but evolved into interpretive interview. Studs Terkel's *Working* (1985) is an example of a particularly free-flowing version of interpretive interview, with almost no structure provided by the interviewer.

7.2 A new field of economics

The introduction of hermeneutic methods into economics would provide economists with tools and standards to enrich current economic methodology by, as Gadamer (1987: 93) has put it, "allowing our subject matter to determine the method of its own access." It would give economists the capability to address the blind spots identified in Part I by grounding the interpretation of their analyses more strongly and convincingly in the actual empirical realities of socio-economic life. Because these methods are significantly different from, and somewhat alien to, the methods of current economic practice, it is my recommendation that a new field be created to develop them and tailor them to the particular needs of economists. To fix terms, I will refer to this proposed new field as "interpretive economics."

---

[4] See, e.g., DeWalt and DeWalt (1998) for a good discussion of various aspects of participant observation.
[5] See, e.g., Levy and Hollan (1998) for a good general description of the strategy of open-ended interview.

In order to be serious about proposing a new field of economics, I will need to specify in detail what that work will consist of, and also to provide concrete examples of what precisely I am proposing. An excellent model for such a proposal is Trygve Haavelmo's "The Probability Approach in Econometrics" (1944), which explained in detail why contemporary statistical work in economics needed to be supplemented with probability theory. The subsequent incorporation of existing work in statistical theory into economic practice resulted in the creation of the field of econometrics.[6]

In the remainder of this chapter, I will provide a sketch of what the work of an interpretive economics field would entail, first through general comments, and then through a discussion of selected examples of such work that has been undertaken both inside and outside of economics.

7.2.1   General comments: the work of the interpretive economics field

The purpose of the interpretive economics field is to develop methods and standards for the use of interpretive analysis in economic research. The field will have three main tasks – which I will denote "theory," "method," and "application" – that mirror the three elements of hermeneutic work outlined above.

Theoretical work in interpretive economics will involve the critical exploration of existing fore-understandings of economic life. The works of Marglin and Sen discussed above are examples of such work, as is Albert Hirschman's *Exit, Voice and Loyalty* (1970), which uses conventional economic understandings of firm behavior as a foil for the presentation of an alternative understanding. From the point of view of economic practice, theoretical interpretive economics work will serve two main functions: (1) an innovative function, by supporting the development of alternative conceptualizations of various aspects of economic life; and (2) an assessment function, by providing a store of information that can be used to assess the plausibility of conceptualizations of economic life employed by past, present, and future analyses. Theoretical interpretive economics will also be relevant to historians of economic thought and to intellectual historians more broadly, as it involves unpacking the manner in which the economy has been (and continues to be) conceptualized.

---

[6] See Morgan (1990). Haavelmo's contribution is dealt with largely in Chapter 8. See also Darnell (1994) for a collection of papers by economists that trace the development of econometric work. Volume II, part II contains papers on the role and method of econometrics, including Haavelmo (1944) and earlier papers that give a flavor of the environment into which Haavelmo introduced his manifesto.

Methodological interpretive economics will involve tailoring existing interpretive social science methods – for example, participant observation and interpretive interview techniques – to the particular needs and challenges of economics. In this, it will be similar to work in econometrics aimed at developing empirical methods (out of statistics and probability theory) for the particular needs of economists, and studying and addressing the particular challenges that arise in applying such methods in economics.

Applied interpretive economics will involve bringing to bear the tools developed in methodological interpretive economics on social phenomena in much the same way that econometric methods and standards are employed in empirical analysis. Indeed, such work would occur alongside econometric analysis as a means of building and justifying appropriate econometric specifications, but applied interpretive economics would become a part of theoretical economic work as well, and for a similar purpose. It would be used to ground economic theories in empirical reality by ensuring that the formal categories they posit are ones that can be shown to be plausible constituents of whatever target world the theory in question is meant to illuminate. This will enhance theoretical analyses and also offer guidance to those who wish to test them in constructing their empirical tests.

These three types of interpretive economics work are, of course, interrelated. In any particular instance of interpretive economics, one is likely to find more than one of the types being pursued. To illustrate both the content of the three types and their interrelation, it will be helpful to turn to some examples.

7.2.2 Examples of interpretive economics work inside and outside of economics

Though interpretive work in economics is not currently common, neither is it completely absent. In addition, interpretive social science analyses performed by non-economists on subjects relevant to economics are also useful as extant examples of the type of work that would be undertaken in an interpretive economics field. Below I will consider examples in each of these sets. With respect to work within economics, I will review Truman Bewley's *Why Wages Don't Fall During a Recession*, Alan Blinder, Elie Canetti, David Lebow, and Jeremy Rudd's *Asking About Prices*, and a recent project by Stephen Marglin and myself on the effectiveness of fiscal stimulus. Outside of economics, I will review a recent work in the anthropology of finance – Vincent Lépinay's (2011) study of the construction and marketing of financial derivatives.

Work within economics

Bewley (1999) is an excellent example of methodological and applied interpretive economics. The purpose of his study was to investigate "why wages don't fall during a recession" – the question contained in the book's title. This economic puzzle – which economists generally call "wage rigidity" – has been studied extensively within economics and has generated several rival theories but no clear consensus as to the cause and implications of wage rigidity. These theories are closely related to (and often bound up with) theories of equilibrium involuntary unemployment, since it is presumed that if wages were perfectly flexible there would be no involuntary unemployment in equilibrium. Examples of existing theories of these phenomena include Shapiro-Stiglitz efficiency wage theory as well as, for example, the "misperceptions" model of Lucas (1972) – which proposes that unemployment rises during a recession because individuals incorrectly conclude that the low level of their own wages is specific to their firm rather than an economy-wide phenomenon which leads them to leave their job in the expectation of finding more lucrative employment elsewhere – and the "Keynesian" theory – which proposes that wages are downwardly rigid because employees are highly sensitive to their relative wage (i.e. compared with others in the economy) and so employers do not cut wages for fear of losing workers.[7]

Bewley's work arose against the background of this abundance of existing work on wage rigidity, and out of his frustration with the failure of current methods to shed ample light on the issue. "Despite intense interest in wage rigidity," he wrote, "little is known about which theories are correct and under what conditions" (Bewley 1999: 4–5). Because Bewley's frustration lay with conventional economic methods themselves and not simply with the extant theories utilizing those methods, he was driven to use unconventional methods of investigation. Interestingly, he seems to have been reluctant to make such a move and reports it almost apologetically. "It is unusual for economists to do surveys of any sort," he wrote, "and I undertook this one because I could think of no other way to answer my questions" (Bewley 1999: 1). This comment highlights the fact that Bewley's study is not in sync with the norms of current economic method.

The non-standard approach Bewley follows in his investigation of wage rigidity provides a good example of interpretive economic research. It is explicitly interpretive in the sense that it follows hermeneutic procedure,

---

[7] Bewley (1999) reviews these and other theories briefly on pp. 3–6. See also Lucas (1972) and Keynes (1936), esp. Chapter 2.

which I summarized above in three steps: (1) choosing or constructing a fore-understanding of the phenomena to be studied; (2a) refining this fore-understanding dialectically through contact with the actual phenomena that is open-ended enough to allow the phenomena to speak for themselves; and (2b) interpreting the phenomena under study utilizing the understanding of their context gained from (1) and (2a).

With respect to step (1), Bewley makes it very clear that the starting point of his investigation was the set of currently accepted (in the mid-late 1990s) economic theories of wage rigidity. As the quotations above indicate, the motivation for his study is his sense that these currently accepted theories are missing important points about wage rigidity. And he devotes considerable effort to developing a detailed picture of this fore-understanding – describing in detail the several different types of extant wage rigidity theories and providing a voluminous bibliography of the academic economic literature covering these theories.

With respect to step (2a), Bewley devotes careful consideration to the development of interpretive investigative techniques and to tailoring existing techniques to his purposes. His goal was to learn about the causes of wage rigidity directly from the experience of those involved in employment and wage decisions. Importantly, however, he approached the development of the precise method for garnering this information openly and with a willingness to allow the experience itself to mold his approach. As with Piore, Bewley's subject matter drove the scope and method of his study. "This study grew from small beginnings," he writes.

Seeking inspiration for theoretical models of wage rigidity, in 1992 I arranged a few interviews with businesspeople. I anticipated making no more than 15 interviews, but found myself drawn into doing more and more, for patterns quickly emerged and respondents were articulate and pre-occupied with the questions that worried me. I persisted until I felt I had learned as much as I could, given my methods and the fact that I was working alone. My last interview was conducted in the Spring of 1994. (Bewley 1999: 20)

Importantly, Bewley's development of an appropriate research method was open-ended without being *ad hoc*. From his detailed account of this process, it is clear that he followed, roughly and informally, a two-stage process in which the first stage consisted in determining the most effective ways to elicit useful information from respondents and in which the second consisted in using these lessons to construct methodological guidelines. These guidelines covered formal/technical issues like sampling methods, but were not limited to such issues. For example, Bewley offers a detailed account of the impact of attitudinal and presentational issues on the type and quality of information elicited from respondents. Especially illuminating are Bewley's comments on the issue of open-ended versus directed questioning. For example:

> Interviews were best when I made it clear to people that they were in charge and that I wanted to hear what they thought I needed to know to understand wage rigidity . . . They revealed most when speaking freely, with few interruptions from me. When I tried a more organized method, insisting on a fixed list of questions, answers were often inconsistent. (Bewley 1999: 23)

This is precisely the type of information elicitation that Friedman (1953) attacked as unhelpful (in his criticism of Meade and Andrews 1938 and Henderson 1938) on the grounds that it did not produce the kind of information that economists really need – i.e. data to test hypotheses. But from Bewley's point of view, his focus on this information is based not upon a misunderstanding of economics but rather upon the belief (consistent with the hermeneutic approach) that one cannot decide *a priori* what are the important categories of economic information.

Bewley adopted an evolutionary approach to his sampling method as well. Recognizing that the types of interviews he wished to conduct would be relatively time-consuming and would require openness on the part of the participant, Bewley understood that he would face a trade-off between randomness of sample and usefulness of data. To obtain a large enough and random enough sample of respondents, he likely would have needed to make his interviews more standardized and less intrusive/time-consuming. He decided that, since introducing such restrictions would have significantly undermined his ability to obtain the type of information he needed, he would sacrifice randomness. In doing so, he understood that the data he gathered would not be analyzable by traditional econometric methods.[8] But, as the purpose of the study was to introduce a different *kind* of information into the study of wage rigidity – precisely the sort of information that is required to address essential compatibility requirement-related issues – this drawback of Bewley's survey method was not a reason to abandon it. Rather, he looked to the use of interpretive survey techniques in sociology and anthropology as a rough guide, and over time developed an interpretive survey technique

---

[8] See Bewley (1999: 26–8). Compare Blinder *et al.* (1998: Chapter 2), in which the authors face the same dilemma but take the opposite route. This is discussed in more detail below.

applicable to the economic subject matter with which he was concerned (Bewley 1999: 20–6).

I should note also that Bewley's methodological interpretive work is not limited only to the method he developed specifically for his wage rigidity study. At the end of his study, he provides several suggestions for the adaptation of the methods he developed to the more focused assessment of particular economic theories of wage rigidity. Specifically, he suggests ways in which the gathering of data, the construction of new hypotheses, and the testing of existing hypotheses could be more fruitfully carried out in light of the methodological lessons he learned in the course of tailoring interpretive methods for use in his own study (Bewley 1999: 464–8).

With respect to step (2b) – the interpretation of the phenomena under study in light of information gleaned from the application of interpretive methods developed in (2a) – Bewley explains in detail how his surveys help to shed light on the strengths and weaknesses of current economic fore-understandings of wage rigidity. And, perhaps most importantly, he proposes a new fore-understanding that bears some resemblance to the work of Solow (1979) and Akerlof (1982), but whose ultimate form incorporates Bewley's new understanding of the relevant and modular-stable categories actually in operation in the realm of phenomena under study.

Most of the space in *Why Wages Don't Fall During a Recession* is taken up by applied interpretive economics; specifically, the reporting of evidence on various subjects – the role of morale, risk aversion, pay structure, layoffs, resistance to pay decreases, etc. – and the assessment of existing economic theories in light of this evidence. Bewley's approach in these chapters is explicitly interpretive: he assesses the information against the fore-understandings of existing theories while being careful not to assign the categories in those fore-understandings priority over the unstructured information gleaned from his surveys. This allows Bewley simultaneously to assess the categories of these fore-understandings while also being open to the development of new categories that have not yet figured in the existing fore-understandings.

It will be helpful to separate the applied interpretive economics work of the Bewley study into two categories: (1) the assessment of existing fore-understandings, and (2) the development of a new fore-understanding. With respect to (1), Bewley found that many of the conventional fore-understandings' posited categories, and relations between those categories, that became untenable and/or seemed to rest on fundamental misunderstandings once actual experience was brought to bear on them. A good example of this is his assessment of what I have been calling Shapiro–Stiglitz efficiency wage theory, and which Bewley refers to as "shirking theory." As discussed above, the shirking theory posits that the rigidity of wages above the market-clearing level may be part of a punishment mechanism on the part of employers to encourage high effort from workers whom they can only imperfectly monitor. The high wage encourages high effort in two ways: (1) it creates unemployment and therefore makes the prospect of being fired more onerous than in an equilibrium with no involuntary unemployment, and (2) it creates a wedge between the pay one receives on the job versus the benefits one gets from being unemployed (which include the benefits of leisure).

Bewley found this theory to be unhelpful in light of the information gathered in his interviews, for two reasons. First, managers called into question the tight connection between effort and pecuniary incentives posited by the theory. Bewley reports that "[a] possible trade-off between productivity and pay level did not occur to them, except in connection with pay cuts or with the trade-off between pay and the quality of new hires … I was told that all workers feel underpaid and soon forget raises" (Bewley 1999: 111). If workers and managers do not view pay levels in the way posited by the theory, then it would be suspect to view correlations between relative wages and productivity, as were examined in Wadhwani and Wall (1991), as supporting shirking theory.

Second, and more importantly, Bewley found that there may be a self-contradictory aspect to shirking theory that arises from a misunderstanding of the actually significant and modular-stable categories of employment relations. Specifically, he found that managers' focus on the importance of worker morale to the good functioning of businesses made it implausible that the incentive mechanisms posited by shirking theory would actually encourage higher worker effort. Virtually all of the individuals with whom Bewley spoke indicated that the main impact of hiring and firing decisions, wage-setting decisions, and disciplinary decisions all flowed through their effect on morale. In Bewley's words, "[m]anagers organize their thinking about their success in dealing with employees around the concept of morale. Good morale is thought to be vital for production, recruitment and retention" (Bewley 1999: 41).[9]

---

[9] Of course, this does not mean that all business decisions are guided primarily by the desire to please employees. Rather, as Bewley documents in great detail, it means that in general managers constantly have the morale of their employees in mind and that their business decisions reflect this concern.

The central role of morale seriously undermines the shirking theory, according to Bewley, because the central mechanism of shirking theory is a disciplinary regime that would significantly negatively affect morale and therefore would be more likely to discourage than to encourage greater effort. Specifically, whereas shirking theory presumes that the pecuniary incentives underlying the efficiency wage system will drive behavior, Bewley's evidence suggests that the effectiveness of the incentive system would likely actually be undermined by its design. The general reaction of managers to Bewley's questions about shirking theory was negative. "It was clear," Bewley reports, "that most businesspeople do not think in the way described by the theory ... Employers believed that in good times most workers do not worry about losing their jobs. Recession and layoffs [that had occurred around the time of Bewley's study] had awakened the fear, a change that managers did not always welcome, finding the anxiety paralyzing and provocative" (Bewley 1999: 111). Significantly, managers generally found implausible the idea that the threat of dismissal would be an effective effort-elicitation device. "Many managers reacted to the [shirking] theory by saying that a threatening atmosphere is bad for the workplace ... A common theme was that productivity is best obtained simply by dealing effectively with subordinates at a personal level, engaging their interest, and taking advantage of the fact that most people naturally want to please and do well" (Bewley 1999: 114–15).

Given the importance of morale in the experience of employment, according to Bewley, the shirking theory seems to be based on categories that are not actually significant or modular-stable in the manner posited by the theory. As such, the theory is more likely to be distortive rather than illuminative as a lens through which to view social activity related to employment and wage-setting policy. It is, thus, not an appropriate lens through which to interpret correlations of relative wages and productivity.

Through his use of interpretive methods to assess current economic theories, Bewley is ultimately able to arrive at a new proposed fore-understanding. Even though he finds the models of Solow (1979) and Akerlof (1982) most attuned to the morale issues he uncovered in his research,[10] he concludes that a new model is necessary to capture these issues adequately; and at the end of his study Bewley offers a formal model of the effect of morale on work effort that can generate predictions regarding unemployment and wage levels.[11] Although the model, considered in isolation, resembles much other economic work it is different from almost all

[10] See Bewley (1999: 415).   [11] See Bewley (1999: 443–62).

current economic work in having been generated by an interpretive investigative and analytic process. As such, Bewley is able to provide an account of the modularity-stability of his categories. Whether or not the account is plausible will rest on judgments about the propriety of his investigative method. Development of the standards for such judgments has not yet been undertaken in economics, and would be one of the central tasks of an interpretive economics field.

It is instructive to contrast Bewley (1999) with another study of price rigidity that is also sensitive to issues of interpretation: Alan Blinder, Elie Canetti, David Lebow, and Jeremy Rudd's (1998) *Asking About Prices: A new approach to understanding price stickiness*. The latter study bears strong similarities to the former in both motivation and approach, but ultimately settles on a more formalized, and less interpretive, information-gathering strategy. Exploring this contrast will provide additional insight into how interpretive economics work could be integrated with current economic methods.

As with Bewley (1999), the starting point of the Blinder *et al.* study is frustration with the inability of standard economic methods to answer a fundamental macroeconomic question despite decades of trying. "In recent decades," the authors write,

> macroeconomic theorists have devoted enormous amounts of time, thought, and energy to the search for better microtheoretic foundations for macroeconomic behavior. Nowhere has this search borne less fruit than in seeking answers to the following question: Why do nominal wages and prices react so slowly to business cycle developments? ... The abject failure of the standard research methodology to make headway on this critical issue in the microfoundations of macroeconomics motivated the unorthodox approach of the present study. (Blinder *et al.* 1998: 3)

Their "unorthodox approach" is to speak with economic actors involved in price-setting in order to "ask about prices," as the title of the book suggests. Like Bewley, the authors are almost apologetic in their appeal to this approach. It is considered only after the standard methods have been shown to have failed abjectly, and even then only with a nod to the traditional skepticism of economists toward such methods.

As with Bewley, the Blinder *et al.* study involves multiple levels of interpretive economics work. The majority of the book is dedicated to critically evaluating the discipline's fore-understandings of price-stickiness. The authors present twelve theories of price-stickiness and critically evaluate them using information gleaned from their survey of economic agents involved in price-setting. And, like Bewley, they are able through this process to draw conclusions regarding which of the theories comports best with the agents' experience. In the vocabulary of my critique, the authors are searching for a plausible modular-stable conceptual map of the economic phenomena surrounding price-setting. The authors do not use this information to construct a new formal model of price-setting, but rather to point out which of the existing models are (in their view) most plausible. As with Bewley, the resulting models do not differ significantly in form from standard economic models. The difference is that they have been more robustly grounded in economic reality by the use of interpretive methods and, thereby, are underlain by a type of evidence of plausibility that is not standard in current economic methodology.

The central difference between the two studies is their investigative method. After weighing the pros and cons of open-ended survey methods and more structured ones, Blinder (who, among the authors, was primarily responsible for the research design) chose the latter. Significantly for our purposes, however, the authors provide a detailed account of how Blinder came to this decision, and their account reveals his sensitivity to the kinds of essential compatibility concerns introduced in Chapter 2. They begin by acknowledging that, due to the wide variety in firm types and the idiosyncrasies of the various theories of price-stickiness,

Blinder was initially skeptical that we could gather the appropriate information via a structured questionnaire ... Hence the original idea was to conduct free-form interviews with a limited number of companies ... In this conception of the study, each interview would have been custom-made on the spot and would have meandered logically down a path dictated by the answers being received. It was just the sort of interview that a team of consultants, called in to advise on pricing strategy, might conduct on their first site visit. (Blinder *et al.* 1998: 48–9)

Blinder felt (initially) that direct dialogue with the agents might be the only way to understand how, if at all, the information gleaned from the interviews corresponded to the categories of the various theories of price-stickiness ostensibly being tested. And although he understood that free-form interviews would be time-consuming and would severely limit the amount of data that could be collected relative to a pre-structured generic survey, he also appreciated that the kind of information he needed might be inaccessible using a more standard (i.e. structured) approach. Indeed, this was the motivating theme of the study.

In the end, pragmatic considerations – i.e. considerations related to the existing norms of economic practice – led Blinder to opt against the free-form interview method in favor of a "tightly structured" and "mechanically" administered survey. He cites specifically the following four advantages of the latter approach: (1) "it yields statistical information which has some claim to generality and can be analyzed by standard statistical techniques," (2) "it is feasible to survey a much larger number of firms," (3) the larger sample size "allows some scope for disaggregation by industry, by firm size, and in other dimensions," and (4) by using the structured approach, "we raise the probability (though certainly not to unity) that the findings will be objective and replicable" (Blinder *et al.* 1998: 49). For the authors, these advantages trumped the interpretive advantages of the free-form approach.

The authors' survey methodology, then, turned out to be more conventional than Blinder's original vision of it. Significantly, however, Blinder's misgivings about the structured approach were not simply shelved. According to the authors, "Blinder wavered [in his decision to use a structured questionnaire] for a long time out of concern that designing a suitable survey instrument might be impossible" (Blinder *et al.* 1998: 53). And this persistent concern led him to take great pains to try to design the questionnaire in a manner that did not simply impose a generic fore-understanding onto the subjects' experience. In crafting the questions, he tried, to the extent possible, to translate his and his co-authors' questions from "technical [academic] journalese into plain English" (Blinder *et al.* 1998: 54). Certainly, the structured format of the questionnaire still did not allow for the course and nature of the questions to be shaped by the respondents. But from the point of view of this book's critique, it is nonetheless important that Blinder had taken the match between the categories of the questionnaire and those of the agents' experience seriously and had documented the steps he took to address it. In the vocabulary of the critique, Blinder was bringing the pragmatic standards of the discipline to bear on the question of what constituted sufficient attention to the considerations of essential compatibility.

Both Bewley (1999) and Blinder *et al.* (1998) are examples of large-scale economic work that grapples directly with the need for an interpretive approach on both the methodological and applied levels. But interpretive economics work need not take the form of comprehensive, multi-level studies. Single-level interpretive economics work could easily take the form of journal length articles. To illustrate, I will briefly review a recent project by

Stephen Marglin and myself (Marglin and Spiegler 2014) that incorporates interpretive methods into an exploration of the effectiveness of the fiscal stimulus in the 2009 American Recovery and Reinvestment Act (ARRA).

The main purpose of the paper was to critically assess a subset of arguments against ARRA's effectiveness based on permanent income hypothesis (PIH), life-cycle hypothesis (LCH), and/or Ricardian equivalence (RE) reasoning. The thrust of these arguments is that temporary fiscal stimulus of any kind is ineffective because agents end up saving most if not all of the temporary stimulus, either because they are engaging in consumption smoothing (PIH, LCH) or because they recognize that they will have to pay back the stimulus in the future through higher taxes (RE).

Several articles appeared in the wake of the ARRA stimulus purporting to demonstrate that it had failed for these reasons.[12] Generally, the evidence adduced in support of this position consisted of statistical analyses showing that once appropriate controls were included there was no positive correlation between the ARRA stimulus and variables such as GDP, employment, or spending. The interpretation of these results was that the stimulus had indeed been saved in some manner, and that this provided support that PIH, LCH, and/or RE dynamics were at work.

Marglin and I sought to critically assess such arguments in part by considering the assumptions that were required to support the authors' favored interpretation of their results, and by exploring the plausibility of those assumptions using interpretive methods. We noted that these interpretations rested on two types of assumptions. The first were "counterfactual assumptions" about what the path of GDP, employment, and/or spending would have been in the absence of ARRA. It is only relative to such a counterfactual assumption that one can assess the impact that ARRA may have had on these variables. The arguments referenced above generally assumed that in the absence of ARRA, the relevant variables would have held steady at their previous levels. The second type of assumptions were "behavioral assumptions" about the spending calculus of stimulus recipients. The authors assumed that a lack of correlation between current spending and current stimulus-related income was evidence of rational consumption smoothing and/or Ricardian equivalence-related saving. These two assumptions, together, formed a bridge between (a) empirical evidence that GDP/expenditure did not increase relative to trend in the several quarters after

---

[12] See, e.g., Barro (2009), Cochrane (2009), Cogan and Taylor (2012), Taylor (2011a), and Uhlig (2010).

ARRA, and (b) the conclusion that the ARRA stimulus failed due to rational saving of the stimulus funds by recipients.

We wanted to critically examine these assumptions by appealing directly to recipients of the stimulus. Obviously, stimulus funds flowed to an enormous pool of economic actors – individual households and public and private institutions of various kinds – and, so, exploring the plausibility of the aforementioned counterfactual and behavioral assumptions in this population as a whole would have meant grappling with the same tradeoffs that faced Bewley and Blinder. Instead, we decided to focus on the behavior of a subset of the total pool – state governments – which had been the particular focus of work by John Taylor and John Cogan. In academic papers, interviews, non-academic articles, and congressional testimony, Taylor and Cogan argued that state governments had engaged in the same kind of expenditure smoothing that the PIH and LCH ascribe to individuals.[13] As such, according to Taylor and Cogan, the stimulus money funneled through the states (like the rest of it) failed to stimulate anything. And this is a significant claim, as this portion of ARRA accounts for roughly one-third of its total outlays (about $250 billion out of a total of $800 billion).[14]

Cogan and Taylor's focus on the state government channel of ARRA significantly narrowed the universe of economic agents to which the counterfactual and behavioral assumptions applied. This made it feasible to appeal directly to the entirety of the subject population to assess the plausibility of these assumptions. We devised a relatively open set of interview/survey questions to pose to the fifty state budget officers, with the goal of ascertaining the extent to which they engage in expenditure smoothing in general and the extent to which, in the particular case of the period during which ARRA funds were administered, they would have been able to maintain their expenditure at the observed levels in the absence of ARRA funding.[15] In line with the spirit of interpretive economics, however, we also wanted to allow the budget officers enough freedom in their answers to introduce elements of their experience that we might not have anticipated.

---

[13] See Taylor (2011a; 2011b) and Cogan and Taylor (2011; 2012).

[14] www.recovery.gov puts the cumulative total of ARRA expenditures at $804 billion, as of February 2013. The $250 billion figure for funds flowing to state governments is our own calculation (Marglin and Spiegler 2014), based on data from the Bureau of Economic Analysis and www.recovery.gov. It includes supplemental Medicaid assistance and funds going to local governments.

[15] We sent the questions along with a cover letter explaining our research to all of the state budget officers via e-mail, offering them the options of answering the questions in writing or through a telephone interview. In one case (Massachusetts), our interview was conducted in-person. The questionnaire is provided in Appendix 7.1.

The results of the interviews/surveys indicated that while the behavioral assumption of an expenditure smoothing motive was valid in some respects, the counterfactual assumption that states would have been able to spend at the observed levels in the absence of ARRA was invalid.[16] With the exception of the few states with significant revenues from fossil fuels, the respondents were very close to unanimous in stating that significant expenditure cuts would have been necessary in the absence of ARRA. This, in turn, cast serious doubt on Cogan and Taylor's interpretation of relatively flat spending data as an indication that the stimulus was ineffective.[17]

It is important to note that some of the doubt cast on Cogan and Taylor's counterfactual assumption comes simply from formal legal and institutional facts about state government budgeting. Constitutional and/or statutory provisions prevent all fifty state governments from borrowing to fund operating budget deficits. As such, one might argue that it would have been possible to judge the plausibility of Cogan and Taylor's counterfactual assumption simply by determining whether the savings states had built up prior to 2009 would have been sufficient to fill their operating shortfalls in the absence of ARRA. This is a calculation that could have been performed without any interpretive methods. Where interpretive methods were needed, however, was in determining whether the actual practice of state budgeting included strategies for creatively circumventing such prohibitions in times of crisis. Many of the questions in our survey aimed at eliciting information precisely on this subject, and we learned (a) that some such strategies are available to budget officers, (b) that there is significant variation across states in their nature and usage, and (c) that even taking such strategies into consideration, it still would not have been possible for the vast majority of the responding states to have avoided significant expenditure cuts in the absence of ARRA.

The evidence gleaned from the state budget officers provides an example of the significance of interpretive considerations as a supplement to the currently standard assessment methods of economics. This evidence provided

---

[16] Of the fifty state budget directors we contacted, we received written responses or had phone interviews with twenty-nine. Obviously, our aim was to collect information from all of the states and we made efforts over a five month period to collect a comprehensive set of responses. Despite these efforts, however, we received no response from twenty-one states. Nonetheless, we feel that our group of respondents is large and comprehensive enough and similar enough to the non-response set in many important demographic aspects to give us some confidence that the responses are not tainted with selection bias. The responding states accounted for 64% of US GDP, 61% of the population, 64% of total state government expenditures, and had an average GDP per capita of $44,307 versus the national figure of $42,447 (all figures from 2009).

[17] We also conducted our own econometric analysis of the data using a different specification than that of Taylor and Cogan which corroborated this conclusion. See Marglin and Spiegler (2014).

a reason to doubt the entire explanatory process of Taylor and Cogan, as the formal model was shown to be mismatched with the subject matter it ostensibly represented. It was not the econometric analysis *per se* that was being called into question, but rather the idea that the econometric analysis was relevant to the question being posed about the economic phenomena under study.

Work outside economics

Interpretive social science work is quite common outside of economics, especially in anthropology and to a lesser extent in sociology and political science. And although such work is generally not performed with an eye toward supporting economic work, it offers a helpful starting point as we imagine how to tailor interpretive methods to meet the needs of an interpretive economics field. In this section, I will briefly review a recent example from the anthropology of finance literature – Vincent Lépinay's (2011) *Codes of Finance: Engineering Derivates in a Global Bank* – that demonstrates the potential for interpretive methods in financial economics.[18]

Broadly speaking, *Codes of Finance* is a close examination of the financial derivatives business from an insider's point of view. Lépinay gained this perspective while working in various areas of the trading operation of a major French bank – which he refers to as "General Bank" for reasons of privacy – from January 2000 to July 2001.[19] He takes as his subject an innovative financial derivative called the "capital guarantee product" (CGP) created by the Bank's "exotics" desk, and shows how the various constituencies that had to deal with the CGP within the bank – traders, salespeople, back-office personnel, accountants, lawyers, and risk management professionals – navigated the challenges of incorporating this new type of product into their routines. The book provides numerous insights into the institutional and cultural life of a trading operation – too many to do justice to in this brief account. For the purposes of discussing the value of the book as an example of how interpretive work can benefit economics, I will focus on just one issue – that of "risk."

Lépinay's portrait of the risks involved in the creation, marketing, and life of the CGP is broad and includes elements that are not generally a part of the

---

[18] Lépinay's book is just one example of a wave of excellent work on the significance of the cultures of economic institutions coming out of anthropology of finance in the past several years. Riles (2011) and Holmes (2013) are two other fine examples.

[19] This employment was undertaken explicitly as field work.

notion of "risk" familiar in financial economics. In particular, he provides a window into what we might call *institutional* risk involved with derivatives – i.e. not simply the financial risk to the enterprise (as measured, for example, through "Value at Risk" (VaR)) as a result of the positions it holds in relation to the security and related hedging instruments, but also the regulatory, legal, and competitive risks associated with valuation and reporting. In brief, Lépinay found the CGP to be highly disruptive to General Bank's business on many levels. Its innovative nature, which was its main advantage and selling point with respect to clients, came with great costs within the organization as the Bank's back-office operations struggled, mostly unsuccessfully, to comprehend its impact on the bank's bottom line and risk profile. The story is revealing and quite relevant to both the recent financial crisis and to ongoing financial reform.

Lépinay relates, for example, the difficulties encountered by General Bank's risk management professionals in comprehending the risk profile of the CGP. These difficulties arose as a result not only of the novelty and relative opaqueness of the product, but also of the risk management professionals' lack of sophistication relative to the traders and financial engineers who created the product. Moreover, both of these sets of problems were endemic to the bank's operations. The culture of the "front office" – i.e. the trading and sales operation – was inherently fast-paced and transaction oriented. Front office personnel needed to think innovatively and move quickly to stay on top of market dynamics and competitive pressures. The "exotics desk" of the trading operation, which created the CGP and was responsible for its maintenance, was focused on meeting and anticipating clients' needs in innovative and non-obvious ways. They were, not surprisingly, less concerned with the difficulties this would engender for the individuals tasked with keeping track – concretely and from moment to moment – of the precise value and risk exposure of the CGP and its related hedges. The risk management personnel, who operated outside of the front office culture, were doubly constrained by their institutional distance from the CGP and the difficulties of comprehending a product that they had had no hand in shaping and whose complexities generally outstripped their analytic capabilities. As a result, they ultimately had to rely on the valuation and reporting techniques suggested to them by the traders and engineers – a practice whose dangers were revealed all too clearly in the financial crisis. The retrospective stories of the credit rating agencies' failure to understand the true risks of collateralized debt obligations is the most public example, but Lépinay's accounts of the operations of General Bank reveal very clearly that this is an endemic problem of financial innovation in general.

Moreover, the problem was part of a self-reinforcing cycle. The front office personnel had a vested interest in retaining a monopoly on the knowledge relating to the value and risk profile of exotic derivatives. This was so not only because it gave them autonomy and raised their stature in the bank, but also because it afforded them the opportunity to pursue trading and reporting strategies that inflated their results (even if only temporarily, for the purposes of compensation accounting) in a manner invisible to their ostensible over-seers. Added to this was the difficulty of attracting and retaining sufficiently sophisticated personnel to the risk management department. Those with such sophistication were generally lured to the faster pace, prestige, and higher earning potential of the front office. The CGP, then, was an exotic instrument not only to investors and regulators, but also to the bank itself. Its creation and marketing (and the creation and marketing of other such "exotic" securities) presented a challenge to the very idea of the bank as a unified corporate entity.

Lépinay's work opens a black box. It allows us to see in fine detail what would otherwise be subterranean influences underlying the economic data that ultimately percolate to the surface – especially those dealing with risk and information. Significantly, it shows us that conceiving of securities simply as loci of conditional and intertemporal resource flows can be misleading. Just as with Credit Default Swaps and Collateralized Debt Obligations – which had their own secret lives – the data held by both the front and back offices of General Bank about the value and risk associated with the CGP only told a part of the story. They did not reveal that General Bank's own risk management and accounting control personnel could not accurately measure the CGP and, therefore, that regulators and the bank's debt and equity investors would not possess the information necessary to accurately assess the bank's value and the risks imposed on it by the exotics desk. They did not reveal the informational power that the CGP's opacity concentrated in the hands of the traders and engineers on the exotics desk. And they did not reveal the extent to which these issues were endemic to the very function of the exotics desk. Lépinay's interpretive research did reveal these issues, and in doing so it provides a unique and valuable set of insights for financial economists and macroeconomists grappling with the complex-ities of modeling the impact of financial innovation on the financial system and the wider economy.

7.3 Ways forward

The four studies reviewed above all yielded economically relevant information using interpretive methods that are non-standard in current economics. Moreover, the authors of the three economic studies pursued these methods explicitly because they found the standard economic methods to be ill-suited to garnering the type of information they sought. Yet, even if one were to agree that the interpretive methods employed had accomplished something important that would have been unlikely if only standard methods had been used, one could still reasonably ask whether this provides support for the idea of a new field devoted to developing interpretive methods and standards for their use. If work such as Bewley (1999) and Blinder *et al.* (1998) can be conducted in the discipline as it is, and if such work has been widely read and accepted as useful by the discipline, then it might seem that the reforms proposed above are superfluous.

There are two principal reasons why this is not the case, and why a new institutional presence to effect these reforms is preferable to the *status quo*. The first is that the concerns expressed in Chapters 2 and 3 about the potential hazards of model-target mismatch are endemic to all mathematical economic modeling, and therefore addressing these concerns should not be optional or supererogatory. Again, the establishment of econometrics as a field provides an apt example. Economists today would insist upon applying the relevant methods and standards of econometrics to any statistical economic analysis, because it is these methods and standards that allow us to properly interpret the quantitative relations underlying the data. And when there are questions about whether a given set of econometric methods and/or standards are, indeed, appropriate, it is to the laws of probability and statistics more broadly (filtered through the field of econometrics) that we appeal. Before such methods and standards were in place it was still acceptable and even laudable for economists to appeal to quantitative data. But without recognition that there is a specific set of concerns that determines the adequate interpretation of such data, we leave ourselves open to mistaking the informational content of such appeals and to underestimating the importance of appealing to the data in an appropriate manner.

We face similar dangers with respect to the evaluation of work on price and wage stickiness. In light of the critique of Chapters 2 and 3, we can see that the concerns of Bewley (1999) and Blinder *et al.* (1998) were *fundamental* to adequately addressing the nature of the phenomena under study.

Any mathematical model-based analysis of these issues that failed to consider whether their model entities referred to modular-stable aspects of the phenomena under study operates under a cloud of possible irrelevancy that could only be addressed using some version of the methods employed by Bewley and Blinder *et al.* Moreover, although the efforts of Bewley (1999) and Blinder *et al.* (1998) to address this issue are laudable, they exist in relative isolation. Their research would likely have been more useful and effective on a discipline-wide level if an ongoing process of generating methods and standards for such analyses had been in place. As a practical matter, this would have meant that in seminar presentations of their work and in the peer review of it questions and suggestions could have been raised to more effectively incorporate their efforts into the broader work of their field. And similarly, other studies addressing these issues would have faced similar questioning and constructive critique, making it less likely that some of the shortcomings that had led to (in the words of Blinder *et al.* 1998) the "abject failure" of the price-stickiness literature could have persisted for as long as they had and become enshrined as part of the discipline's conventional wisdom on the subject.

The second principal reason why an institutional presence is desirable is that the discipline currently does not possess expertise in the use of interpretive methods, and it is important that we incorporate these methods in a manner that is not *ad hoc*. Lépinay (2011) provides a useful example. Interpretive interview and survey methods are sufficiently close to some of the current standard economic practices that one could imagine economists incorporating such methods organically. Bewley (1999) and Blinder *et al.* (1998) attest to this. But methods like participant observation are more alien to current economic practice. Although many economists have first-hand experience with the phenomena they study, gleaned either through working in various kinds of economic institutions or through field work, immersion for the explicit purpose of generating *experiential* "data" is virtually unheard of. To the extent that economists inject their personal experience into their research, it is generally done informally and given a back seat to the information gleaned through more formal channels (e.g., existing data sets or original data generated through formal survey procedures). And this is not accidental. Rather, it is part of an epistemological stance that devalues such non-formally gleaned information. And while there may be good reasons to be suspicious that such information can be subject to various kinds of biases, such suspicions must be weighed against the biases introduced by blinding ourselves *a priori* to potentially relevant, even crucial, sources and types of information about the economy. As Blinder's struggles with these competing imperatives suggest, we need not (indeed, *must* not) merely throw up our hands in the face of the possible dangers of such non-formally gleaned information. The more appropriate response is to consider in a systematic way how we can benefit from these information sources in a manner consonant with the overall goals and principles of economics. Doing so on a discipline-wide level requires a discipline-wide approach. This is precisely what an interpretive economics field would produce.

Conclusion

In this chapter, I have argued that the essential compatibility requirement-related problems raised in Chapters 2 and 3 cannot be addressed adequately with the methods of current mainstream economics, and therefore necessitate the introduction of new methods. Specifically, I have argued that interpretive investigative methods (in the hermeneutic sense of "interpretive") will be necessary to garner the type of information necessary to address these issues. The deployment of these methods in economics will involve three types of work, which I have called "theoretical," "methodological," and "applied." The first of these involves the construction of fore-understandings of economic phenomena, the second involves the development of interpretive methods (or the tailoring of existing methods) to assess and refine fore-understandings, and the third involves applying these methods. The ultimate goal of this work is to aid economics in the determination of modular-stable categories and dynamics of social life that can be proper inputs into mathematical modeling exercises. Toward that end, I have proposed the establishment of a new field in economics – interpretive economics – to focus exclusively on these issues. In this respect, the field of econometrics is a good guide to what I have in mind. Econometrics arose out of the recognition that early use of statistics in economics did not properly reflect its connection to an underlying probability theory. The task of the new field was to develop statistical methods in economics that were properly embedded in probability theory, and to develop standards for assessing the proper use of statistics. Just as econometrics supports the formal empirical analysis function of economics, so would an interpretive economics field support the design and execution of economic modeling more broadly.

Four examples of interpretive economics work were reviewed – three from within economics, and one from the anthropology of finance. Taken together, these examples are suggestive of what an interpretive approach to economics might look like.

Appendix 7.1 State Budget Officer Questionnaire from Marglin and Spiegler (2014)

1. What would have been the consequences for current and capital spending had no ARRA money come to [your state]?
2. Again, assume that no ARRA money had come to [your state]. In this case, would your capital budgeting process have required you to reduce capital expenditures in response to worsening economic conditions?
3. Outside of the general fund (and stabilization funds) were there other options for funding current budget deficits that might have arisen without ARRA? (*For example, special funds from other public or quasi-public agencies not included in the general fund, but that can be drawn on by the state? Revenue anticipation notes or similar instruments?*)
4. Is it possible for [your state] to borrow to finance operating-budget deficits?
5. In your experience, did the maintenance of effort provisions (MOE) attached to ARRA funding significantly restrict [your state]'s flexibility regarding how to use the funding?
6. In [your state], is there any flexibility with regard to classifying expenses as "current" or "capital"?
7. In [your state], is any portion of the capital budget typically funded from the operating budget (i.e., using current revenues as opposed to bonds)?
8. With regard to ARRA funding for capital projects, to the extent you received such funding, did it fund new incremental capital spending, or did it just act as a replacement funding source?

Conclusion

It is a fundamental challenge of empiricist science that we must assess the merits of our theories and models without any purely objective means of doing so. The set of lenses through which we theorize about and model our subject matter are the same lenses through which we identify what will count as "data" of/about the subject matter. If these lenses fundamentally distort or render imperceptible important aspects of the subject matter, then our theories and models will in a sense be detached – we will be exploring the implications of a version of the subject matter that comports with our conceptual map, but we will not know the extent to which that conceptual map reproduces that of the subject matter in the relevant respects. In order to ensure that such detachment has not occurred (or, retrospectively, to detect when it has), we must, in a sense, go "behind the model" – that is, we must use some other mode of access to the subject to ascertain whether important information about the latter has indeed been distorted or rendered imperceptible by the model.

The central difficulty in doing so is that we do not know *a priori* precisely what kind of information we will need to accomplish this task, as the subject matter under study may turn out to be constituted in a manner that we had not anticipated. As such, it is crucial that we develop and maintain the capacity to be sensitive to relevant information about the subject matter in whatever form it may become manifest, and that we incorporate this sensitivity into our methods.

The financial crisis of 2008–09 was an object lesson in both the importance and the difficulty of this task. It demonstrated that even apparently extensively vetted models that enjoy wide acceptance on the basis of their performance in econometric testing can possess substantial and inherent blind spots. And it demonstrated, further, how a failure to remain sufficiently attuned to the particular circumstances of the target subject matter – especially those circumstances that may lie outside the conceptual map of our models – allows such blind spots to persist.

The testimony of Sidney Winter at the 2010 Congressional hearing on the failures of DSGE modeling in the lead-up to the crisis helpfully illustrates this point. Winter argued that in order to have adequately understood the economy of the late 1990s and 2000s, it would have been necessary to understand the peculiar business practices that had arisen in mortgage-related industries out of the nexus of political, regulatory and commercial factors discussed above in Chapter 5. These changes in mortgage-related business practice were, he argued, "central to the distinctive features of THIS crisis" (Winter 2010: 21; emphasis in original).

To assess the "cause" of the crisis *without* reference to mortgage-related business practices would seem to be a bold exercise in hypothetical history. However sound and factual such an account might be with respect to interest rates, asset bubbles, speculative psychology and other matters, it has a weak claim to being about the Financial Crisis of 2008. (Winter 2010: 22; emphasis in original)

The problem with mainstream economic analysis in the lead-up to the crisis, according to Winter, was not just that it failed to recognize the importance of these evolving business practices in the crisis, but further, and more importantly, that the methods employed in these analyses actually prevented economists from learning that they were important in the first place. The reason for this imperviousness to relevant information, Winter charged, was an *a priori* commitment to formal modeling that resulted in an insufficient sensitivity to the evolving nature of the target subject matter. The proper response to this failure, in Winter's view, cannot be to leave our existing modeling practice essentially intact and simply seek to incorporate (or create new models of) features of financial markets that we now know to have been important and that were missed. Rather, we must address the deeper problem of the epistemic insensitivity of our current practice and cultivate the capacity to be "attentive to the available evidence on the phenomena and prepared to concede it presumptive validity" (Winter 2010: 22). We must, that is, be able to hear what the phenomena have to say when they speak for themselves.

The financial crisis was a particularly spectacular example of how detached models leave us vulnerable to blindsiding, and how a detached model can pass through the screen of our current standards of assessment. But as I have tried to show in this book, susceptibility to such failures is a general feature of mathematical modeling practice in economics.

Mathematical economic modeling, like all scientific modeling, is an inherently indirect means of illuminating a subject. Questions or puzzles about the subject are addressed not through direct exploration of the subject but rather through exploration of a model. The modeler translates the initial question about the target into an (ostensibly) analogous question about the model, then constructs a "model narrative" that traces out a solution to the question in the model, and, finally, translates the model narrative back into the terms of the target subject, creating a "target narrative" that (ostensibly) constitutes an answer to the initial question about the target. The illumination of the target in this process is accomplished by projecting selected aspects of the internal structure of the model onto the target – that is, by re-imagining the target as though it were organized according to the logic of the model, and considering what answer(s) to the initial question this re-organization affords.

As I argue in Chapter 1, however, a crucial assumption underlies this means of illumination. In order for the model narrative to imply parallel dynamics in the target, it must be the case that the implied narrative is a *possible* narrative for the target. That is, it is necessary that the solution to the initial question about the target implied by the model narrative does not depend upon the target's possessing properties that it does not plausibly possess. It is only when the model narrative meets this condition that the model can be deemed an "apt representation" of the target for the purposes of the modeling exercise in question.

In Chapters 2 and 3, I considered what the requirements of apt representation imply for the kind of modeling most prevalent in economics – namely, mathematical modeling of social phenomena – with Chapter 2 focusing on theoretical modeling exercises (i.e. those that do not include rigorous analysis of data) and Chapter 3 focusing on empirical modeling exercises (i.e. those that do include rigorous analysis of data). I began by arguing that the illuminative process of scientific modeling is best understood as essentially metaphorical. Like metaphors, models provide insight by drawing on three types of analogy with their targets: (1) positive analogy, i.e. the ways in which the two entities are similar; (2) negative analogy (or disanalogy), i.e. the ways in which they are dissimilar; and (3) neutral analogy, i.e. the ways in which the entities may possibly be similar. We first satisfy ourselves (by considering the positive and negative analogies) that there is enough relevant similarity and sufficiently little relevant dissimilarity between the model and the target for their conjunction to be fruitful, and then we see what insight can be gained from thinking of the neutral analogies as positive analogies.

In order for a model to be an apt representation of its target, I argued, certain key properties of the model – those which I called "essential" properties – must belong to the set of neutral analogies; that is, they must be properties that are at least possibly shared by the target. *Which* of the properties are essential is determined jointly by the nature of the model and target and the purposes of the modeler in the modeling exercise in question. Specifically, the essential properties of the model are those which are necessary for the construction of the model narrative(s) deployed in the modeling exercise, and the essential properties of the target are those which are the focus of the question or puzzle the modeling exercise is meant to address. If, in a given modeling exercise, any of the essential properties reside in the realm of negative analogy, then the model narrative cannot validly be interpreted as a possible narrative for the target – indeed, it cannot validly be interpreted as a narrative about the target at all. Thus, the absence of essential negative analogies between model and target is a necessary condition for the aptness of the model with respect to the modeling exercise in question. When model and target meet this condition, they are "essentially compatible."

In the remainder of Chapter 2, I argued that in mathematical economic modeling the essential compatibility condition can be satisfied only when: (a) the objects under investigation are plausibly *stable, modular,* and *quantitative*, with no qualitative differences among instantiations of each type; and (b) the relations between them are plausibly *fixed* and *law-like* throughout the context under study in the modeling exercise. This conclusion derives from the fact that the model narratives of mathematical economic modeling exercises are mathematical narratives, and the properties referenced above are constitutive of mathematical objects *qua* mathematical objects. These properties, therefore, are essential properties of mathematical model narratives as such (in the sense that if a model object or objects were not to possess these properties, then a model narrative that included this object/these objects would be uninterpretable as a mathematical narrative). For the essential compatibility condition to be satisfied, then, the target objects must also possess these properties. If they do not, then the model will be inherently inapt.

I concluded the discussion in Chapter 2 by considering an objection to this claim; namely, that it is misguided as a claim about theoretical models on the grounds that: (1) it unduly restricts the freedom of theoretical modelers to engage in possibly counterfactual but nonetheless illuminating thought experiments, and (2) that concerns about the empirical adequacy of a theoretical model are properly the province of empirical modeling exercises. I argued that we should resist this objection for two reasons. The first is that the division of labor between theoretical and empirical models it suggests is too starkly drawn. While theoretical economic modeling exercises do not involve econometric analysis of data, they still ultimately refer to the social world and are justified on the basis of their ability to represent (or to develop tools to help us represent) aspects of that world, however loosely. Theoretical modeling exercises may vary in how much they foreground the questions about the target world that ultimately motivate the exercise, but some recourse of this kind is implied whenever these exercises are presented as economically relevant (as opposed to simply mathematical exercises). This suggests that part of good practice in theoretical modeling must be explicit consideration of what the essential properties of the model imply with respect to the potential scope of applicability of the model.

The second reason to resist the objection, as I discuss in Chapter 3, is that the aptness of empirical models depends upon essential compatibility with their targets for precisely the same reasons (and in precisely the same manner) as is the case for theoretical models. Empirical and theoretical modeling exercises follow the same illuminative process. In both, a motivating question about some aspect of the social world is explored through analysis of a mathematical model (i.e. a purely quantitative representation). Significantly, economic data are quantitative representations of the underlying social objects of interest – just as the variables and parameters of theoretical models are – and are thus model objects. Recognizing this allows us to see that inferences about the data are entirely *model* narratives. And as such they can provide answers to questions about the social world only to the extent that the model (*including* the data) is essentially compatible with the target. Thus econometric analysis, in itself, is neither an adequate means of assessing the aptness of a model nor a means of escaping the necessity of establishing the essential compatibility of a model and its target. Concretely, what this means is that econometric analysis of data in an empirical modeling exercise is not in itself sufficient to establish the merits of the model in question as a generator of insight into the target. Without independently exploring the extent to which the model (including the data) is essentially compatible with the target phenomena of interest, we cannot know the extent to which the results of the empirical modeling exercise can validly be interpreted as being *about* the target. Chapters 4 and 5 were devoted to illustrating the foregoing through examples from the literature.

In the final two chapters of the book, I considered how the need to establish essential compatibility of mathematical economic models and their targets might best be addressed. In Chapter 6, I argued that doing so will require substantive reforms to current economic methodology.

As discussed in Chapters 2 and 3, the logic of mathematical economic modeling presumes the essential compatibility of model and target, in the sense that when the two are not essentially compatible we cannot validly interpret inferences from the model as possible inferences about the target. In light of this, we must use methods other than mathematical modeling to explore the extent to which essential compatibility holds in any given modeling exercise. The appropriate methods for doing so, I argued, will necessarily be "hermeneutic" or "interpretive," as what is required is an exploration of the meaning of actions undertaken by agents who simultaneously create and are subject to the norms that establish that meaning. Because general, discipline-wide standards for using interpretive methods in this way do not currently exist in economics, it will be necessary to build this capacity into the discipline.

In Chapter 7, I described methodological reforms aimed at accomplishing this task and provided examples of the kind of work the reforms would entail. Centrally, I proposed the development of a new field within the discipline – "interpretive economics" – the primary aim of which would be to develop methods and standards for assessing the essential compatibility (or lack thereof) of social phenomena of interest to economists with mathematical models. As essential compatibility is a property applicable at the level of the modeling exercise, the purpose of this field would not be to produce conclusions about the mathematical compatibility of various aspects of social experience in general, but rather to develop the capacity to make such assessments with respect to individual modeling exercises.

Broadly speaking, work in the interpretive economics field would be of three types: "theoretical," "methodological," and "applied." Theoretical interpretive economics would involve the critical investigation of current understandings of economic phenomena. From the point of view of economic practice, this work would serve two main functions: (1) an innovative function – by supporting the development of alternative conceptualizations of various aspects of economic life; and (2) an assessment function – by providing a store of information that can be used to assess the plausibility of conceptualizations of economic life employed by past, present, and future analyses. Methodological interpretive economics would involve tailoring existing interpretive social science methods – for example, participant observation and interpretive interview techniques – to the particular needs and challenges of economics. As such, it would be similar to work in econometrics aimed at developing empirical methods (out of statistics and probability theory) for the particular needs of economists, and studying and addressing the particular challenges that arise in applying such methods in economics. Applied interpretive economics would involve bringing to bear the tools developed in methodological work on social phenomena in much the same way that econometric methods and standards are employed in empirical analysis.

The chapter concluded with a discussion of the desirability of considering interpretive economics as constituting a new subfield of economics. As I have tried to show in this book, mathematical economic modeling is an inherently incomplete mode of engagement with economic phenomena. We cannot be confident that the inferences we draw from mathematical economic models will be relevant to – let alone capable of generating insight into   the social phenomena they are meant to illuminate without independently establishing the essential compatibility of the model with its ostensible target. The near-exclusive reliance of contemporary economics on mathematical modeling means that this is a ubiquitous concern and, therefore, one that should be addressed comprehensively. Moreover, this task will necessarily involve developing and adapting interpretive investigative and analytic methods that are not currently a standard part of the toolkit of economics. It is important that we incorporate these methods in a manner that is not *ad hoc*, but rather systematically and in a manner consonant with the overall goals and principles of economics. Doing so on a discipline-wide level requires a discipline-wide approach.

References

Acemoglu, Daron 2005. "Understanding institutions," presentation slides, Lionel Robbins Lectures, http://econ-www.mit.edu/faculty/acemoglu/selected, accessed September 19, 2008.

Acemoglu, Daron and James A. Robinson 2006. *Economic Origins of Dictatorship and Democracy*. Cambridge, UK; New York: Cambridge University Press.

Aiyagari, S. Rao 1994. "On the contribution of technology shocks to business cycles," *Federal Reserve Bank of Minneapolis Quarterly Review* 18(3): 22–34.

Akerlof, George A. 1982. "Labor contracts as partial gift exchange," *Quarterly Journal of Economics* 97(4): 543–69.

    2011. "Rising to the challenge: equity, adjustment and balance in the world economy," Panel discussion, Institute for New Economic Thinking Conference, Bretton Woods, New Hampshire, April 10.

Akerlof, George A. and Robert J. Shiller 2009. *Animal Spirits: How Human Psychology Drives the Economy and Why It Matters for Global Capitalism*. Princeton, NJ: Princeton University Press.

Allied Social Sciences Association 2009. 'Panel discussion: recent financial crisis', ASSA Annual Meeting, January 3, www.aeaweb.org/webcasts/2009/Recent_Financial_Crisis_Jan_3_2009/Player.php.

    2010. "Panel discussion: how should the financial crisis change how we teach economics?" ASSA Annual Meeting, January 3, Part 1, www.aeaweb.org/webcasts/2010/fin_crisis_1/. Part 2, www.aeaweb.org/webcasts/2010/fin_crisis_2/.

Almond, Gabriel A. and Sidney Verba 1963. *The Civic Culture: Political Attitudes and Democracy in Five Nations*. Princeton, NJ: Princeton University Press.

Ashraf, Nava, James Berry, and Jesse M. Shapiro 2010. "Can higher prices stimulate product use? Evidence from a field experiment in Zambia," *American Economic Review* 100(5): 2383–413.

Audi, Robert J. (ed.) 1999. *The Cambridge Dictionary of Philosophy*. Cambridge, UK; New York: Cambridge University Press.

Bailer-Jones, Daniela M. 1999. "Tracing the development of models in the philosophy of science," in Lorenzo Magnani, Nancy Nersessian, and Paul Thagard (eds.) *Model-Based Reasoning in Scientific Discovery*. Dordrecht: Kluwer, pp. 23–40.

    2002. "Models, metaphors and analogies," in Peter Machamer and Michael Silberstein, eds., *The Blackwell Guide to the Philosophy of Science*. Oxford, UK; Malden, MA: Blackwell Publishers, pp. 108-27.

2003. "When scientific models represent," *International Studies in the Philosophy of Science* 17(1): 59–74.

Bajaj, Vikas 2006. "Mortgages grow riskier, and investors are attracted," *New York Times*, September 9, www.nytimes.com/2006/09/06/business/06place.html, accessed November 10, 2014.

Barro, Robert J. 1974. "Are government bonds net wealth?" *Journal of Political Economy* 82(6): 1095–117.

1997. *Determinants of Economic Growth: A Cross-Country Empirical Study*. Cambridge, MA: MIT Press.

2009. "Voodoo multipliers," *Economists' Voice* 6(2), article 5.

Barthes, Roland 1982. "Introduction to the structural analysis of narratives," in S. Sontag (ed.) *A Roland Barthes Reader*. London: Vintage, pp. 251–95.

Baumol, William J. 1986. "Productivity growth, convergence, and welfare: what the long-run data show," *American Economic Review* 76(5): 1072–85.

Beales, Richard and Gillian Tett 2005. "How rating agencies navigate the lucrative waters of structured finance," *Financial Times*, London edn, July 28, p. 23.

Bernanke, Ben S. 2004. "The great moderation," remarks by Governor Ben S. Bernanke at the meetings of the Eastern Economic Association, Washington, DC, February 24, www.federalreserve.gov/Boarddocs/Speeches/2004/20040220/, accessed July 1, 2012.

2010. "Implications of the financial crisis for economics," remarks at the conference co-sponsored by the Center for Economic Policy Studies and the Bendheim Center for Finance, Princeton University, Princeton, NJ, September 24, 2010, www.federalreserve. gov/newsevents/speech/bernanke20100924a.htm, accessed July 1, 2012.

Besley, Tim and Peter Hennessy 2009. "The global financial crisis – why didn't anybody notice?" *British Academy Review* 14: 8–10.

2010. "Financial and economic horizon-scanning," *British Academy Review* 15: 12–14.

Bewley, Truman F. 1999. *Why Wages Don't Fall During a Recession*. Cambridge, MA: Harvard University Press.

Black, Max 1962. *Models and Metaphors*. Ithaca, NY: Cornell University Press.

1993. "More about metaphor," in Andrew Ortony (ed.) *Metaphor and Thought*, 2nd edn. Cambridge, UK; New York: Cambridge University Press, pp. 19–41.

Black, R.D. Collison, A.W. Coats, and Craufurd D.W. Goodwin (eds.) 1973. *The Marginal Revolution in Economics: Interpretation and Evaluation*. Durham, NC: Duke University Press.

Blanchard, Olivier J. 2008. "The state of macro," National Bureau of Economic Research Working Paper No. 14259.

Blinder, Alan S., Elie R.D. Canetti, David E. Lebow, and Jeremy D. Rudd 1998. *Asking about Prices: A New Approach to Understanding Price Stickiness*. New York: Russell Sage Foundation.

Blomberg, Brock and Joseph E. Harrington, Jr. 2000. "A theory of rigid extremists and flexible moderates with an application to the US Congress," *American Economic Review* 90(3): 605–20.

Botticini, Maristella and Aloysius Siow 2003. "Why dowries?" *American Economic Review* 93(4): 1385–98.

Boumans, Marcel 1999. "Built-in justification," in Mary S. Morgan and Margaret Morrison (eds.) *Models as Mediators: Perspectives on Natural and Social Science*. Cambridge, UK; New York: Cambridge University Press, pp. 66–96.

2005. *How Economists Model the World into Numbers*. London: Routledge.

Burtless, Gary 1995. "The case for randomized field trials in economic and policy research," *Journal of Economic Perspectives* 9(2): 63–84.

Burton, Peter, Shelley Phipps, and Lori Curtis 2002. "All in the family: a simultaneous model of parenting style and child conduct," *American Economic Review* 92(2): 368–72.

Buiter, Willem 2009. "The unfortunate uselessness of most 'state of the art' academic monetary economics," http://voxeu.org/index.php?q=node/3210, accessed February 28, 2014.

Caballero, Ricardo J. 2010. "Macroeconomics after the crisis: time to deal with the pretense-of-knowledge syndrome," *Journal of Economic Perspectives* 24(4): 85–102.

Cappelli, Peter and Keith Chauvin 1991. "An interplant test of the efficiency wage hypothesis," *Quarterly Journal of Economics* 106(3): 769–87.

Case, Karl E. and Robert J. Shiller 2003. "Is there a bubble in the housing market?" *Brookings Papers on Economic Activity* (2): 299–342.

Cassidy, John 2010a. "Interview with Eugene Fama," *The New Yorker*, January 13, www.new yorker.com/online/blogs/johncassidy/2010/01/interview-with-eugene-fama.html, accessed September 6, 2011.

2010b. "Interview with John Cochrane," *The New Yorker*, January 13, www.newyorker.com/online/blogs/johncassidy/2010/01/interview-with-john-cochrane.html, accessed September 6, 2011.

Cavendish, Henry 1798. "Experiments to determine the density of the Earth," *Philosophical Transactions of the Royal Society of London* 88: 469–526.

Chang, Ha-Joon 2006. "Understanding the relationship between institutions and economic development: Some key theoretical issues," UNU-WIDER Research Paper, World Institute for Development Economics Research.

Chari, V.V. 2010. Testimony before the Committee on Science and Technology, Subcommittee on Investigations and Oversight, US House of Representatives, *Building a Science of Economics for the Real World: Hearing Before the Subcommittee on Investigation and Oversight, Committee on Science and Technology, US House of Representatives*, 111th Congress, Second Session, July 20, Washington, DC: Government Printing Office, pp. 32–7.

Chari, V.V. and Patrick J. Kehoe 2006. "Modern macroeconomics in practice: how theory is shaping policy," *Journal of Economic Perspectives* 20(4): 3–28.

Cochrane, John H. 2009. "Fiscal stimulus, fiscal inflation, or fiscal fallacies?" http://faculty.chicagobooth.edu/john.cochrane/research/papers/fiscal2.ht, accessed June 24, 2012.

2011. "Why did Paul Krugman get it so wrong?" *Economic Affairs* 31(2): 36–40.

Coddington, Alan 1975. "The rationale of general equilibrium theory," *Economic Inquiry* 13(4): 539–58.

Cogan, John F., Tobias Cwik, John B. Taylor, and Volker Wieland 2009. "New Keynesian versus Old Keynesian government spending multipliers," National Bureau of Economic Research Working Paper 14782.

Cogan, John F. and John B. Taylor 2011. "Stimulus has been a Washington job killer," *Wall Street Journal*, October 4, p. A21.

2012. "What the government purchases multiplier actually multiplied in the 2009 stimulus package," in Lee. E. Ohanion, John B. Taylor, and Ian J. Wright (eds.) *Government Policies and the Delayed Economic Recovery*. Stanford, CA: Hoover Institution Press.

Cohen, Jessica and Pascaline Dupas 2010. "Free distribution or cost-sharing? Evidence from a randomized malaria prevention experiment," *Quarterly Journal of Economics* 125(1): 1–45.

Colander, David 2005a. "The future of economics: the appropriately educated person in pursuit of the knowable," *Cambridge Journal of Economics* 29(6): 927–41.

2005b. "The making of an economist redux," *Journal of Economic Perspectives* 19(1): 175–98.

2009. Testimony before the Committee on Science and Technology, US House of Representatives, *The Risks of Financial Modeling: VaR and the Economic Meltdown*, September 10. Washington, DC: Government Printing Office, pp. 127–41.

2010. Testimony before the Committee on Science and Technology, Subcommittee on Investigations and Oversight, US House of Representatives, *Building a Science of Economics for the Real World: Hearing Before the Subcommittee on Investigation and Oversight, Committee on Science and Technology, US House of Representatives*, 111th Congress, Second Session, July 20, Washington, DC: Government Printing Office, pp. 39–45.

Colander, David, Michael Goldberg, Armin Haas, Katarina Juselius, Alan Kirman, Thomas Lux, and Birgitte Sloth 2009. "The financial crisis and the systemic failure of the economics profession," *Critical Review* 21(2–3): 249–67.

Colander, David, Richard Holt, and Barkley Rosser 2004. "The changing face of mainstream economics," *Review of Political Economy* 16(4): 485–99.

Colander, David, Peter Howitt, Alan Kirman, Axel Leijonhufvud, and Perry Mehrling 2008. "Beyond DSGE models: toward an empirically based macroeconomics," *American Economic Review* 98(2): 236–40.

Commons, John R. 1924. *Legal Foundations of Capitalism*. New York: Macmillan.

1934. *Institutional Economics: Its Place in Political Economy*. New York: Macmillan.

Contessa, Gabriele 2007. "Scientific representation, interpretation, and surrogative reasoning," *Philosophy of Science* 74: 48–68.

Courcelle-Seneuil, J.-G. 1858. *Traité theoretique et pratique d'économie politique*, 2 vols. Paris: Guillaumin.

Darnell, Adrian C. (ed.) 1994. *The History of Econometrics*, 2 vols. Aldershot, Hants, UK: Edward Elgar.

Davidson, Paul 2009. *The Keynes Solution: The Path to Global Economic Prosperity*. New York: Palgrave Macmillan.

Davis, Douglas D. and Charles A. Holt 1993. *Experimental Economics*. Princeton, NJ: Princeton University Press.

Davis, John B. 2007. "The turn in economics and the turn in economic methodology," *Journal of Economic Methodology* 14(3): 275–90.

Dell'Ariccia, Giovanni and Robert Marquez 2006. "Lending booms and lending standards," *The Journal of Finance* 61(5): 2511–46.

DeLong, J. Bradford 1987. "Have productivity levels converged? Productivity growth, convergence, and welfare in the very long run," National Bureau of Economics Working Paper #2419. Cambridge, MA: National Bureau of Economic Research.

Dennis, Ken 1982a. "Economic theory and the problem of translation: part one," *Journal of Economic Issues* 16(3): 691–712.

1982b. "Economic theory and the problem of translation: part two," *Journal of Economic Issues* 16(4): 1039–62.

Dequech, David 2002. "The demarcation between the 'old' and the 'new' institutional economics: recent complications," *Journal of Economic Issues* 36(2): 565–72.

DeWalt, Kathleen M. and Billie R. DeWalt 1998. "Participant observation," with C.B. Wayland, in H. R. Bernard (eds.) *Handbook of Methods in Cultural Anthropology*. Walnut Creek, CA: AltaMira.

Diamond, Douglas W. and Raghuram G. Rajan 2005. "Liquidity shortages and banking crises," *The Journal of Finance* 60(2): 615–47.

Dixit, Avinash, Gene M. Grossman, and Faruk Gul 2000. "The dynamics of political compromise," *Journal of Political Economy* 108(3): 531–68.

Domar, E. D. 1946. "Capital expansion, rate of growth, and employment," *Econometrica* 14(2): 137–47.

Duflo, Esther and Abhijit Banerjee 2011. *Poor Economics: A Radical Rethinking of the Way to Fight Global Poverty*. New York: PublicAffairs.

Duhem, Pierre 1954. *The Aim and Structure of Physical Theory*, 2nd edn. trans. Philip P. Wiener. Princeton, NJ: Princeton University Press.

Dupas, Pascaline 2014. "Short-run subsidies and long-run adoption of new health products: evidence from a field experiment," *Econometrica* 82(1): 197–228.

Eatwell, John and Murray Milgate 2011. *The Rise and Fall of Keynesian Economics*. New York: Oxford University Press.

Ericsson, Jan and Olivier Renault 2006. "Liquidity and credit risk," *Journal of Finance* 61(5): 2219–50.

Faccio, Mara, Ronald W. Masulis, and John J. McConnell 2006. "Political connections and corporate bailouts," *Journal of Finance* 61(6): 2597–635.

Fang, Hanming 2001. "Social culture and economic performance," *American Economic Review* 91(4): 924–37.

Farmer, J. Doyne and Duncan Foley 2009. "The economy needs agent-based modeling," *Nature* 460(6): 685–6.

Finkelstein, L. 1975. "Fundamental concepts of measurement: definition and scales," *Measurement and Control* 8: 105–10.

Fisher, Irving 1911. *The Purchasing Power of Money: Its Determination and Relation to Credit, Interest and Crises*. New York: Macmillan.

Friedman, Milton 1953. *Essays in Positive Economics*. Chicago: University of Chicago Press.

1991. "Old wine in new bottles," *Economic Journal* 101(January): 33–40.

Gadamer, Hans-Georg 1987. "The problem of historical consciousness," in Paul Rabinow and William M. Sullivan (eds.) *Interpretive Social Science: A Second Look*, Berkeley, CA: University of California Press.

1989. *Truth and Method*. New York: Continuum.

Gallegati, Mauro and Matteo G. Richiardi 2011. "Agent based models in economics and complexity," in Robert A. Myers (ed.), *Complex Systems in Finance and Econometrics*. Berlin: Springer, pp. 30–53.

Geertz, Clifford 1973. *The Interpretation of Cultures: Selected Essays*, New York: Basic Books.

Gibbard, Allan and Hal R. Varian 1978. "Economic models," *Journal of Philosophy* 75: 664–77.

Giere, Ronald N. 1979. *Understanding Scientific Reasoning*. New York: Holt, Reinhart & Winston.

  1988. *Explaining Science: A Cognitive Approach*. Chicago: University of Chicago Press.

  1999. *Science Without Laws*. Chicago: University of Chicago Press.

  2004. "How models are used to represent reality," *Philosophy of Science* 71(December): 742–52.

Gintis, Herbert 2006. "The evolution of private property," *Journal of Economic Behavior and Organization* 64(1): 1–16.

Glaeser, Edward L., Joseph Gyourko, and Raven E. Saks 2005. "Why have housing prices gone up?" *American Economic Review* 95(2): 329–33.

Glaeser, Edward L. and Andrei Shleifer 2003. "The rise of the regulatory state," *Journal of Economic Literature* 41(2): 401–25.

Godfrey-Smith, Peter 2006. "The strategy of model-based science," *Biology and Philosophy* 21: 725–40.

Goodman, Allen C. and Thomas G. Thibodeau 2008. "Where are the speculative bubbles in US housing markets?" *Journal of Housing Economics* 17: 117–37.

Gorton, Gary and Lixin Huang 2004. "Liquidity, efficiency, and bank bailouts," *American Economic Review* 94(3): 455–83.

Groenewegen, John, Frans Kerstholt and Ad Nagalkerke 1995. "On integrating new and old institutionalism: Douglass North building bridges," *Journal of Economic Issues* 29(2): 467–76.

Grossman, Gene M. 1986. "Strategic export promotion: a critique," in Paul R. Krugman (ed.), *Strategic Trade Policy and the New International Economics*. Cambridge, MA: MIT Press, pp. 47–68.

Guala, Francesco 2005. *The Methodology of Experimental Economics*. Cambridge, UK; New York: Cambridge University Press.

Guiso, Luigi, Paola Sapienza, and Luigi Zingales 2006. "Does culture affect economic outcomes?" *Journal of Economic Perspectives* 20(2): 23–48.

Haavelmo, Trygve 1944. "The probability approach in econometrics," *Econometrica* 12(supplement): iii–vi, 1–115.

Hacking, Ian 1983. *Representing and Intervening: Introductory Topics in the Philosophy of Natural Science*. Cambridge, UK; New York: Cambridge University Press.

Hahn, F.H. 1970. "Some adjustment problems," *Econometrica* 38(1): 1–17.

Hands, D. Wade 2001. *Reflection Without Rules: Economic Methodology and Contemporary Science Theory*. New York and Cambridge, UK: Cambridge University Press.

Hanssen, F. Andrew 2004. "Is there a politically optimal level of judicial independence?" *American Economic Review* 94(3): 712–29.

Harrod, R.F. 1939. "An essay in dynamic theory," *Economic Journal* 49(193): 14–33.

Hausman, Daniel 1984. "Why look under the hood?" in Daniel Hausman (ed.), *The Philosophy of Economics: An Anthology*. New York: Cambridge University Press.

  1992. *The Inexact and Separate Science of Economics*. Cambridge, UK; New York: Cambridge University Press.

Hausman, Daniel (ed.), 1984. *The Philosophy of Economics: An Anthology*. New York: Cambridge University Press.

Heckman, James J. and Jeffrey A. Smith 1995. "Assessing the case for social experiments," *Journal of Economic Perspectives* 9(2): 85–110.

Heidelberger, Michael 1993. "Fechner's impact for measurement theory," *Behavioral and Brain Sciences* 16: 146–8.

Henderson, H.D. 1938. "The significance of the rate of interest," *Oxford Economic Papers* 1: 1–13.

Herfel, William E., Wladyslaw Krajewski, Ilkka Niiniluoto, and Ryszard Wójcicki (eds.) 1995. *Theories and Models in Scientific Processes, Poznan Studies in the Philosophy of the Sciences and Humanities* 44. Amsterdam: Rodopi.

Hess, Gregory D. and Athanasios Orphanides 2001. "War and democracy," *Journal of Political Economy* 109(4): 776–810.

Hesse, Mary B. 1963. *Models and Analogies in Science*. London: Sheed & Ward.

1966. *Models and Analogies in Science*. Notre Dame, IN: University of Notre Dame Press.

Himmelberg, Charles, Christopher Mayer, and Todd Sinai 2005. "Assessing high house prices: bubbles, fundamentals and misperceptions," *Journal of Economic Perspectives* 19(4): 67–92.

Hirschman, Albert O. 1970. *Exit, Voice and Loyalty: Response to Decline in Firms, Organizations, and States*. Cambridge, MA: Harvard University Press.

Hodgson, Geoffrey 1988. *Economics and Institutions*. London: Polity Press.

1999. "Structures and institutions: reflection on institutionalism, structuration theory, and critical realism," presented at European Association for Evolutionary Political Economy conference, Prague.

2007. "Evolutionary and institutional economics as the new mainstream?" *Evolutionary Institutional Economics Review* 4(1): 7–25.

2008. "After 1929 economics changed: will economists wake up in 2009?" *Real-World Economics Review* 48: 273–8.

2009. "The great crash of 2008 and the reform of economics," *Cambridge Journal of Economics* 33: 1205–21.

Holmes, Douglas R. 2013. *Economy of Words: Communicative Imperatives in Central Banks*. Chicago: University of Chicago Press.

Hoover, Kevin D. 2001. *Causality in Macroeconomics*. New York: Cambridge University Press.

2005. "The methodology of econometrics," available at http://public.econ.duke.edu/~kdh9/Source Materials/Research/econometric_methodology_plus_abstract.pdf, accessed August 1, 2014.

Hughes, R.I.G. 1997. "Models and representation," *Philosophy of Science* 64 (Supplement. Proceedings of the 1996 Biennial Meetings of the Philosophy of Science Association, Part II): S325–S336.

Hutchison, T.W. 1938. *The Significance and Basic Postulates of Economic Theory*. London: Macmillan.

Iacoviello, Matteo 2005. "House prices, borrowing constraints, and monetary policy in the business cycle," *American Economic Review* 95(3): 739–64.

Ireland, Peter N. 2004. "A method for taking models to the data," *Journal of Economic Dynamics and Control* 28: 1205–26.

Jevons, W. S. 1958. *The Principles of Science: A Treatise on Logic and Scientific Method*, 2nd edn. Intr. by Ernest Nagel. New York: Dover Publications.

1965. *The Theory of Political Economy*, 5th edn. reprint of the 1957 edition. New York: Augustus M. Kelley.

Johnson, Simon and James Kwak 2010. *13 Bankers: The Wall Street Takeover and the Next Financial Meltdown*. New York: Pantheon.

Juselius, Katarina and Massimo Franchi 2007. "Taking a DSGE model to the data meaningfully," *Economics* 1, 2007(4), available at http://dx.doi.org/10.5018/economics-ejournal.ja.2007-4, accessed August 1, 2014.

Kehoe, Timothy J. and David K. Levine 2001. "Liquidity constrained markets versus debt constrained markets," *Econometrica* 69(3): 575–98.

Keynes, J. M. 1936. *The General Theory of Employment, Interest, and Money*. London: Macmillan.

Kiyotaki, Nobuhiro and John Moore 1997. "Credit cycles," *Journal of Political Economy* 105(2): 211–48.

Krishnan, C.N.V., P.H. Ritchken, and J.B. Thomson 2005. "Monitoring and controlling bank risk. does risky debt help?" *Journal of Finance* 40(1): 343–78.

Krugman, Paul 2009. "How did economists get it so wrong?" *New York Times Magazine*, September 2, www.nytimes.com/2009/09/06/magazine/06Economic-t.html, accessed August 31, 2014.

Krusell, Per and Anthony A. Smith, Jr. 1998. "Income and wealth heterogeneity in the macroeconomy," *Journal of Political Economy* 106(5): 867–96.

2006. "Quantitative macroeconomic models with heterogeneous agents," in R. Blundell, W. Newey, and T. Persson (eds.) *Advances in Economics and Econometrics: Theory and Applications*. Econometric Society Monographs 41. Cambridge: Cambridge University Press, pp. 298–340.

Kuhn, Thomas S. 1996. *The Structure of Scientific Revolutions*, 3rd edn. Chicago: University of Chicago Press.

Kydland, Finn E. and Edward C. Prescott 1982. "Time to build and aggregate fluctuations," *Econometrica* 50(6): 1345–70.

Lakatos, Imre 1978. *The Methodology of Scientific Research Programmes*. Cambridge, UK: Cambridge University Press.

Langlois, Richard N. 2003. "The vanishing hand: the changing dynamics of industrial capitalism," *Industrial and Corporate Change* 12(2): 351–85.

Lawson, Tony 1997. *Economics and Reality*. London; New York: Routledge.

2003. *Reorienting Economics*. London; New York: Routledge.

2009. "The current economic crisis: its nature and the course of academic economics," *Cambridge Journal of Economics* 33: 759–77.

Layard, Richard and Stephen Nickell 1986. "Unemployment in Britain," *Economica* 53(210 Supplemental Issue on Unemployment): S121–S169.

LeBaron, Blake and Leigh Tesfatsion 2008. "Modeling macroeconomies as open-ended dynamic systems of interacting agents," *American Economic Review* 98(2): 246–50.

Leijonhufvud, Axel 2009. "Out of the corridor: Keynes and the crisis," *Cambridge Journal of Economics* 33: 741–57.

Leontief, Wassily 1971. "Theoretical assumptions and nonobserved facts," *American Economic Review* 61(1): 1–7.

Lépinay, Vincent A. 2011. *Codes of Finance: Engineering Derivatives in a Global Bank*. Princeton, NJ: Princeton University Press.

LeRoy, Stephen F. 2004. "Rational exuberance," *Journal of Economic Literature* 42(3): 783–804.

Levy, Robert I. and Douglas W. Hollan 1998. "Person-centered interviewing and observation," in H. Russell Bernard (ed.) *Handbook of Methods in Cultural Anthropology*. Walnut Creek, CA: AltaMira.

Lucas, Robert E. 1972. "Expectations and the neutrality of money," *Journal of Economic Theory* 4(2): 103–24.

2003. "Macroeconomic priorities," *American Economic Review* 93(1): 1–14.

Lycan, William G. 1999. "Philosophy of language," in Robert J. Audi (ed.) *The Cambridge Dictionary of Philosophy*. Cambridge, UK; New York: Cambridge University Press, pp. 673–6.

Machamer, Peter and Michael Silberstein (eds.) 2002. *The Blackwell Guide to the Philosophy of Science*. Oxford, UK; Malden, MA: Blackwell Publishers.

MacIntyre, Alasdair 1978. "Is a science of comparative politics possible?" in *Against the Self-Images of the Age: Essays on Ideology and Philosophy*. Notre Dame, IN: University of Notre Dame Press.

Mäki, Uskali 1992. "On the method of isolation in economics," *Idealization IV: Intelligibility in Science: Poznan Studies in the Philosophy of the Sciences and the Humanities* 26: 37–51.

1994. "Reorienting the assumptions issue," in Roger E. Backhouse (ed.) *Economists and the Economy: The Evolution of Economic Ideas*, 2nd edn. New Brunswick, NJ: Transaction Publishers, pp. 236–56.

2005. "Models are experiments, experiments are models," *Journal of Economic Methodology* 12(2): 303–15.

2009a. "MISSing the World: models as isolations and credible surrogate systems," *Erkenntnis* 70: 29–43.

2009b. "Models and truth," in *EPSA Epistemology and Methodology of Science*, Mauricio Suárez, Mauro Dorato and Miklós Rédei, eds. Dordrecht: Springer, pp. 177–87.

Marglin, Stephen A. 1974. "What do bosses do? The origins and functions of hierarchy in capitalist production," *Review of Radical Political Economics* 6(2): 60–112.

1975. "What do bosses do? Part II," *Review of Radical Political Economics* 7(1): 20–37.

Marglin, Stephen A. and Peter Spiegler 2014. "Did the states pocket the Obama stimulus money? Lessons from cross-section regression and interviews with state officials," *Political Economy Research Institute Working Paper #371*.

Maskin, Eric and Jean Tirole 2004. "The politician and the judge: accountability in government," *American Economic Review* 94(4): 1034–54.

McCleary, Rachel M. and Robert J. Barro 2006. "Religion and economy," *Journal of Economic Perspectives* 20(2): 49–72.

McCloskey, Deirdre N. 1990. *If You're So Smart: The Narrative of Economic Expertise*. Chicago: University of Chicago Press.

McCloskey, Donald N. 1983. "The rhetoric of economics," *Journal of Economic Literature* 21(2): 481–517.

Mead, Margaret 1953. *Coming of Age in Samoa: A Psychological Study of Primitive Youth for Western Cultures*. New York: Modern Library.

Meade, J.E. and P.W.S. Andrews 1938. "Summary of replies to questions on effects of interest rates," *Oxford Economic Papers* 1: 14–31.

Mill, John Stuart 1972. *The Collected Works of John Stuart Mill, Volume XVII, The Later Letters of John Stuart Mill 1849–1873, Part IV*. Francis E. Mineka and Dwight N. Lindley (eds.) Toronto: University of Toronto Press; London: Routledge and Kegan Paul. http://oll.libertyfund.org/titles/254#lf0223-17_footnote_nt_1141_ref, accessed April 2, 2015.

   1974. *A System of Logic Ratiocinative and Inductive: Being a Connected View of the Principles of Evidence and the Methods of Scientific Investigation*. J.M. Robson (ed.). Introduction R.F. MacRae. Toronto: University of Toronto Press.

Mirowski, Philip 2013. *Never Let a Good Crisis Go to Waste: How Neoliberalism Survived the Financial Meltdown*. New York: Verso.

Moore, Jr., Barrington 1966. *Social Origins of Dictatorship and Democracy: Lord and Peasant in the Making of the Modern World*. Boston, MA: Beacon Press.

Morgan, Mary S. 1990. *The History of Econometric Ideas*. Cambridge, UK: Cambridge University Press.

   1997. "The technology of analogical models: Irving Fisher's monetary worlds," *Philosophy of Science* 64 (Supplement. Proceedings of the 1996 Biennial Meetings of the Philosophy of Science Association. Part II: Symposia papers): S304–S314.

   2001. "Models, stories and the economic world," *Journal of Economic Methodology* 8(3): 361–84.

   2008. "Models," in Steven N. Durlauf and Lawrence E. Blume (eds.) *The New Palgrave Dictionary of Economics*, 2nd edn. London: Palgrave Macmillan.

Morgan, Mary S. and Margaret Morrison (eds.) 1999. *Models as Mediators: Perspectives on Natural and Social Science*. Cambridge UK; New York: Cambridge University Press.

Morgenson, Gretchen 2007. "Crisis looms in mortgages," *New York Times*, March 11, p. A1.

Morley, James 2010. "James Morley on the failure of 'modern' macroeconomics," *Brad DeLong's Grasping Reality*, June 27, http://delong.typepad.com/sdj/2010/06/james-morley-on-the-failure-of-modern-macroeconomics.html, accessed September 6, 2011.

Morrison, Alan D. and Lucy White 2005. "Crises and capital requirements in banking," *American Economic Review* 95(5): 1548–72.

Mulligan, Casey B. 2009. "Is macroeconomics off track?" *The Economists' Voice* 6: Article 6.

Murphy, Kevin M. and Andrei Shleifer 2004. "Persuasion in politics," *American Economic Review* 94(2): 435–9.

North, Douglass C. 1990. *Institutions, Institutional Change and Economic Performance*. Cambridge, UK: Cambridge University Press.

   1991. "Institutions," *Journal of Economic Perspectives* 5(1): 97–112.

Ortalo-Magné, François and Sven Rady 2006. "Housing market dynamics: on the contribution of income shocks and credit constraints," *Review of Economic Studies* 73(2): 459–85.

Page, Scott E. 2010. Testimony before the Committee on Science and Technology, Subcommittee on Investigations and Oversight, US House of Representatives, *Building a Science of Economics for the Real World: Hearing Before the Subcommittee on Investigation and Oversight, Committee on Science and Technology, US House of Representatives*, 111th Congress, Second Session, July 20, Washington, DC: Government Printing Office, pp. 29–32.

Peart, Sandra J. 1995. "'Disturbing causes,' 'noxious errors,' and the theory-practice distinction in the economics of J.S. Mill and W.S. Jevons," *Canadian Journal of Economics* 28(4b): 1194–211.

Peek, Joe and James A. Wilcox 2006. "Housing, credit constraints and macro stability: the secondary mortgage market and reduced cyclicality of residential investment," *American Economic Review* 96(2): 135–40.

Piore, Michael 1979. "Qualitative research techniques in economics," *Administrative Science Quarterly* 24(4): 560–9.

Popper, Karl R. 1968. *The Logic of Scientific Discovery*. London: Hutchinson.
  1969. *Conjectures and Refutations*. London: Routledge & Kegan Paul.
  1994. *The Myth of the Framework: In Defence of Science and Rationality*. M. A. Notturno (ed.) London: Routledge.

Quigley, John M. and Steven Raphael 2005. "Regulation and the high cost of housing in California," *American Economic Review* 95(2): 323–8.

Quine, W.v.O. 1963. *From a Logical Point of View*, 2nd edn. New York: Harper & Row.

Reddy, Sanjay G. 2013. "Randomise this! On poor economics," *Journal of Agrarian Studies* 2(2), www.ras.org.in/randomise_this_on_poor_economics.

Riles, Annelise 2011. *Collateral Knowledge: Legal Reasoning in the Global Financial Markets*. Chicago: University of Chicago Press.

Rodrik, Dani 1999. "Democracies pay higher wages," *Quarterly Journal of Economics* 114(3): 707–38.

Rodrik, Dani, Arvind Subramanian, and Francesco Trebbi 2004. "Institutions rule: the primacy of institutions over geography and integration in economic development," *Journal of Economic Growth* 9(2): 131–65.

Samuelson, Paul A. 1947. *Foundations of Economic Analysis*. Cambridge, MA: Harvard University Press.

Sargent, Thomas 2010. "Interview with Thomas Sargent," *The Region*, September, Federal Reserve Bank of Minneapolis, www.minneapolisfed.org/publications_papers/pub_display.cfm?id=4526.

Scheinkman, José A. and Wei Xiong 2003. "Overconfidence and speculative bubbles," *The Journal of Political Economy* 111(6): 1183–219.

Schneider, Martin and Aaron Tornell 2004. "Balance sheet effects, bailout guarantees and financial crises," *Review of Economic Studies* 3: 883–913.

Sen, Amartya 1999. *Development as Freedom*. New York: Alfred A. Knopf.

Sethi, Rajiv 1996. "Evolutionary stability and social norms," *Journal of Economic Behavior and Organization* 29(1): 113–40.

Shapiro, Carl and Joseph E. Stiglitz 1984. "Equilibrium unemployment as a worker discipline device," *American Economic Review* 74(3): 433–44.

Shiller, Robert J. 2007. "Understanding recent trends in house prices and home ownership," Proceedings: Housing, Housing Finance and Monetary Policy Symposium, Federal Reserve Bank of Kansas City, www.kansascityfed.org/publicat/sympos/2007/PDF/Shiller_0415.pdf.

Sims, Christopher A. 1980. "Macroeconomics and reality," *Econometrica* 48(1): 1–48.
  2007. "On the fit of New Keynesian Models: comment," *Journal of Business and Economic Statistics* 25(2): 152–4.

Skidelsky, Robert 2009. *Keynes: The Return of the Master*. New York: Public Affairs.

Smets, Frank and Rafael Wouters 2007. "Shocks and frictions in US business cycles: a Bayesian DSGE approach," *American Economic Review* 97(3): 586–606.

Smith, Margaret Hwang and Gary Smith 2006. "Bubble, bubble, where's the housing bubble?" *Brookings Papers on Economic Activity* (1): 1–50.

Smith, Vernon L. 1976. "Experimental economics: induced value theory," *American Economic Review* 66(2): 274–9.

1982. "Microeconomic systems as an experimental science," *American Economic Review* 72(5): 923–55.

Smith, Yves 2011. *Econned: How Unenlightened Self Interest Undermined Democracy and Corrupted Capitalism*. London: Palgrave Macmillan.

Snowdon, Brian and Howard R. Vane 1999. *Conversations with Leading Economists: Interpreting Modern Macroeconomics*. Cheltenham, UK; Northampton, MA: Edward Elgar Publishers.

Solow, Robert M. 1956. "A contribution to the theory of economic growth," *Quarterly Journal of Economics* 70(1): 65–94.

1957. "Technical change and the aggregate production function," *Review of Economics and Statistics* 39(3): 312–20.

1979. "Another possible source of wage stickiness," *Journal of Macroeconomics* 1(1): 79–82.

2010. "Testimony before the Committee on Science and Technology, Subcommittee on Investigations and Oversight, US House of Representatives," *Building a Science of Economics for the Real World: Hearing Before the Subcommittee on Investigation and Oversight, Committee on Science and Technology, US House of Representatives*, 111th Congress, Second Session, July 20, Washington, DC: Government Printing Office, pp. 12–15.

Spiegler, Peter 2012. "The unbearable lightness of the economics-made-fun genre," *Journal of Economic Methodology* 19(3): 283–301.

Spiegler, Peter and William Milberg 2009. "The taming of institutions in economics: The rise and methodology of the *new*, new institutionalism," *Journal of Institutional Economics* 5(3): 289–313.

2013. "Methodenstreit 2013? Historical perspective on the contemporary debate over how to reform economics," *Forum for Social Economics* 42(4): 311–45.

Stevens, S.S. 1959. "Measurement, psychophysics, and utility," in C. West Churchman and Philburn Ratoosh (eds.) *Measurements: Definitions and Theories*. New York: Wiley.

Stockhammer, Engelbert and Ozlem Onaran 2012. "Wage-led growth: theory evidence and policy," Political Economy Research Institute Working Paper No. 300, www.peri.umass.edu/fileadmin/pdf/working_papers/working_papers_251-300/WP300.pdf.

Suárez, Mauricio 2004. "An inferential conception of scientific representation," *Philosophy of Science* 71: 767–79.

Summers, Lawrence 2011. "A conversation on new economic thinking with Larry Summers and Martin Wolf," video recording, Institute for New Economic Thinking Conference, Bretton Woods, NH, April 8, http://ineteconomics.org/video/bretton-woods/larry-summers-and-martin-wolf-new-economic-thinking.

Suppe, Frederick 1989. *The Semantic Conception of Theories and Scientific Realism*. Urbana and Chicago, IL: University of Illinois Press.

Suppes, Patrick 1960. "A comparison of the meaning and uses of models in mathematics and the empirical sciences," in *Studies in the Methodology and Foundations of Science: Selected papers from 1951 to 1969*. Dordrecht: D. Reidel.

1962. "Models of data," in Ernest Nagel, Patrick Suppes, and Alfred Tarski (eds.) *Logic, Methodology and Philosophy of Science: Proceedings of the 1960 International Congress*. Stanford, CA: Stanford University Press, pp. 252–61.

1967. "What is a scientific theory?" in Sidney Morgenbesser (ed.) *Philosophy of Science Today*. New York: Basic Books, pp. 55–67.

Swoyer, C. 1981. "Structural representation and surrogative reasoning," *Synthese* 87: 449–508.

Taylor, Charles 1985. "Interpretation and the sciences of man," in *Philosophy and the Human Sciences: Philosophical Papers 2*. Cambridge, UK: Cambridge University Press.

Taylor, John B. 2011a. "An empirical analysis of the revival of fiscal activism in the 2000s," *Journal of Economic Literature* 49(3): 686–702.

2011b. "The 2009 stimulus package: two years later," testimony before the Committee on Oversight and Government Reform, Subcommittee on Regulatory Affairs, Stimulus Oversight and Government Spending, US House of Representatives, February 16, http://media.hoover.org/sites/default/files/documents/2009-Stimulus-two-years-later.pdf, accessed June 24, 2012.

Taylor, Lance 2010. *Maynard's Revenge: The Collapse of Free Market Macroeconomics*. Cambridge, MA: Harvard University Press.

Terkel, Studs 1985. *Working: People Talk About What They Do All Day and How They Feel About What They Do*. New York: Viking Penguin.

Tett, Gillian 2005a. "Innovative ways to repackage debt and spread risk have brought higher returns but have yet to be tested through a full credit cycle: not everyone believes buyers are fully aware of the potential downside," *Financial Times*, London edn, April 19, p. 17.

2005b. "Why more opacity is dangerous for financial markets," *Financial Times*, London edn, October 21, p. 19.

Tinbergen, J. 1935. "Suggestions on quantitative business cycle theory," *Econometrica* 3(3): 241–308.

Tuck, Richard 1979. *Natural Rights Theories: Their Origin and Development*. Cambridge, UK: Cambridge University Press.

Uhlig, Harald 2010. "Some fiscal calculus," *American Economic Review* 100(2, Papers and Proceedings of the One Hundred Twenty Second Annual Meeting of the American Economic Association): 30–4.

US House Committee on Science and Technology 2010. *Building a Science of Economics for the Real World*, July 20, www.gpo.gov/fdsys/pkg/CHRG-111hhrg57604/pdf/CHRG-111hhrg57604.pdf, accessed August 1, 2014.

US Senate Committee on Homeland Security and Governmental Affairs 2011. *Wall Street and the Financial Crisis: Anatomy of a Financial Collapse*, www.hsgac.senate.gov//imo/media/doc/Financial_Crisis/FinancialCrisisReport.pdf, accessed August 1, 2014.

Van Fraassen, Bas 2000. *The Scientific Image*. Oxford: Oxford University Press.

Van Order, Robert 2006. "A model of financial structure and financial fragility," *Journal of Money, Credit and Banking* 38(3): 565–85.

Veblen, Thorstein 1912. *The Theory of the Leisure Class: An Economic Study in the Evolution of Institutions*. New York: Macmillan.

1915. *The Theory of Business Enterprise*. New York: Charles Scribner's Sons.

1919. "Why is economics not an evolutionary science?" in Thorstein Veblen, *The Place of Science in Modern Civilization*. New York: Cosimo.

Wadhwani, Sushil B. and Martin Wall 1989. "The effects of unions on corporate investment: Evidence from accounts data," Centre for Labour Economics, London School of Economics, Discussion Paper No. 355.

1991. "A direct test of the efficiency wage model using UK micro-data," *Oxford Economic Papers*, New Series 43(4): 529–48.

Weisberg, M. 2007a. "Who is a modeler?" *British Journal of the Philosophy of Science* 58: 207–33.

2007b. "Three kinds of idealization," *Journal of Philosophy* 104(12): 639–59.

Williamson, Oliver E. 1975. *Markets and Hierarchies: Analysis and Antitrust Implications.* New York: The Free Press.

1985. *The Economic Institutions of Capitalism.* New York: The Free Press.

2000. "The new institutional economics: taking stock, looking ahead," *Journal of Economic Literature* 38(3): 595–613.

Winter, Sidney G. 2010. "Testimony before the Committee on Science and Technology, Subcommittee on Investigations and Oversight, US House of Representatives," *Building a Science of Economics for the Real World: Hearing Before the Subcommittee on Investigation and Oversight, Committee on Science and Technology, US House of Representatives* 111th Congress, Second Session, July 20, Washington, DC: Government Printing Office, pp. 15–27.

Woodward, Jim 1989. "Data and phenomena," *Synthese* 79(3): 393–472.

Worsley, Peter 1968. *The Trumpet Shall Sound: A Study of "Cargo" Cults in Melanesia,* 3rd edn. New York: Schocken.

Index

abstraction, 3, 9, 124
  in Dynamic Stochastic General Equilibrium
    models, 7–8
Acemoglu, Daron, 95, 99–114, 115, 116, 117, 118,
    137, 139
agent-based computational economics (ACE), 133,
    138, 141
Aiyagari, S. Rao, 122
Akerlof, George A., 13, 138, 141, 179, 181
Allied Social Sciences Association (ASSA), 133
Almond, Gabriel A., 160
American Economic Association, 8
American Economic Review, 130
American Recovery and Reinvestment Act
    (ARRA), 184–188, 194
analogy, 54–55
  negative, 54–55, 57–60, 197
    essential negative, 57–60, 62, 121,
      125–127, 198
  neutral, 54–55, 57, 59, 60, 197
  positive, 54, 57, 60, 89, 197
Andrews, P.W.S., 162–163, 178
anthropology, 171, 178
  of finance, 175, 188–190
Aristotle, 2
Arrow, Kenneth, 13
Ashraf, Nava, 91
as-if, 40–41, 149, 157–163
Autorité des Marchés Financiers, 130

Bailer-Jones, Daniela M., 15, 37
Bajaj, Vikas, 129
Banerjee, Abhijit, 91
Bank of International Settlements, 130
Barro, Robert J., 34, 98, 185
Barthes, Roland, 38
Baumol, William J., 19
Bayesian updating, 148
Beales, Richard, 129
behavioral economics, 133, 134, 138, 141
Bernanke, Ben S., 123, 137

Berry, James, 91
Besley, Tim, 133
Bewley, Truman F., 64, 65, 165, 175, 176–183, 184,
    186, 191–193
Black, Max, 46, 54, 57
Black, R.D. Collison, 99
Blanchard, Olivier J., 120
Blinder, Alan S., 175, 178, 182–184, 191–193
Blomberg, Brock, 108
Botticini, Maristella, 108
Boumans, Marcel, 38, 70, 74, 75, 76
British Academy, 133
British Classical School, 1
Buiter, Willem, 7, 120, 121, 122, 127
Bureau of Economic Analysis, 21, 186
Burtless, Gary, 90
Burton, Peter, 108

Caballero, Ricardo, 7, 9, 123, 124, 138, 140
Cairnes, John Elliot, 1, 2
Canetti, Elie R.D., 175, 182–184
Cappelli, Peter, 151–155
cargo cult, 159
Case, Karl E., 131
Cassidy, John, 134
catalog of correspondences, 50, 82, 85, 86, 87, 92,
    104–105, 113, 148, 153, 156, 169, 170
Cavendish, Henry, 5
Chang, Ha-Joon, 98
Chari, V.V., 120, 122, 123, 131, 134
Chauvin, Keith, 151–155
Coats, A.W., 99
Cochrane, John H., 125, 134, 135, 185
Coddington, Alan, 124
Cogan, John F., 72, 185, 187–188
Cohen, Jessica, 91
Colander, David, 2, 95, 131, 133, 139, 140
collateralized debt obligation (CDO), 127, 128,
    189, 190
Commons, John R., 114
complexity, 3, 6, 7, 87, 122, 124, 133, 138–141

Printed in the United States
By Bookmasters